NOT FOR RESALE

ONE
BRIEF
SHINING
MOMENT

WILLIAM
MANCHESTER

REMEMBERING
KENNEDY

ONE
BRIEF
SHINING
MOMENT

Little, Brown and Company
Boston · Toronto

Books by William Manchester

Biography

Disturber of the Peace: The Life of H. L. Mencken
A Rockefeller Family Portrait: From John D. to Nelson
Portrait of a President: John F. Kennedy in Profile
American Caesar: Douglas MacArthur, 1880–1964
The Last Lion: Winston Spencer Churchill; Visions of Glory: 1874–1932

History

The Death of a President: November 20–November 25, 1963
The Arms of Krupp, 1587–1968
The Glory and the Dream: A Narrative History of America, 1932–1972

Essays

Controversy: And Other Essays in Journalism, 1950–1975

Fiction

The City of Anger
Shadow of the Monsoon
The Long Gainer

Diversion

Beard the Lion

Memoirs

Goodbye, Darkness
One Brief Shining Moment: Remembering Kennedy

COPYRIGHT © 1983 BY WILLIAM MANCHESTER

ALL RIGHTS RESERVED. NO PART OF THIS BOOK MAY BE REPRODUCED IN ANY FORM OR BY ANY ELECTRONIC OR MECHANICAL MEANS INCLUDING INFORMATION STORAGE AND RETRIEVAL SYSTEMS WITHOUT PERMISSION IN WRITING FROM THE PUBLISHER, EXCEPT BY A REVIEWER WHO MAY QUOTE BRIEF PASSAGES IN A REVIEW.

FIRST EDITION

The author is grateful to the following for permission to quote song lyrics:
  Lines from ''Camelot'' by Alan Jay Lerner and Frederick Loewe. Copyright © 1960, 1961 by Alan Jay Lerner and Frederick Loewe. Chappell & Co., Inc., owner of publication and allied rights throughout the world. International copyright secured. ALL RIGHTS RESERVED. Used by permission.
  Lines from ''Hooray for Hollywood,'' lyrics by Johnny Mercer, music by Richard Whiting. © 1937 (renewed) Warner Bros. Inc. All rights reserved. Used by permission.
  Lines from ''September Song'' by Kurt Weill and Maxwell Anderson. Copyright © 1938 by DeSylva, Brown & Henderson, Inc. Copyright renewed, Chappell & Co., Inc. and Hampshire House Publishing, owners of publication and allied rights. International copyright secured. ALL RIGHTS RESERVED. Used by permission.

Library of Congress Cataloging in Publication Data

Manchester, William Raymond, 1922–
  One brief shining moment.

  1. Kennedy, John F. (John Fitzgerald), 1917–1963.
2. Presidents—United States—Biography. 3. United
States—Politics and government—1945–
I. Title. II. Title: 1 brief shining moment.
E842.M29 1983   973.922'092'4   [B]   83-17590
ISBN 0-316-54491-4

RRD

Published simultaneously in Canada by Little, Brown & Company (Canada) Limited

PRINTED IN THE UNITED STATES OF AMERICA

To
Dave Powers
Who Fought with Him
upon Saint Crispin's Day

Thou Sir Launcelot, there thou lyest, thou that were never matched of erthely knyghtes hande. And thou were the courteoust knyght that ever bare shield. And thou were the trewest frende that ever bestrade horse. And thou were the trewest lover of a synful man that ever loved woman. And thou were the kyndest man that ever strucke with swerde. And thou were the goodlyeste persone that ever came emonge press of knyghtes. And thou were the mekest and the gentlest that ever ete in halle emonge ladyes. And thou were the sternest knyghte to thy mortal foe that ever put speare in the reste.

— Sir Thomas Malory
Le Morte d'Arthur
1469

CONTENTS

AUTHOR'S NOTE

This is not a scholarly work. It is instead a recollection of high summer written in the autumn of life, a tribute to a man I knew and an inquiry into why his memory should be cherished. Readers searching for objective appraisals of Kennedy must look elsewhere. I was not and am not entirely uncritical of his performance. The race to put a man on the moon was, I thought, completely unjustified; my argument was that the money would be better spent clearing slums. You will find omissions. This book is not a history. It is, quite simply, a book about him. In my opinion he was an exceptional man. Denied his chance at greatness, he was cut down after 1,037 days in the White House. Nevertheless, he left an enduring legacy: an example of how a life should be lived. His story may be read for both pleasure and profit.

He had as many names as he had identities. At his confirmation he became John Fitzgerald Francis Kennedy. Most American Catholics abandon their confirmational names, and he was no exception. To friends and relatives he was simply Jack. His fellow PT-boat skippers (Peter Tares) in the Solomons called him Shafty because of his frequent gripe, "I've been shafted," which, emerging from his Boston/Harvard euphonium, was transformed into *shahfted*. In 1946 he became, as he himself wryly put it, the Candidate. Congressman Kennedy followed and was, after six years, succeeded by Senator Kennedy; eight more years passed and on January 20, 1961, he became President Kennedy. His wife called him Bunny; his sister Eunice and his brother Bob, in serious moments, Johnny. The Pentagon knew him as Chief — short for Commander in Chief. To his staff he was sometimes the Tiger; to headline writers, JFK. With friends, the situation determined the form of address. If his only companion was an old acquaintance, he would be Jack, but if an outsider or even a servant entered, he became Mr. President.

Though I first met him in 1946, and was frequently alone with him during his White House years, with Kenneth O'Donnell, his appointments secretary, or another presidential aide, phoning to tell me when to be where, I have tried to remain offstage as much as possible. I was, after all, a mere spectator. Sometimes I have donned the traditional cloaks of anonymity ("The President told a friend"; "Kennedy said privately") but my chief device is the second person ("If you entered the Oval Office that morning, you learned . . ."). The "you" may be the author of this book, or O'Donnell, or Dave Powers, or Arthur Schlesinger, or one of Kennedy's sisters, or any of nearly 150 other men and women who, over the years, have shared with me their recollections and observations — some of which have been previously published. My purpose here is to re-create the past for the reader. If I have been successful, you should feel not only that these events happened, but that they are happening as your eye roves down the page, and that you, "you" — not the author or any other source — are actually there.

My debt to these sharers of memories and thoughts is so immense that I shall not try to sort out and specify my gratitude. Instead, I set down their names here, a roll of gallant and admirable people. They are: members of President Kennedy's family — Joseph P. Kennedy, Jacqueline Kennedy, Robert F. Kennedy, Edward M.

Kennedy, Eunice Kennedy Shriver, Jean Kennedy Smith, and Joe and Ann Gargan; the President's relatives by marriage — Hugh Auchincloss, Janet Auchincloss, Ethel Kennedy, Joan Kennedy, Stanislaus Radziwill, Sargent Shriver, and Stephen Smith; school, college, and navy friends — K. LeMoyne Billings, Paul B. Fay, Jr., James A. Reed, George "Barney" Ross; presidential staff, members of the Kennedy administration, political advisers and associates — John Bailey, George Ball, Charles E. Bohlen, Henry Brandon, Jerry Bruno, McGeorge Bundy, George G. Burkley, Christine Camp, Chester V. Clifton, John B. Connally, Jr., Michael Cook, C. Douglas Dillon, Ralph Dungan, Henry H. "Joe" Fowler, John Kenneth Galbraith, Mary Gallagher, Barbara Gamarekian, Richard N. Goodwin, Jim Greenfield, Edwin O. Guthman, Milton Gwirtzman, Averell Harriman, Fred Holdborn, U. Alexis Johnson, Nicholas deB. Katzenbach, Evelyn Lincoln, John Macy, Dean F. Markham, John McCone, Godfrey McHugh, George J. McNally, Jack McNally, Robert S. McNamara, Bill D. Moyers, Daniel B. Moynihan, Angela Novello, Lawrence F. O'Brien, P. Kenneth (later Kenneth P.) O'Donnell, Mary Ann Orlando, David Powers, Timothy J. Reardon, Jr., George Reedy, Dean Rusk, Pierre Salinger, Arthur M. Schlesinger, Jr., Tazewell Shepard, Theodore C. Sorensen, Arthur Sylvester, Andrew T. Hatcher, Llewellyn Thompson, Nancy Tuckerman, Pamela Turnure, Sue Vogelsinger, Jerome B. Wiesner, and Willard Wirtz; friends, associates, writers, and commentators — Letitia Baldridge, Charles Bartlett, Martha Bartlett, Carmine Bellino, Benjamin C. Bradlee, Tony Bradlee, David Brinkley, Sir Denis W. Brogan, James M. Burns, Jan Burns, Douglass Cater, Richard Cardinal Cushing, Angier Biddle Duke, Robin Duke, David Hackett, Walter Lippmann, Joe McCarthy, Mary McCrory, Bunnie Mellon, Walter I. "Bill" Pozen, Richard H. Rovere, Eric Sevareid, Mrs. Tazewell Shepard, Hugh Sidey, Merriman Smith, Mrs. Potter Stewart, Maxwell Taylor, William Walton, and Theodore H. White; Washington dignitaries and acquaintances — Nicole Alphand, Hale Boggs, Jack S. Brooks, Joan Douglas, William O. Douglas, Dwight D. Eisenhower, J. William Fulbright, Arthur J. Goldberg, J. Edgar Hoover, Hubert H. Humphrey, Mrs. Lyndon B. Johnson, Mike Mansfield, John W. McCormack, Sir David Ormsby-Gore, Elizabeth Pozen, Albert Thomas, John W. Walsh, Earl Warren, Byron White, and Ralph Yarborough; Secret Service agents — Gerald A. Behn, Gerald S. Blaine, Bob Foster, Bill Greer, Clinton J. Hill, Roy Kellerman, Sam Kinney, and Emory P. Roberts; and members of the Air Force One crew and the Kennedy household staffs in the White House and the Hyannis Port Compound — Joseph Ayres, Rita Dallas, Joseph D. Giordano, Lewis Hanson, Jacqueline Hirsch, Providentia Marades, George D. Miller, John J. "Muggsy" O'Leary, James Sasser, Maude Shaw, James Swindal, George Thomas, and J. Bernard West.

None of the above, of course, is answerable for a word in this book. The responsibility is mine alone.

I am profoundly grateful to my editor, Roger Donald, whose suggestions and advice have always been invaluable, but in this book were absolutely indispensable; to Ellen Panarese, for her help in picture research; to Alan Goodrich and the staff of the John F. Kennedy Library in Boston; to Irwin Glusker, who designed the book; and — last but never least — to Melissa Clemence, my copy editor, who had better not predecease me.

W. M.

Wesleyan University
Middletown, Connecticut
August 5, 1983

ONE
BRIEF
SHINING
MOMENT

THEN

All this happened long ago, and millions of Americans now of voting age have no memories of the Kennedy years. They are startled when told that once there was a President — the youngest man ever elected to the office — who was the idol of American youth. Students of the 1950s had been written off as the silent generation; they had made it clear that they wanted no part of the political process. Yet by the third year of the Kennedy presidency, a poll of campuses reported that the Peace Corps was the country's "most admired institution" and the civil service reported a sharp increase in college applicants.

Students were not yet wearing their hair long — the arrival of the Beatles was a few months away — and student interest in hairstyles was largely confined to that of the White House occupant; the president of Chatham College told a reporter that students "can't help feeling some sense of identity with a Commander in Chief who has to have a special haircut to look the part." At the same time, high school girls studied his wife and copied her gestures, her style, her formfitting slacks, and her preference for pink (sometimes called "hot pink"). After Dallas all that would change. Lyndon Johnson succeeded to the presidency, but not to Kennedy's youthful constituency.

JFK's impact was not confined to youth. He inspired in countless Americans of all ages — and both parties — a zeal for achievement, a yearning to test the ancient Athenian maxim that genuine pleasure can be found only in the pursuit of excellence. Unlike most politicians, he never pretended to be a commoner. In his first Massachusetts election his opponents were introduced, one after the other, as Bostonians who had "come up the hard way." Jack took his turn at the microphone and began: "I'm the one who didn't come up the hard way." He was an elegant cum laude graduate of Harvard, a man both cool and concerned, witty and profound, profane and highly eloquent, a Pulitzer Prize winner with a subtle mind and a passion for cutting through clichés. In a single speech he would thread his remarks with quotes from Pericles, Swift, Emerson, Faulkner, and Goethe. He enjoyed playing host at small dinners for scientists, poets, musicians, and intellectuals — Isaac Stern, Igor Stravinsky, Pablo Casals, Robert Frost, W. H. Auden, Paul Tillich, and Allen Tate. "What a joy," said Steinbeck, "that literacy is no longer prima facie evidence of treason." Like many national leaders, Kennedy was thin-skinned about criticism, but he encouraged dissent. If you called on the President one rainy evening in 1962, you saw an elderly scientist, the winner of two Nobel Prizes, picketing the White House in a Ban-the-Bomb demonstration. Inside the Oval Office you mentioned it to Kennedy. He immediately sent the pickets an urn of coffee, boxes of doughnuts, and an invitation to the demonstration's leaders to come inside and state their case. Shortly thereafter he presented the double laureate with a presidential award. Edmund Wilson was similarly honored — even though he had refused to pay his taxes in protest against Pentagon policies.

Abroad, a United States Information Agency poll reported, the prestige of the United States was at an all-time peak. JFK had been decorated for heroism in the war, and his courage was unquestioned; twice he faced down the Russians, over Berlin in 1961 and during the Cuban missile crisis a year later. But his foreign policy was what he called his "Strategy of Peace." In pursuit of it, he carried on a secret correspondence with Nikita Khrushchev, set up the "hot line" between Moscow and Washington, negotiated the test-ban treaty, and established the Arms Control and Disarmament Agency. In the Congo he played the role of peacemaker. Anticipating unrest in Latin America, he founded the Alianza, the Alliance for Progress. His great failure, of course, was Vietnam. But he repeatedly refused to send combat units, and particularly draftees, to Southeast Asia. In Kennedy's last year, seventeen U.S. volunteer advisers were killed in Vietnam. After his assassination, 58,655 Americans died there, most of them conscripts. As Hegel observed, quantitative differences may be so great that they become qualitative.

Ironically, JFK was regarded as antibusiness. Actually, big business — represented by U.S. Steel's Roger Blough — attacked *him*. Kennedy had midwifed a contract with steelworkers, who withdrew demands for higher wages as a dike against inflation. Then the executives of Big Steel, sandbagging the President, boosted their prices by six dollars a ton. The workers felt betrayed; so did the President. He threatened antitrust investigations, the cancellation of tax relief for the industry, and the loss of Pentagon contracts. Three days later the manufacturers surrendered unconditionally. Subsequently, speaking at Yale, the President tried to dispel myths about hostility between industry and government, but the Old Blues simply glowered. They believed that he was robbing the rich.

In reality, Kennedy was enriching the rich, and doing it the only way that counts — by enriching the country. He had studied economics with Walter Heller, and his annual presidential budgets were less than $100 billion. His was the first administration to hold inflation to 3.5 percent while business boomed. During each of his thirty-four months in the White House, all economic indexes increased steadily and the stock market soared. U.S. trade expanded abroad. Ninety-four percent of the labor force was employed; mortgages were between 5 and 5.25 percent; a postage stamp cost a nickel; factory wages were at a new high. Some ninety thousand Americans were then millionaires — and each year the figure was growing by five thousand. Under Kennedy, U.S. investments abroad had leapt from $12 billion to $80 billion. But perhaps his most appealing legacy lies in his compassion. He belonged to one of the wealthiest families in the United States, and he had not seen the misery of rock-bottom American poverty until the West Virginia Democratic primary in the spring of 1960. Deeply

THE IDOL OF AMERICAN YOUTH

moved, he made his first official act as President the issuance of an executive order doubling the food rations for four million needy Americans. Later he launched Medicare and strengthened social security.

His ultimate social issue became civil rights. After Martin Luther King had spoken at the Lincoln Memorial, telling his vast, rapt audience, "I have a dream that one day, on the red hills of Georgia, sons of former slaves and the sons of former slaveowners will be able to sit down together at the table of brotherhood," Kennedy welcomed him to the White House, gripped his hand, and said, "*I* have a dream — the *same* dream." He mounted a militant campaign to enforce desegregation laws, and when the governor of Alabama defied him, Kennedy called out troops. On June 19, 1963, JFK sent a comprehensive and far-reaching civil rights bill to Congress, thereby becoming the first President since Lincoln to put the full force of his office behind racial equality. Gallup reported that, as a result, his popularity plummeted to 59 percent. Kennedy ignored the backlash. He asked the country if when Americans claimed that theirs was the land of the free, they meant "that we have no second-class citizens except Negroes; that we have no class or caste system, no ghettos, no master race except with respect to Negroes?" The question, he said, was a "moral issue." Meeting with black leaders in the Oval Office he said: "This could cost me the election, but we're not turning back." Prodded by Lyndon Johnson, Congress passed the legislation during the national mourning which followed his death. But while Kennedy lived, it was a political millstone around his neck.

His last presidential days were strikingly different from the present time, illuminated by different celebrities. Konrad Adenauer, David Ben-Gurion, and Harold Macmillan had just retired from office. Mme Ngo Dinh Nhu, the sharp-tongued sister-in-law of South Vietnam's despotic president, excoriated the Kennedy administration for its insistence on Vietnamese land reform and its refusal to defend her mandarin family with American marines and GIs. "The Tiger Lady," as the press called her, was particularly angry at David Halberstam, a young *New York Times* correspondent who was convinced that the Saigon regime was doomed. Halberstam's most eminent and most faithful reader was the President of the United States.

The same people who hated the President wanted to impeach Earl Warren, and their anger at the Supreme Court reached a new high when the Court outlawed reading of the Lord's Prayer or verses from the Bible in U.S. public schools. Another Court ruling held that lawyers must be provided for indigent defendants. There was a suspicion that the President and the chief justice were in collusion. They were. Both believed, in Kennedy's inaugural words, that "if a free society cannot help the many who are poor, it cannot save the few who are rich." All this had impact abroad. Kennedy's duel with Big Steel had left a deep impression on leftist reformers in Central America, who had believed that their only hope lay in guerrilla warfare. Anti-Americanism temporarily vanished in the European Left. In Berlin, Willy Brandt frankly patterned his political campaigns on those of the American President. Anthony Sampson wrote in the London *Observer* that "Nenni, the old Italian firebrand socialist, cannot now contain his praise for Kennedy."

These were locust years for Ronald Reagan. He was narrating *The Truth about Communism*, playing host for the weekly television drama "Death

Valley Days," and appearing in his last film, a remake of *The Killers*. In the 1962 congressional elections Reagan had campaigned for John Rousselot, a leading spokesman for the John Birch Society. Richard Nixon, having lost the last California gubernatorial election, was also in political exile. On November 22, 1963, he was an attorney representing Pepsi-Cola. He had addressed a convention of bottlers in Dallas, and left Love Field just two and a half hours before the arrival of Air Force One, bearing the President and his party. Six months before Dallas, Nelson Rockefeller had been the GOP front-runner, but when he divorced his wife to remarry, the spotlight shifted to Barry Goldwater. Earlier in the week of JFK's Texas trip, Goldwater had declaimed that the New Frontier had produced "1,026 days of wasted spending, wishful thinking, unwarranted intervention, wishful theories, and waning confidence." Reporters asked the President to reply. "Not yet," he said, grinning; "not yet," but plainly he relished the prospect of running against the Arizonan.

The nation's First Lady had returned on October 17 from an extended cruise aboard Aristotle Onassis's yacht. Jackie's frequent travels had honed Republican wits — "Good night, Mrs. Kennedy, wherever you are" — and joining her husband on his Texas trip had been, in some respects, an act of contrition. Her elegance hadn't helped his campaigns for lesser offices, but voters plainly regarded her as a magnificent First Lady.

The big stories of 1963, before Dallas, were the March on Washington by 300,000 blacks and whites supporting civil rights; the President's "*Ich bin ein Berliner*" speech in the shadow of Walter Ulbricht's infamous wall; Gordon Cooper's twenty-two orbits of the earth; the four-straight World Series victory of the Dodgers over the Yankees; the tremendous harvest of American farmers and the failure of Soviet crops; and the tracing of botulism deaths to canned tuna.

Selectric typewriters first appeared in 1963; so did Valium, postal zip codes, Weight Watchers, Webster's *Third*, Instamatic cameras, polyethylene, Polaroid color packs, Detroit models featuring sleekly sloping rear windows — "fastbacks" — and the expansion of a chain of hamburger shops called McDonald's. Julia Child appeared on television for the first time; so did the new "Tonight Show," with Johnny Carson. Direct distance dialing was available to less than half of Bell subscribers. The first issue of the *New York Review of Books* appeared on September 26, coincident with a report that Manhattan pollution was approaching toxic levels. Color television was still a rarity — four years would pass before the networks switched to full color. On September 2, 1963, however, CBS Evening News increased its nightly show from fifteen to thirty minutes, and NBC followed suit a week later. These developments were to have profound implications for news coverage of the coming Vietnam War.

But in 1963 all that lay in the future. It was a time of whimsical, ingenious TV commercials. Piels beer was presenting the Return of Bert and Harry. Hertz dropped drivers into convertibles. Popular songs were "If I Had a Hammer"; the Beatles' first success, "I Wanna Hold Your Hand"; and two Peter, Paul, and Mary hits: Bob Dylan's "Blowin' in the Wind," and "Puff the Magic Dragon" ("A dragon lives forever, but not so little boys"). Americans were reading *Silent Spring*, *The Group*, *The American Way of Death*, *Franny and Zooey*, *Thunderball*, *Catch-22*, *Calories Don't Count*, and Victor

Lasky's paste-up philippic, *JFK: The Man and the Myth*. In movie theaters they were enthralled by *Tom Jones* or bored by *Last Year at Marienbad*.

In London a cabinet minister named John Profumo faced disgrace; he had lied to the House of Commons in denying his sexual romps with Christine Keeler, 1963's most distinguished prostitute. (The story fascinated President Kennedy; he couldn't get enough of it.) Richard Burton and Elizabeth Taylor, having fallen in love during the filming of *Cleopatra*, were divesting themselves of their spouses and planning an early wedding. *Look, Life,* and the *Saturday Evening Post* were flourishing, but in none of them would you find the words *hippie, superstar, Super Bowl, freak out, mind-blowing, joints, roach, tune in, turn-off, put-down, rip-off, love-in, flower power, Day-Glo art, psychedelic,* or *vibes*. The Watergate office and apartment complex was under construction near the State Department in Washington. President Kennedy's funeral procession would pass it on Monday, November 25, 1963.

T he country, having lost a President, mourned, then healed. But if you had been close to him, if you had lost an old friend as well as a President, you were permanently scarred. You never knew when a pang would come, or what would set it off — a young woman dressed in black, perhaps, or a little boy playing soldier; a sailboat, a yelping game of touch football, a rocking chair — any of these could touch off the pain, and in your nightmare's memory you would hear the broken roll and dreadful stutter of the muffled drums, the harsh voice of the old cardinal from Southie as he rasped the ritualistic

> *Agnus Dei, qui tollis peccata*
> *mundi, dona eis requiem.*

The years of grief were ineluctable. Yet the time has come to grope for the meaning of that shocking, endless, deeply moving four-day weekend when we each died a little. The President's death was tragic, but his life had been a triumph, and that is how he should be remembered, and celebrated, now.

WE HAPPY FEW

His first hurrah was heard in Boston less than six months after the war. Jack was one of ten candidates in a free-for-all primary, running for Jim Curley's seat in the Eleventh Congressional District. Old, broke, down on his luck, and under a court order to repay forty-two thousand dollars he had stolen from Boston, the "Purple Shamrock" — a.k.a. "The Master" — had decided to resign from Congress and repossess his office in Boston's city hall. On November 2 the Shamrock won the mayoralty in a landslide. Through some unfortunate misunderstanding he was soon back in the dock, however, accused of using the U.S. mails to defraud. Convicted, he governed the city from a cell.

Some grasp of Boston's traditional Irish politics is necessary to understand what Jack Kennedy was up against. During the nineteenth century, in one eight-year period, 1,186,000 immigrants arrived from Ireland. The economy couldn't digest them. Employment agencies hung out signs: IRISH NEED NOT APPLY, or HELP WANTED — NO IRISH. Even after the newcomers had been established for a generation, newspapers carried two society pages, one for Yankee Protestants and the other for Irish Catholics. President Kennedy was the first Irishman to be appointed a Harvard overseer — his father, also a son of Harvard, had been unsuitable — and even the President was ineligible for membership in Boston's Somerset Club. Once at a Beacon Hill cocktail party you remarked to a Kennedy sister that the cobblestones in Louisburg Square were charming. "Those aren't cobblestones," she said bitterly. "They're Irish heads."

Irishwomen took in wash, or went into service. The brightest Irishmen ran for office, and they transformed Boston politics into rollicking vaudeville. One of the gayest entertainers was Jack Kennedy's grandfather John F. Fitzgerald, otherwise known as "Honey Fitz," "Fitzie," or, by the Shamrock, the "Little General." Honey Fitz's signature was "Sweet Adeline," sung with a false-tooth lisp. Once he sang it in Spanish to a crowd of Latin Americans. Shortly thereafter FDR visited Boston. Fitzie was standing on the curb when Roosevelt spotted him and cried joyfully, *El Dulce Adelino!* Like Curley, Fitzie became mayor of Boston, and the two men waged a long, complicated, Byzantine struggle for control of the city. Neither won. The party was unmanageable; a maxim went: "Massachusetts Democrats have a thousand leaders and no followers."

Fitzie, like many of his colleagues, was not above fraud. In one congressional fight — significantly, Boston elections are called fights — voters were given stickers to paste their candidate's name on the ballot. Fitzie had a man in the printing plant who saw to it that there was no stickum on the back of his opponent's stickers. They all fell off the ballots.

Jack was actually present the last time the Shamrock slipped his stiletto into Fitzie. Jack, a friend, and Teddy Kennedy were standing across from the statehouse. Teddy was carrying a green book bag, and he asked his grandfather to hold it while he ran into the drugstore for a candy bar. Fitzie was still holding the bag when Curley, swinging down the street, spotted him. "Ah!" he cried cheerfully. "I see you're still carrying your burglar's tools!"

This was the stage upon which Jack, as serious a man as ever entered politics, had to make his debut. Everyone was looking for another Master, an engaging rogue and public featherbedder who would keep the voters rolling in the aisles while he slipped his hand in the till. They expected a young Curley who would accuse his rivals of contributing to Planned Parenthood, and, when asked to appoint Endicott Peabody Saltonstall to a minor post, inquire: "All three of them?"

Kennedy was sometimes blunt and frequently profane. Like all sailors (and marines) he had learned the language of obscenity and lapsed into it when aroused and among men who understood. Referring to the remark the *New York Times* reported that he had made while battling the steel industry, he recalled: "I didn't call businessmen sons of bitches, I called them pricks." Years later, when Jackie was present, he labeled a newspaper columnist a "Charlie-Uncle-Nan-Tare." His wife asked, "My goodness, what's a Charlie-Uncle-Nan-Tare?" Kennedy changed the subject. He shrank from the promiscuous camaraderie of the Shamrocks and Fitzies, but forced himself to perform like an old campaigner. He would shake hands until his own had swollen a whole glove size because he knew it must be done. Shy and reserved rather than folksy, he was ill at ease in such political haunts as Sully's Tavern, or the bar of the old Bellevue Hotel, across from the statehouse. His distaste for campaign clichés and high-pressure politicking was obvious. To working-class constituents his sophisticated wit was baffling and, at times, patronizing. He didn't even look old enough to be a congressman. When a Japanese warship cleaved his torpedo boat in half he had been badly hurt; ever since a prewar football injury his spine had been painful, and the sea action had consigned him to a life of incessant pain. In Chelsea Naval Hospital his weight had dropped below 140 pounds. His gauntness and his thick, bushy hair emphasized his boyishness.

In his role as the Candidate, he refused to discuss patronage. Others in the race were promising the moon, but Jack believed that people supported him because they thought he would make a good congressman. That was to be his attitude throughout his career. As President he discovered an incompetent employee and asked an aide, "What's he doing in the government?" The aide replied: "His imagination was fired by your eloquence, your dedication, your zeal." Kennedy nodded shortly. "Yes, that happens," he said, "but would you please explain what he's doing in the government?"

He had been born in the Boston suburb of Brookline on May 29, 1917. In 1926, however, his father, Joseph P. Kennedy — always known to family and friends as "the ambassador" — rather than live with the Hub's prejudice against the Irish, moved his family to New York. They spent their summers on Cape Cod and winters at Palm Beach, which became Joe and Rose's voting address in 1934. Although born in Brookline, Jack knew little about Boston, and even less about its politics. He learned the importance of joining the Holy Name parade, Charlestown's Bunker Hill parade, and, in South Boston (Southie), the Saint Patrick's Day parade, always led by three-hundred-pound Knocko McCormack, the future Speaker's nephew, straddling a rented truck horse. In Southie, Jack marched with other members of VFW Post 5880, which had been named for his brother Joe Jr., who had been killed in August 1944 after volunteering for a dangerous mission in Europe. But there is more to politics than parades. Jack had to reach the key pols, and he didn't even know who they were. It took him three months to discover that Mother Galvin was not a woman, but Bill Galvin, a ward leader who had been rechristened because of his many kindnesses to the people of Charlestown.

But Kennedy was eager to learn; he always would be. Standing atop the old Boston El one afternoon, he was shown a panoramic view of the Eleventh Congressional District. At that height, about sixty feet, you could see East Boston, the birthplace of both his father and his grandfather. The North End, where his mother was born, was now mostly Italian; the East End was still solidly Irish. Looking down, Jack could see the Charlestown longshoremen, freight handlers, truck drivers, and stevedores on the dock. Speaking softly, almost to himself, he said: "These are the kind of people I want to represent."

The pros didn't believe he'd make it. Dan O'Brien, a powerful ward boss, studied him contemptuously and said: "You're not going to win this fight. You're a carpetbagger. You don't belong here." The other pols agreed. How could a millionaire's son, a Harvard man whose address was room 306 at the Bellevue, beat nine popular Bostonians, including an ex-WAC major who campaigned in uniform and two Italians, both named Joseph Russo? (Later a *third* Joseph Russo threw his hat in the ring; his slogan was "Vote for the One in the Middle.") The bosses' scorn grew when they heard of Kennedy's "Junior Brains Trust." The trustees were his school and service friends: Torbert Macdonald, who had been his roommate in Weld Hall, on the Yard; Ben Smith, another Harvard classmate; LeMoyne Billings, who had roomed with him at Choate; and such PT skippers as Jim Reed and Paul B. Fay, Jr., a.k.a. Red Fay, a.k.a. the Redhead, a.k.a. Grand Old Lovable. In fact, these pals were not completely ineffective. And even if they had been completely feckless, their presence signified one of three Kennedy political principles. Traditional pols, as he would later explain, practiced exclusivity. What the voters didn't know couldn't hurt office seekers. Kennedy preferred what he called *in*clusivity. If someone wanted to help, he was given a job; participants would convert their friends and relatives. Eventually, during his last Massachusetts fight, he had 21,286 volunteers. Another Kennedy tactic was underdoggery. If you expected 30 percent of the vote, you told the press you anticipated 20 percent; when the returns came in you would express delighted surprise and claim a sweep, even a landslide. Last, there was hallmanship: never hire a hall unless you are absolutely certain that every seat will be occupied. Cameramen love to photograph empty seats. It was

*JFK's paternal grand-
parents: Mary Hickey
Kennedy (circa 1890)
and state senator P. J.
Kennedy*

FOREBEARS

*JFK's maternal grandparents: John
F. Fitzgerald ("Honey Fitz"; circa
1907) and Mary Josephine Hannon
Fitzgerald*

*Mayor Honey Fitz at Old Home Week
parade, July 29, 1907, flanked by
Edward Everett Hale (l) and Master Fiske
of Boston Latin School (r)*

A beach party in 1907: P. J. Kennedy, Rose Fitzgerald, and Honey Fitz are respectively second, third, and fourth from the left, Joseph P. Kennedy, Sr. (JFK's father), is second from the right

Mayor Honey Fitz handing out Christmas baskets to the needy, 1911

Honey Fitz and P. J. Kennedy at a fox hunt in North Carolina, 1911

The Hannon family: Rose is at bottom, center; her mother, Mary Josephine, is at extreme right

much better to have a smaller room overflowing. That way, people would say next day: "I went to the Kennedy rally and couldn't get a seat — it was packed."

The real key to that first postwar primary in the Eleventh was — as in all his elections thereafter — the Candidate himself. He was still the self-effacing, self-deprecating tyro then, but in time he would be recognized as a master politician. Already he was studying the Eleventh, ward by ward. After he became a senator the district would be represented by Thomas P. "Tip" O'Neill, Jr. Analyzing the returns in 1952 and 1958, when Tip ran for Congress and Jack for the Senate, Kennedy found that a precinct had given him four more votes than O'Neill. Together they examined the voting list and discovered that his extra votes came from a family of French-Canadians who disliked Tip. On January 20, 1961, Kennedy's first day as President, he spotted O'Neill across an inaugural ballroom. "Hey, Tip," he shouted, "how many votes did you get in the North Cambridge precinct — and how many did I get?" Tip yelled back the returns. Kennedy grinned widely: "That Lefebre family is still voting against you!"

Early in 1946, however, he was no professional. And he knew it. He turned, as he always had, to his father. Joe Kennedy's name was no asset in an election; he was remembered as the isolationist ambassador in London who had been willing to abandon England and whom Roosevelt had been forced to fire. No man who had failed America's greatest Democratic President was likely to arouse enthusiasm in Boston or any other Democratic stronghold. But Joe could work behind the scenes; he possessed a powerful intellect, over two hundred million dollars, and friends in the right places. The ambassador's first cousin was Joe Kane — they always addressed each other as "Cousin Joe" — a bald, crusty, cynical, wise politico who had spent most of his life in a cafeteria near city hall, sitting over a coffee cup, keeping his ears open. Cousin Joe put the arm on Cousin Joe, and Kane made his first contribution to Jack's faltering campaign with a slogan: "The New Generation Offers a Leader — John F. Kennedy." Kane recruited Bill Sutton, a shrewd campaigner just out of the army, and Sutton in turn urged Jack to call on Dave Powers, another veteran, who had sold newspapers at the Charlestown Navy Yard before the war, ushered at five Saint Catherine's masses every Sunday, coached parochial school teams, and knew just about every voter in Charlestown by his first name.

On the bitter evening of Monday, January 21, 1946, Jack climbed the steps of the three-decker tenement at 88 Ferrin Street, Charlestown, to the top-floor Powers home. Inside, Dave was sipping a beer and enjoying the leisure of the 52-20 Club — twenty dollars a week for fifty-two weeks for job-hunting veterans. At the first knock Dave opened the door and saw a skinny youth who held out his hand and said: "My name is Jack Kennedy. I'm a candidate for Congress." Dave explained that he was virtually committed to another man in the race and that he thought Kennedy a lost cause. Nevertheless, he agreed to accompany him Saturday evening to a meeting of Gold Star Mothers in Charlestown's American Legion Hall.

Curley had said, in a misanthropic mood, "There are only two political issues in Boston: 'All Ireland must be free' and 'Trieste belongs to Italy.'" That Saturday, in the Legion Hall, Kennedy proved the Master's contempt wrong, and he did it in the presence of Powers, the best and brightest of Boston's rising political generation. Jack spoke only ten minutes. He talked of the sacrifices made during the war, the need for lasting world peace, and the responsibilities of the veterans who had survived. *Politics* was not a bad word, he said. Serious politicians should be honored; without them, democracy would not work. Citing his favorite book, *Pilgrim's Way,* he quoted John Buchan's definition of democracy as "primarily an attitude of mind, a spiritual testament" in which politics was "still the greatest and most honorable adventure." He then said: "The complacent, the soft, the self-indulgent societies will be swept away with the debris of history." To permit that would "betray all the brave men who gave their all for freedom." He paused and ended gently: "I think I know how all you mothers feel. You see, my mother is a Gold Star Mother, too."

Women rose and surged toward the platform, grasping his hand, smiling with tears in their eyes, telling one another that Jack was just like their Kevin, or Mike, or Patrick. To Dave it was a revelation. Until then the chief political tribute to vets had been the Purple Shamrock standing on the steps of the city hall, leading his followers in a weepy chorus of "My Buddy." Jack was offering something new, exciting, and powerful. Outside, Kennedy asked him how it had gone. Powers replied: "You were terrific. I've never seen such a reaction." Jack asked: "Then you'll be with me?" Dave held out his hand and said: "I've already started working for you."

Dave's first job was to rent a vacant third-floor office at 18 Tremont Street as Kennedy headquarters. Thereafter this office and the third floor of the Bellevue were the eyes of Jack's developing storm. Dave began registering veterans and mailing each of them a *Reader's Digest* reprint of John Hersey's "Survival," an account of Kennedy's gallantry which had originally appeared in the *New Yorker.* Jack felt uneasy — "There's something wrong about parlaying a sunken PT boat into a congressional seat" — but Powers told him it was too good a card to be left unplayed. Dave pointed out that Jack's valor lay, not in the loss of his boat, but in saving his crew and bringing them back safely through Japanese waters, 150 miles from U.S. bases. He had been decorated for "extremely heroic conduct," when, "unmindful of personal danger," he had rescued PT-109's men on the night of August 1–2, 1943. His citation ended: "His courage, endurance, and excellent leadership contributed to the saving of several lives and was in keeping with the highest traditions of the United States Naval Service."

Jack's amateurs and Kane's pros were working in tandem now, and a roll call of their names, like names chiseled on a war monument, brings back memories of comradeship, ebullience, and absolute loyalty to the Candidate: Dobie, McLaughlin, Kelly, Dalton, McGoff in the Boston wards; Reardon and MacDonald in Somerville; Billings, Dalton, Droney, and Healey in Cambridge; Ward and Broderick in Brighton; Sutton in Charlestown; Rosetti and De Marco in the Italian North End; in the West End, Grace Burke, who, despite her femininity, could have survived with the toughest in a Pier Six brawl. Most days their expectations were high, but there were gloomy moments. Ferrin Street was enemy territory. Another candidate — a former Curley aide — was popular there, and every time Powers went home his neighbors heckled him. "Never mind, Dave," Jack said with a smile. "Years from now you can say you were with me on Saint

THE
EARLY
YEARS

Rose Kennedy holding Bobby, with Joe Jr. and Jack beside her

Joe Kennedy, Sr., holding Joe Jr. and Jack

Joe Jr. and Jack

The family at their Boston home in 1934 (from the left): Edward, Jean, Robert, Patricia, Eunice, Kathleen, Rosemary, John, Rose, and Joe Sr. (Joe Jr. is not shown)

Bobby, Jack, Eunice, Jean, Joe Sr., Rose, Pat, Kathleen, Joe Jr., and Rosemary

Jack with his sisters Rosemary, Kathleen, and Eunice at the Cape

Dexter School picture, 1927;
Jack is in first row, far right

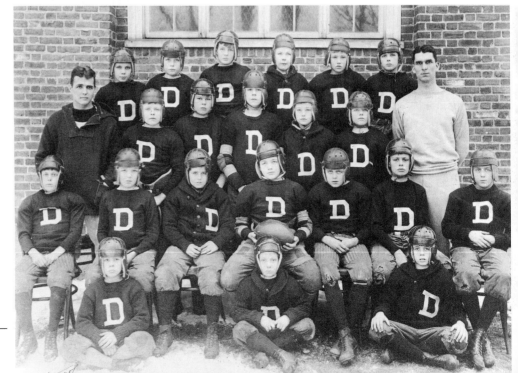

The Dexter School football team;
Jack is in first row, far right, Joe Jr.
is in second row, third from left

A senior at Choate, 1935

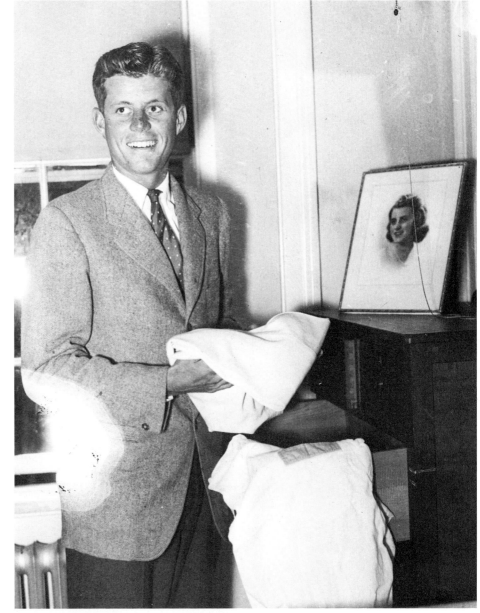

Freshman at Harvard

The family at Hyannis Port, 1937

Crispin's day." Dave stared at him blankly. Jack quoted the splendid passage, editing it slightly to conceal the author's national origin:

This story shall the good man teach his son;
And Crispin Crispian shall ne'er go by,
From this day to the ending of the world,
But we in it shall be remembered;
We few, we happy few, we band of brothers;
For he, to-day, that sheds his blood with me,
Shall be my brother; be he ne'er so vile,
This day shall gentle his condition:
And gentlemen in safe homes now abed,
Shall think themselves accurs'd they were not here;
And hold their manhoods cheap, while any speaks
That fought with us upon Saint Crispin's day.

Jack had been Harvard '40, and there were still characters who remembered him as the most inquisitive student in Arthur Holcombe's upperclass course, Government 7. If, while crossing Boston Common, you met a wartime acquaintance who had been one of Kennedy's classmates, and told him you were curious about the city's newest fledgling politician, you were led to the nearby Bellevue and introduced. It was a very brief introduction. Kennedy was on his way to a rally. Your fleeting impression was of a thick shock of chestnut hair and oddly opaque blue eyes: hooded, friendly but impenetrable. There was the usual vet-to-vet banter; you had been a marine on Guadalcanal when he was stationed at a base for PT boats (or "Peter Tares," as he called them) on nearby Tulagi, another Solomons island visible from the Canal. Kennedy admired the marines — "the first team," he called them — and he suggested that you return in the afternoon. Mornings, he said, he was out of touch. By 6:00 A.M. each day he was standing beside cold, dark factory gates, or waterfront docks, or at the Charlestown Navy Yard, shaking hands with arriving workmen. At 8:15, when the last of them had punched his time card, he would have breakfast in a diner. At nine o'clock he was back on the job, making calls in the tenements like a door-to-door salesman, astounding and then delighting housewives. Afternoons would be spent strolling down streets, shaking hands in groceries, meat markets, taverns, department stores, fire stations, police stations, and barbershops. Four o'clock would find him back at the factories and docks, greeting men who had finished their shift. Back at the Bellevue he would rest. Evenings would be spent in a whirlwind tour of at least a half-dozen house parties, the typical volunteer hostess being a typist, switchboard operator, or schoolteacher who would gaze at him with starstruck eyes while he sipped Cokes and nibbled sandwiches, stealing furtive glances at his watch.

The Purple Shamrock had never done that. In Boston it was unheard of. (But hearing about it, Curley became the only veteran politician in the state to predict a Kennedy victory.) Jack spent one day each week in one of the district's communities — Cambridge on Mondays, Somerville on Tuesdays, Brighton on Wednesdays, and so forth. His mother and sisters held tea parties open to the public; over a thousand women had turned out for the first of them, at Cambridge's Hotel Commander. Nothing was taken for granted. The evening before election day Kennedy and several friends were tooling down Arlington Street when Kennedy saw an old lady dead ahead, trying to cross the street. "Stop!" ordered the Candidate. He leapt out and helped the woman hobble over to the opposite curb. When he returned, somebody in the backseat blurted out: "Jesus, you really *do* want them all, don't you?"

The best time to find him at the hotel was just before dinner. The door to 306 was usually ajar. You put your head in, feeling like an intruder, and uneasily called out his name. His cordial, if starchy, accent greeted you from the bathroom. ("I'm in *heah*.") With the possible exception of Winston Churchill, Jack may have taken more baths than any politician in history. It wasn't that he felt unclean; long soaks in hot baths relieved his back pains. It was an odd place for serious conversation, but since he showed no embarrassment, sitting there and talking to him soon seemed natural. In the '52 campaign he would acquire a board stretched across the bathtub, bearing his safety razor, shaving soap, and a book rest, but in those early days he juggled toiletries and volumes from time to time, not always successfully, with the result that one or two books were always drying out. On the floor that afternoon were copies of Lord David Cecil's *Young Melbourne* and Alfred Duff Cooper's *Talleyrand*, both spread open. As you entered he had been reading Bulwer-Lytton, whom he quoted with approval: "When it is not necessary to change it is necessary not to change." It is doubtful that any twentieth-century American politician has been more well read. These "tub talks," as they came to be called, performed a useful service for him: they took his mind off contemporary politics; shoptalk was tacitly forbidden, though the authors he read occasionally proved useful on the stump. Sometimes, bored with campaigning, Jack would alter lines familiar to him but not, he knew, to his audience: "Scollay Square is lovely, dark and deep/But I have promises to keep/And miles to go before I sleep."

Ideas intrigued him, provided they worked; pure theory would start him fiddling with the razor, a sure sign of irritation. His manner was wry yet engaging; his intellect penetrating, inquisitive, analytic, but pragmatic. You felt from the outset that he was genuinely interested in you and your opinions. Before the war, he told you, he had started carrying a little black loose-leaf notebook in which he would write phrases worth remembering. He still had it. In the tub he would quote Andrew Jackson: "One man with courage makes a majority." "Courage" appeared often in the little book and in his conversations; that and drive ("*vigah*") were, he thought, man's most admirable qualities. "Everyone admires courage," he would say, "and the greenest garlands are for those who possess it."

Despite his illnesses and his weight loss, you could see, as he gingerly stepped from the tub, favoring his back, that he was a well-built man: six feet tall, with tousled hair, a straight mouth, skin coarsened by the sea; the first trace of furrows across his brow and around his eyes, lines that would later deepen; and those extraordinary eyes, which, if he felt hostile or be-

WORLD WAR II

Lieutenant John F. Kennedy in the Solomon Islands

The crew aboard PT-109

Being decorated for heroism, June 1944

Members of the PT-109 crew in Hyannis Port, 1944

trayed, could be riveting, even intimidating. His shoulders and arms were muscular, his legs solid; if he could build his weight up to 170 pounds, you thought, he would have the build of a light-heavyweight boxer. He was, you sensed, a nice guy who would never finish last.

Later he would become a fashion plate, but in those days he wore mismatched socks, rumpled shirts and jackets, neckties badly knotted; brown shoes and a blue suit. His hands were — and would always be — the key to his anxiety. This was particularly true in public speaking. The audience never saw it; from out there he seemed to be a model of poise. But if you were behind him on the platform, you could see both hands trembling, even shaking. If he was restless, which was often, he would pull up his socks, or toy absently with a phone, or arrange items on a desk and then rearrange them, or tap his upper lip lightly with his index finger, or brush the hair over his forehead with the full palm of his hand. It was at about this time that someone said: "Jack doesn't sit in a chair; he bivouacs in it." Slouching deeply in the seat, he would prop up his feet on a table or whatever piece of furniture was handy, flicking his fingernails over his teeth or tucking in his tie, even when it wasn't out.

Barney Ross, a fellow PT veteran, said: "The word for Jack is *Go.*" It was true, even when he didn't appear to know where he was going. If you asked him a question he hadn't expected, or didn't want to answer, he would quickly say, "What?" and turn away. One issue in that campaign, seldom resolved until the last moment, was when or where to eat. Suddenly he would realize that he was hungry and had to do something about it. Stumping the district, he usually ate hamburgers and drank frappes, as Bostonians call milk shakes. Later, in his father's home, you would discover that the cook always kept a huge tureen of clam chowder for him in the kitchen; he could devour bowls of it with a zeal and speed that can only be called gluttonous. During drinks before parties he would limit himself to a daiquiri or a scotch and water, which he would sip from time to time and never finish. The only wine he couldn't resist was Dom Pérignon.

When he entered a room with his curious gait, half lope and half glide, women perked up and patted their hair. If on the prowl for a playmate he seldom left, so to speak, empty-handed; in Lem Billings's words, "Jack always had lots of girls and did quite well with them." But when running for office, his serious side was in complete control, and he became the despair of hostesses. Once handed a drink, he would head for a fellow guest who could increase the Candidate's knowledge or help advance his career. Some people found this offensive. His ambition was so very naked; they wished he would camouflage it a little. Later, as President, he would. But young men headed for the top are often unattractive. If Jack found himself stuck with a bore he simply turned on his heel and walked away. And he had a disconcerting habit of reaching into his pocket, just as dinner was about to begin, and popping a caramel or a chocolate into his mouth. While campaigning, his only decent meal was breakfast: fresh orange juice to wash down a vitamin pill, two four-and-a-half-minute boiled eggs, four strips of broiled bacon, toast, and coffee. On Fridays, unless he was among close friends, the bacon was omitted.

If you were on the town with him, you quickly discovered that he couldn't pass a newsstand without buying the latest editions. Folding the

paper lengthwise, he would devour the print, his eyes sweeping down columns at unbelievable speed. His absorption was total. You had to keep your eye on his coat and his black alligator briefcase; he was always leaving them behind. At least once a day he would borrow your pencil or comb. And he never seemed to have any money. The party's fund-raising drives embarrassed him, but he never hesitated to lean on a friend. He would ask you for a dollar to buy a newspaper and then keep the change. In church he would whisper: "I want them to know I'm a generous candidate. Slip me a ten." It took him so long to repay a loan that you considered charging him interest. Once his mother, who was campaigning for her son, spent a trip in a cab describing Jack's virtues to the cabbie. When she reached her destination he told her she owed him her fare and another $1.85. Rose indignantly asked why. He said: "Because your son took this cab last night, and when we got there he found he was broke."

He was the world's worst loser. If he had to pay off he carried on as though he were coughing up the national debt. In golf, on the first tee, he explained his complicated system of side bets, which only he understood, and which almost guaranteed that he would come out ahead. Here was a man who, under the terms of his father's trust fund, had become a millionaire while still in boarding school, and could raise almost any sum of money with a phone call, manipulating stakes of dimes and quarters. He liked Monopoly for a while but then tired of it, as he later tired of backgammon, charades, Chinese checkers, and bridge, all for the same reason: he couldn't always come out ahead. Once you asked him if he minded you quitting games. He grinned. "Not if you're winning." Another time, during a checker game, with you clearly ahead, he suddenly erupted in a tremendous cough and the pieces scattered all over the floor. "Oh shit," he said. "Now we'll have to start all over again." Furious, you accused him of violating moral parameters. He asked you to repeat that; then he wrote it down in his little black book.

His favorite diversion was motion pictures, and like many of his generation, he considered *Casablanca* the greatest picture of all time. But on entering a theater he had to hunt for a seat behind an empty seat. Sitting at a movie, in a chair, on a couch, in a cab — anywhere — was difficult for him because of his back. He required a prop for his knees, and he needed to change position every few minutes. If a movie bombed, his pain threshold was low and he would whisper: "Let's haul our ass out of here." He never left a good one, though. His favorites that year were *The Lost Weekend*, *The Bells of Saint Mary's*, and *Henry V*. When Laurence Olivier cried, "We happy few," Jack gripped your arm and whispered: "Terrific!"

Compared with his senatorial campaigns of 1952 and 1958, not to mention his drive for the presidency in 1960, his congressional fight of 1946 was clumsy and amateurish. Many of Kane's old-timers, irritated by Jack's Ivy Leaguers, quit in disgust. His first radio speech — there was, of course, no TV — was almost canceled because he didn't reach the studio until the last minute. He was so disorganized that the appearance of his name on the ballot was technically illegal. One of the Tremont Street volunteers had asked casually: "Jack, when did you file your nomination papers?" The Candidate was stunned. "My God," he gasped, "they haven't been filed." It was 6:30 P.M.; the deadline had passed at 5:00 P.M., and the appropriate office was closed. Desperate phone calls were made, money changed hands — all funds had to come from the ambassador's assistant Edward Moore, who demanded that requisitions be submitted in triplicate — and a clerk opened the office so that Jack could complete the necessary forms and pay the fee. People put up with this sort of thing because they found his charm irresistible. His mother, however, was another matter. For weeks Joe Kane had been begging Jack to wear a hat; his youth was a handicap, Joe argued, and a hat would make him look older. After trying on every sample in a shop, he left wearing one. It had taken so long that he was very late for a rally. His mother stood at the lectern, holding the audience. When he finally turned up, he pointed to his head and asked Rose: "How do I look?" She replied witheringly: "You would have looked a lot better two hours ago."

Jack's problem, from the day he entered the race, had been his father. Opponents accused Kennedy of trying to buy a congressional seat. (Those who had to fill out Ed Moore's forms knew that if Joe was buying, he was buying on the cheap.) Jack's instinct, when challenged, was to attack. Just as he would rout anti-Catholic bigots in 1960, now he struck back at his accusers in Boston. His eyes blazing, he turned on one tormentor: "I don't have to apologize for myself or any of the Kennedys. I'm running for Congress. Let's stick to that. If you want to talk about my family, I'll meet you outside." His most dramatic moment came when he was heckled by Joe O'Toole, a notorious Curley henchman. "Where do you live?" O'Toole shouted. "New York? Palm Beach? Not Boston. You're a goddamned carpetbagger." In a voice like a file Jack replied: "Listen, you bastard [*bahstard*]. Nobody wanted to know where my brother was from when he volunteered for the mission that cost him his life. Nobody asked my address when I was on PT-109."

Until then he had resembled a British aristocrat seeking to represent a working-class constituency. Paul Dever said, "Jack is the first Irish Brahmin." In fact, he was an anglophile, and in many ways resembled a member of Britain's upper class. But he was proud of being one hundred percent Irish. "The rest of you," he later told a group of friends in the White House, "are mongrelized." Someone couldn't resist asking: "And your children?" "What?" he said hurriedly and raised another subject. His answer to O'Toole had been a magnificent non sequitur, but his anger was also Irish, and that was why the audience cheered it. His daring was Irish, and so were his wit; his love of politics, lost causes, and outrageous practical jokes; his toughness; and his romantic view of history. By the middle of May the voters were beginning to sense that. Here was an Irishman who wasn't ashamed of his Harvard degree, who never asked, "How's Mother? Tell her I said hello," and never appeared at wakes unless he had known the man well. Francis Russell, the Boston political writer, noted that after "half a century of oafishness . . . this attractive, well-spoken, graceful, witty, Celtic, Harvard-bred, and very rich young man was what every suburban matron would like her son to be. In fact, many of them came to see Jack *as* their son."

He was the first politician with something to say to voters under twenty-five. (A later study showed that if everyone over thirty had stayed away from the polls in that first campaign, his landslide would have been historic. Jack immediately proposed that the voting age be lowered to nine.) Finally, he had learned to enjoy greeting strangers and asking for their vote.

It surprised him; it surprised his family, too. One day his father was in East Boston's Maverick Square when he saw his son emerge from a car across the street and head for a group of tough blue collar workers on the corner, offering his hand, identifying himself, and asking for their support. The ambassador said: "I never thought he had it in him." Arthur Krock said afterward: "He made himself over; he became a new man."

Primary day was June 18. As the first returns came in it was clear that Kennedy was on his way. He came out of Boston with 10,170 votes, increased his lead by over 4,000 votes in Brighton, and outscored the Italians in their North End stronghold. Overall, he had doubled the vote of his closest competitor. Now that he represented the Eleventh District — Boston was so heavily Democratic that the general election was a formality — he decided to live in it. He acquired a rather faded four-room apartment at 122 Bowdoin Street, around the corner from the Bellevue. Rose arrived to put down carpeting. Joe Murphy, the building's janitor, seemed always at hand, ready to brew an acceptable cup of coffee, and the furniture, though shabby, was comfortable. There were rumors that a remarkable number of attractive, well-bred young Boston women found their way to 122 Bowdoin. You once asked Jack the secret of his romantic triumphs. With that charming tact he reserved for friends, he said: "Some guys have got it, and some haven't. You haven't got it." It was the kind of answer the question had deserved. Jack would lay it on you that way, enjoy your discomfort, and then give you something you had always wanted and never dared to ask for. In this case it was an invitation to spend a weekend in Hyannis Port, the fief of his father, the powerful, ruthless, and unbelievably opulent Joseph P. Kennedy.

To Jack, Hyannis Port was Home. Even when, in his last year as President, curious tourists made life there unbearable, he rented a sprawling, weathered cottage on nearby Squaw Island, in walking distance across a causeway from the Compound. He needed the Cape; needed, as he put it, "to feel the salt in my face." In that summer when he was resting after his primary victory, the Compound, as the nation would come to know it during the Kennedy presidency, did not exist. Hyannis Port comprises about a hundred roomy, solidly built, shingled or clapboard homes, separated from one another by low stone New England walls or manicured hedges. The ambassador's home, near the juncture of Scudder and Irving avenues, was known to its WASP neighbors as "the Irish house." He had acquired it in 1929. Later, after Jack and Bobby had acquired the two homes contiguous to it, the Irish house became the Big House, and the barbered lawn within the triangle became a playground for Kennedys of all ages and their guests — a Compound. But in 1946 the only Kennedy house there was their father's. Sided unpretentiously in white clapboards with green shutters, it was nevertheless vast: there were seventeen rooms and quarters for servants. The beach was a few feet away. Various craft, including Jack's sailboat *Victura*, were tethered to the wharf. Gulls wheeled overhead, darting down when they spotted food below; gray feathery tufts of beach rushes curtsied softly in a sighing breeze. As you alighted from the congressman-elect's

*Campaigning
on crutches*

FIRST
ELECTION

The new congressman

Three generations:
Honey Fitz, Joe Sr.,
and JFK

*Relaxing in Hyannis Port
after his victory*

Celebrating with parents and grandparents

convertible you thought that Hyannis Port must be an ideal place for relaxation.

You could not have been farther wrong. If you had known what lay ahead, you would have spent a week *training*. Around the house members of the Kennedy tribe darted back and forth, playing tag, kick-the-can, and, of course, touch football, all with a teeth-grinding physical tenacity, pushing themselves to the limits of endurance, and sometimes beyond the pale of fair play, in order to win. Win what? It didn't matter; they had been raised to compete, to finish *first*. Rose, who seemed to be completely dominated by the ambassador, explained serenely: "My husband is quite a strict father; he likes the boys to win at sports and everything they try. If they don't win, he will discuss their failure with them, but he doesn't have much patience with the loser." That was putting it gently. If they lost, and he felt they hadn't made their best effort, they would be sent from the dinner table in disgrace. Jack and his older brother, Joe Jr., had been entered in swimming races when they were so small their heads were invisible from the shore. Their father would give them a pep talk beforehand: "Come in a winner; second place is no good."

In most families, boys are warned not to pick on their younger brothers. Joe Kennedy believed in muscular laissez-faire. Joe Jr. was not only older, he was taller, stronger, and, as Jack recalled, had "a pugnacious personality. Later on it smoothed out, but it was quite a problem in my boyhood." Rose said: "Joe was so much stronger than Jack, and if there was a physical encounter, Joe really whacked him." Jack was the same; when Teddy was small, he was afraid to leave his bedroom, because he knew Jack was waiting to smack him over the head with a pillow. A friend of the ambassador's later recalled that the Kennedy sons "were always knocking themselves out. I can remember when one or the other of the boys would be picked up unconscious; they were always bandaged and bruised all over." After a collision between Jack and Joe Jr., Jack had to be sent to the hospital for twenty-eight stitches.

All this, of course, was a violation of every accepted principle in modern child-raising. Yet everyone who came to know them was struck by the abiding love between parents and children, between brothers and sisters. And it is doubtful that, had Jack Kennedy been raised by a conventional father, he could have survived the sinking of his boat in the Solomons. His older brother died a hero's death in Europe; he himself became a congressman, senator, and President. One of his younger brothers became an outstanding attorney general before his election to the Senate; the other brother, also a senator, will be regarded as a presidential contender for the rest of his life, unless, of course, he is actually elected.

The immediate consequence of their upbringing was behavior that produced astonishment among their peers. Jack, in the Harvard infirmary, really sick with the grippe, sneaked out evenings to swim forty laps in the college pool, hoping to make the varsity swimming team. He failed, but, as he explained later, "I tried, I participated, and that's what mattered." Bobby, the only Kennedy to make the Harvard football team, broke his leg yet kept playing until Kenny O'Donnell, the team captain, had him carried, protesting, from the field. John Tunney, Teddy's law-school roommate, was standing on a sidewalk with him, and they were tossing a football back and forth, when Ted suggested they try a little contact. Tunney thought he was joking. The next thing he knew, he was flattened. "I couldn't believe it," Tunney recalls. "There we were in our street clothes . . . throwing each other on the concrete with full tackles!"

Three of the Kennedy sisters — Pat, Eunice, and Jean — were in their late teens or early twenties, throbbing with energy and ready for the next game, whatever it was. Rosemary, twenty-eight and retarded, was in a Wisconsin convent; her father, furious when told of her handicap, had dismissed psychiatrist after psychiatrist until, finding them unanimously against him, he agreed to have her institutionalized. He never spoke of her; it almost seemed as though he regarded her condition as a stain on his honor. Another sister was in Europe: Kathleen ("Kick"), Jack's favorite. Against the wishes of both families — the groom's parents were relentless Protestants — Kick had married the heir to a dukedom. Shortly afterward he had been killed while fighting on a Normandy beachhead. Kick herself later died in a European plane crash. The ambassador, who could salvage distinction even from death, said: "If my daughter Kathleen and her husband had lived, I would be the father of the Duchess of Devonshire and the father-in-law of the head of all the Masons in the world."

In rare deference to Rose's wishes, the ambassador had agreed to send the girls to parochial schools, but they were just as aggressive as their brothers. You had always thought of one-hand touch football as a safe, graceful sport. In Hyannis Port you learned otherwise. Kennedy touch rules were simple. There was to be no blocking. The defensive team could not cross the line of scrimmage until the quarterback had the ball in his hands. Then you could rush him. But the offense could pass the ball at any time, anywhere, either backward or forward. Bobby was there that weekend, having been discharged from the navy on Memorial Day; despite his father's vehement protests, he had joined up as an enlisted man when Joe Jr. was killed. He and Jack were opposing quarterbacks. You were on Jack's side, and in the huddle he said, "We'll try the perfect Melacreamo." You said, "The *what?*" He explained: "I'll center the ball to you and fake downfield. Bobby will think I'm going down for a pass. You drop deep, and I'll come back for a lateral. Eunice will be too late rushing, and before Bobby can run in to take you, you'll be down and clear for a pass." It actually worked. He threw you a perfect strike and you scored. You felt elated until you saw the dangerous glint in Bob's eye. Thereafter the game got much more physical; the girls kicked, screamed, scratched and clawed. Bobby seemed to have seventeen elbows. No blocking, my eye; the members of this eminent family were committing fouls that would have disqualified them in pro games. There was something Dantesque about it, evocative of being tossed about by sinister forces. In the end Bobby won. Later you learned that he *always* won. He always had the best plays, and his need to win seemed even greater than Jack's.

Their father came out to greet his new guest and watch the last few plays. A slender, erect man with sandy hair combed straight back and horn-rimmed glasses which gave him an owlish appearance, he clapped as Bobby broke free and ran for the winning touchdown. The ambassador said: "He hates like me." It wasn't true. Bob was certainly a ferocious fighter. You ought to know: once he battered you unmercifully. But he didn't *hate* you.

He was a lover, not a hater. He loved justice, and ultimately would love needy Americans, migrant fruit pickers, wetbacks — people whose votes were negligible, but who deserved security and dignity. He was naturally gentle; he established immediate rapport with children; and it was Bob, not the liberal professors in his brother's administration, who became its conscience. During the Cuban missile crisis, when the President's advisers were leaning toward a surprise air strike, Bob ended the discussion, estimating civilian casualties and saying: "For a hundred and seventy-five years we have not been that kind of people."

Nevertheless, he was a tremendous competitor. After he married Ethel — who became a great wide receiver — he put each of his children in the internecine battles almost as soon as they could walk. "Let's win this one big," he would tell them, or, "Let's try for a record"; and "Kennedys aren't scared," and "Kennedys don't cry." (This last maxim was challenged by Sargent Shriver, who married Eunice. Sarge entered the Compound to find his little son in tears, with his cousins chanting: "Kennedys don't cry." Sarge swept up his child and told him, "Shrivers cry. Bawl as long as you want.") Ethel, on the other hand, became "more of a Kennedy than the Kennedys" — the highest accolade the tribe could bestow. Jackie was hopeless at all outdoor games. Eventually she broke an ankle playing touch and retired permanently, but not before she had contributed to family lore. In a huddle she had asked: "Just tell me one thing. If I get the ball, which way do I run?"

Dave Hackett, Bob's best friend at Milton, once drew up a list of rules for people visiting the Kennedys. His suggestions for touch were: "Run madly on every play, and make a lot of noise. Don't appear to have too much fun, though. They'll accuse you of not taking the game seriously enough. . . . Don't criticize the other team, either. It's bound to be full of Kennedys, too, and the Kennedys don't like that sort of thing. . . . To become really popular you must show raw guts. To show raw guts, fall on your face now and then. Smash into the house once in a while going after a pass. Laugh off a twisted ankle or a big hole torn in your best suit. They like this. It shows you take the game as seriously as they do."

Touch was only the beginning. You were also expected to sail, swim, play softball, tennis, and golf on Hyannis Port's nine-hole course; to give concise opinions on the girls' dresses and hairstyles, and bone up for the coming dinner conversation. Gossip was out; so were jokes; so was money: "Big businessmen are the most overrated men in the country," the ambassador told you. "Here I am, a boy from East Boston, and *I* took 'em. So don't be impressed." Instead, you were expected to discuss current affairs. To be fully prepared, you should have read all the latest newsmagazines, journals of opinion, and, if possible, the *Congressional Record*. That was the warm-up. The main bout came after dessert. Each week the ambassador assigned a topic for the following weekend. That week it was the essays in *The Federalist* favoring ratification of the U.S. Constitution. Each member of the family was assigned a part: Hamilton, Jefferson, Madison, and so on. It was assumed that anyone invited to Hyannis Port was brilliant, gifted, talented, cheerful, amusing, energetic, and informed. In the family lexicon, no tag was more derogatory than "He's a very ordinary type," or "She's very common." At the end all participants were congratulated — "terrific" was always an O.K. word — and the singing would start. It was always spontaneous. This was the one place in the world where Jack felt completely uninhibited. His voice was flat and unmelodic, but that was true of the others, too. He would croon his two favorites: "Blue Skies" and "Bill Bailey, Won't You Please Come Home?" Others would be encouraged to volunteer; if none did, the sing-along would end with everyone harmonizing in the family anthem: "Heart of My Heart."

One moment they were sentimental; a moment later they became tough, even cruel. A guest was invited, urged, and finally forced to give a speech. The instant you stopped protesting and started speaking the catcalls would begin, and the family would boo and hiss until you sat down, feeling baffled and betrayed. Jack had been nicknamed "Rat Face" at Choate, and he spent the rest of his life getting even. Charlie Bartlett was "Duckwalker," Ben Bradlee became "Boston Blackie," and another acquaintance — it stung, but was right on the money — was "Assless Manchester." A Harvard professor objected because a *New York Times* piece had called him arrogant. Jack said: "Why not? Everybody else does." The ambassador instinctively distrusted anyone who had more than one drink before dinner, so naturally, your first evening there, Jack said to his father: "My friend would like a second martini." And your first and last experience as his crew in a sailboat race was very unsettling. He began taunting you even before you were under way: "Who's going to pull up the jib, Bill? I've got the mainsail and the race starts in two minutes, so *who's going to pull up the jib, Bill?*" A skillful skipper keeps other skippers guessing over when he is going to come about. But if a crewman doesn't know when it's coming, he can get clouted by the boom. So the skipper should shout the warning "Hard alee!" You were in the middle of Nantucket Sound when without notice the *Victura* came about and the boom was upon you. You took the only available option; you leapt over the side. Luckily you grabbed a line and hoisted yourself back aboard. Afterward, you called the future President of the United States a mick, a Paddywhack, a son of a bitch, and a Peter-Roger-Item-Charlie-King. He just laughed and said: "Didn't you hear my command? I just said, 'Yeah.' That was it." You don't believe he said anything. You think the *bahstard* wanted to see you swim halfway across the Sound.

How did they get that way? One explanation is that their rich Republican Hyannis Port neighbors had always ostracized them. As a result, they had to create their own social enclave. Another reason is their extraordinary father. When Joe Kennedy turned and gave you his undivided attention, the effect was electrifying: your spine pricked; you could almost feel your hair standing on end. This was a dynamic, elemental force. It had nothing to do with intellect, wisdom, or good judgment. You quickly found that you disagreed with him on almost every issue of substance. He was anti-Semitic. He thought blacks were subhuman. Foreign aid was money down a rathole. Defending Berlin was absurd. Assuring Western Europeans that Americans would fight beside them if the Russians lunged across their frontiers was irresponsible; the United States should withdraw into a Fortress America and let the rest of the world go to hell. But his was not a lone voice. Millions of his countrymen felt the same way. What set the ambassador apart was the way he handled his children, particularly his sons. He sent Joe Jr. and Jack to study under Harold Laski in the London School of

Economics. "Laski is a nut and a fellow traveler," he said. "But I figured . . . it was time for them to hear other points of view." He settled ten million dollars on each child, "so they can tell me to go to hell." Once he felt Jack was taking the wrong stand in Congress on a vital issue. He begged his son to switch. Jack shook his head and the ambassador beamed. "You see?" he said. "He can spit in my eye if he wants to!"

The ambassador's remarkable career began when, at the age of eight, he began peddling candy and peanuts on Boston excursion boats. He worked his way through Harvard ('12), took an office on State Street, Boston's Wall Street, and became a bank president at the age of twenty-five. Then he went to New York, where he became a wizard of such stock dodges as market rigging, matched orders, margin manipulation, and washed and short sales. By the ingenious deployment of his money he multiplied his fortune again and again, until it was measured in hundreds of millions of dollars.

Wealth can't change a man's background. During a Hyannis Port bull session that first summer after the war, one of Jack's new friends hinted that the ambassador might not appreciate the average person's point of view. "What do you mean?" Joe flared. "I happen to be the most average guy in this whole outfit." And in some ways he was. Unlike Jack, he wasn't the son of a millionaire. Although spectacularly successful as a financier, he hadn't acquired status until President Roosevelt, anxious to stamp out the very practices which had made Joe rich, appointed him to the Securities and Exchange Commission. He became acceptable, but he was still the outsider: improper, scheming, imperious, defiant, romantic, with keen instincts — some paternal, some political, some sexually chauvinistic. He liked to play classical music during negotiating sessions. Once two of his business associates protested. Joe replied: "You dumb bastards don't appreciate culture."

He cherished two ambitions. One was to become the first Irish-American ambassador to the Court of St. James's. Roosevelt made that possible. The second was to see one of his sons inaugurated as President of the United States. He had assumed it would be Joe Jr. When news of the boy's death reached him he wept inconsolably for hours. Before that, the family had assumed that Jack would become a teacher or a writer. Clearly he was the family intellectual. He began reading the *New York Times* daily at the age of fourteen. At about that time a family friend visited him at the Choate School and found him reading *The World Crisis*, Winston Churchill's six-volume history of World War I. He was interested in foreign affairs. Twice he and a friend — first Lem Billings, then Torbey Macdonald — toured prewar Europe. In Germany he met a young man he would one day appoint to the Supreme Court, a Rhodes scholar, Byron "Whizzer" (*Whizzah*) White. Jack was in London when a Nazi submarine torpedoed the British liner *Athenia* with 1,418 aboard, including 300 Americans. The ambassador sent Jack — then twenty-one and still a Harvard student — to interview the American survivors in Glasgow. They demanded that the U.S. Navy convoy them home. That was impossible, Jack explained, but he assured them that every reasonable precaution would be taken for their return. The general impression was that he had handled a difficult situation with tact and poise. Back in Massachusetts he turned his senior thesis into a book, *Why England Slept*. Henry Luce wrote the introduction, and it sold ninety thousand copies.

JFK and Bobby watch as their sister Eunice leaves the American embassy for Buckingham Palace to be presented at court

Father and son on their way to Paris

EUROPEAN APPRENTICESHIP

At an embassy reception

Recuperating from a bout of jaundice, London, 1937

Belgium, 1939

Juggling on the streets of Amsterdam

With German soldiers, 1937

*At The Hague with
Lem Billings*

Piazza San Marco, Venice

JFK's first visit to a night-club, the "400 Club" in London, 1939

Egypt, 1939

*The Kennedy family at the
coronation of Pope Pius XII*

*JFK and friends at the
Lido in Venice*

*The author and
his reviews*

When he was graduated cum laude, with magna cum laude on his thesis, the ambassador cabled: TWO THINGS I ALWAYS KNEW ABOUT YOU ONE THAT YOU ARE SMART TWO THAT YOU ARE A SWELL GUY LOVE DAD.

Had his older brother lived, Jack would never have entered politics. The converse was not true, however. The death of Joe Jr. did not necessarily mean that Jack would step into his place. He was hesitant, and when he made his choice the family wasn't at all sure it was wise. His health had been erratic since childhood; he had suffered through serious cases of scarlet fever and appendicitis, and he had almost died of diphtheria. In the Solomons he had picked up malaria; afterward, diagnosticians found that he suffered from jaundice, hepatitis, and an adrenal insufficiency. He was deaf in his left ear, allergic to dogs, and afflicted with a sensitive stomach for which fast food, inescapable during a political fight, was an irritant. Later he needed glasses to read, although, like most politicians, he rarely wore them in public. Once he was admitted to a hospital with a temperature of 106 degrees and little hope of survival. He lived with pain, though only those who knew him well could tell when he was suffering. To Boston, to Massachusetts, to the United States, and eventually to the world, he seemed to be the symbol of eternal youth — wiry and agile, with the profile of a Lindbergh and the glowing health of a Merriwell. This image was a triumph of will.

In the end, of course, the decision to enter politics was Jack's. The ambassador tried to project a hardheaded image, but his children knew him to be highly emotional. They had seen the depth of his grief after Joe Jr. died, and it would reappear when, learning of Kick's death, he flew to a village in southern France to identify her body. He played the role of the stern patriarch, but in his eyes his children could not err. Once, after an important appearance on television, Jack was anxious for a balanced appraisal of his performance. He talked to his father on the phone, and said afterward: "I still don't know how I did. If I had slipped and fallen on the floor, he would have said, 'The graceful way you picked yourself up was terrific.'" As Jack's eminence grew, and he rose in the eyes of the world, a subtle changing of the guard took place between father and son until, when Joe's power to speak became inhibited, the ambassador told the family: "You do what Jack says." Well before that, the two of them had enjoyed an easy equality. Periodically the ambassador would review bills charged to him, decide that the family was living beyond his means, and lecture his children at the dinner table. Unless this hemorrhage stopped, he warned, their own children would be destitute. Once he singled out Ethel, waving a sheaf of charge accounts at her until she fled, weeping. Bobby rose, his face taut as a winched halyard, and ran after her. When they returned, the tension was still there. Jack broke it. He told Bob: "We've found the solution. Dad's just got to go out and make more money."

OUR FRIENDS
WERE DEARER THEN

Hindsight distorts memories, particularly our recollections of men in public life. Although Kennedy was elected President in 1960 by only 49.7 percent of the popular vote, by June 1963, pollsters found that 59 percent of the electorate recalled voting for him — a figure which, after his death, jumped to 65 percent, meaning that over ten million voters had edited their memories. An extraordinary number of Bostonians now recall having prophesied, in 1946, that Kennedy would rise from congressman to senator and thence to the presidency. And thousands of others, while not claiming to have predicted it, believe that his political future was preordained, the work of destiny, a part of some grand design as inevitable as the stars turning in their courses.

Of course, it wasn't like that at all. Kennedy's drive and political instincts had a lot to do with it, but so did luck. It was pure chance, for example, that Martin Luther King was jailed in Atlanta on October 19, 1960, and that Jack impulsively called Coretta King to express his concern. Yet without that call he wouldn't have received 70 percent of America's black vote, providing him with the margin he needed to beat Nixon. (King's father told the press that he had been against Kennedy because he was a Catholic, but he now supported him. Jack, amused, said: "Imagine Martin Luther King's father being a bigot!" He paused, and added dryly: "But we all have fathers, don't we?")

On January 3, 1947, he took his congressman's oath, and defying convention, refused to call on the dean of Massachusetts congressmen, John W. McCormack, and pledge allegiance to him. As a freshman member of the House Labor Committee he filed a separate report on the Taft-Hartley bill disagreeing with both Republican and Democratic members, criticized the Truman administration's trade policies and budget appropriations, became the only member of the Massachusetts congressional delegation who refused to petition for Curley's pardon, and then attacked the sacred veterans' lobby for opposing low-cost housing. The ambassador was particularly pleased with some other things Jack was saying because Joe himself thought they needed saying. They were right-wing dogmas, popular with Republicans but heresy to Harry Truman, who was a dangerous enemy with a long memory. Kennedy denounced Truman's Point-Four Program; he was against all foreign aid. He told the House that at Yalta a "sick" Roosevelt,

The congressman inspecting the Boston waterfront

on the advice of General George Marshall, "gave" the Kurils and other strategic points to the Soviet Union. The administration had tried to force Chiang into an alliance with Mao, he said. Truman had even treated Mme Chiang with "indifference," if not "contempt." The State Department had squandered America's wartime gains by listening to such advisers as Owen Lattimore. "This," Kennedy concluded, "is the tragic story of China. . . . What our young men saved, our diplomats and our President have frittered away."

Later Kennedy said of these speeches, "I'd just come out of my father's house and these were the things I knew." But the longer he stayed in Washington, and the less he saw of his father, the more dedicated to liberal causes he became. He changed his mind about foreign aid. He kept in touch with the political leaders and the ward bosses at home. The longshoremen and freight handlers, all union men, were outraged by Taft-Hartley, a "bosses' bill." Kennedy believed their grievances were justified and debated the issue with another freshman congressman, Richard M. Nixon of the Twelfth California District. He also debated another newcomer, the still obscure Senator Joe McCarthy of Wisconsin, on the need for public housing. Kennedy fought loyalty oaths, and noted that any mossbacks who had voted for him in the past must have been "under the impression that I am my father's son." Joe Kennedy had a tyrannical manner, a soft heart, a quick temper, a tendency to bully, and a way of exaggerating loves and hates. Jack was calm, patient, civil, reasonable, and given to understatement. Yet he was by far the tougher of the two. If a member of the family appealed to the ambassador, he would yield. Jack never gave an inch. His winning smile was deceptive; under that charm he could be hard, ruthless, and even, at times, unscrupulous.

Politics was his trade now, and he went at it, in his own words, "flat out, all out." He had to wade through stacks of documents; therefore he took a speed-reading course. He wondered why most voters were indifferent to, or suspicious of, the pope, and to find out, he read Buchan's 1934 study of Cromwell and Paul Blanshard's best-selling (but anti-Catholic) *American Freedom and Catholic Power*. A few days after his election he had met his old professor Arthur Holcombe, who congratulated him, told him he had voted for him, and suggested he spend an afternoon attending Holcombe's graduate seminar in American politics. Between a dozen and twenty bright Harvard students would attend a two-hour session. Jack would talk first about political realities. Then they would question him for an hour. Kennedy did it, enjoyed it, and came back to the Yard every year until he entered the White House. Then the Holcombe sessions bore rich fruit. It was there, on his old campus, that he learned the techniques he later used to master televised presidential press conferences.

In Georgetown, among his new friends, was Bill Walton, then the *New Republic*'s Washington correspondent. They met through a girl; both were bachelors and Walton's service as a paratrooper instantly qualified him for Kennedy friendship. Moreover, in London he had known both Joe Jr. and Kick. He lived on nearby N Street and they were frequently together. Yet Walton had no idea that Jack was rich. Only the family and a few close friends knew that Kennedy contributed all his salaries, as congressman and later as senator and President, to charities, dividing them among Protestant,

Jewish, and Catholic causes and such organizations as the Boy and Girl Scouts, with the understanding that the gifts receive no publicity.

In political fights Kennedy avoided ostentation — telethons, full-page newspaper advertisements, billboards. He never played host at Washington's lavish cocktail parties, and seldom attended them as a guest. All Walton knew in those years was that his friend lived in a rented house and drove an ordinary car — later, when his wife gave him a white Jaguar, he returned it. "It was only if you went to Hyannis Port and saw all the boats there," Walton recalls, "that you became aware that there was a lot of dough in the family." Kennedys, particularly Jack, judged other people by their appearance, but it never occurred to them that they themselves might be so appraised. If it had, Jack might have become a far more successful congressman.

As it was he was unprepossessing. In many ways he seemed to be in his late teens. His mother sent the family cook down to put some meat on him — she failed — and then Rose herself arrived to supervise the redecoration of his home. At the ambassador's request Arthur Krock reluctantly parted with his valet, George Thomas, to look after Joe's boy. In the halls of Congress, Jack was often taken for a tourist. His wardrobe didn't help; he often entered the House wearing a rumpled seersucker jacket and khaki trousers. Sunday afternoons he would slip into a sweat shirt and sally out to the sweeping greensward around the Washington Monument, looking for a game of touch. Once, when you were in Washington covering Whittaker Chambers's testimony before the House, Jack met you at Union Station and drove you to the Hill, where he parked in front of a No Parking sign. "This is what Hamlet means by the insolence of office," he said gaily. A dour policeman appeared and started writing a ticket, observing that congressional plates did not convey immunity to congressmen's sons. Even after Kennedy had been elected to the upper house, a guard once waved him away from a phone, saying, "Sorry, son. These are reserved for senators." And when Jack tried to board a presidential train in Springfield, Massachusetts, he was thrown off by James J. Rowley — later chief of President Kennedy's Secret Service.

Jack and Jacqueline Lee Bouvier, the extraordinary beauty who was about to enter his life, were very much on the minds of Washington matchmakers. Both were Roman Catholic, upper-class, and exceptionally attractive. Charlie Bartlett of the Chattanooga *Times* and his new wife, Martha, thought they should meet. Charlie had nearly brought it off at his brother's wedding. He had alerted Jack and had Jackie in tow when she fell into conversation with Gene Tunney. Jack, unaccustomed to waiting for a girl, departed alone. Now, early in the spring of 1952, Martha took over, inviting Jack and Jackie to dinner. Kennedy was preoccupied with political developments in Massachusetts; Miss Bouvier was packing for Europe. All present later agreed that nothing memorable was said. As they were leaving, Jack asked her, in that shy way he had, "Shall we go somewhere for a drink?" Before she could reply, she saw a young man crouched in the backseat of her car, one of several suitors who followed her around. It was one of those inexplicable situations. She spread her hands in a helpless gesture; under the circumstances, she really couldn't go somewhere for a drink. Kennedy, rejected for the second time, huffed off.

But he was interested. He called Charlie the next day with a few questions and learned that she was the daughter of divorced parents, her father a stockbroker and a member of Newport society. She was a 1947 alumna of Miss Porter's exclusive finishing school in Farmington, Connecticut. (The school yearbook noted her ambition: "Not to be a housewife.") Having studied at Vassar, at the Sorbonne, and at George Washington University, she was fluent in Spanish, Italian, and French. Mastery of foreign languages impressed Jack. He himself couldn't do it, though being a Kennedy, he never quit trying — at the time of his death he was taking French lessons, hoping to carry on an intelligent conversation with Charles de Gaulle. He called Jackie and asked if she could translate some French documents dealing with Southeast Asia. She could; she did. During the early 1950s she translated several pieces for him, including articles on the French struggle in Indochina. Kennedy was almost certainly the first American politician since Franklin Roosevelt — who had fiercely believed and argued that the French colonies in Indochina should be granted full independence — to speak out in support of native nationalism there. In 1951 he had visited the area and, impatient with the routine briefing at the American embassy in Saigon, had asked sharply why Vietnamese peasants should fight to keep their country in the French empire. Back in Washington, Kennedy declared: "In Indochina we have allied ourselves to the desperate effort of a French regime to hang on to the remnants of empire." To do this "through reliance on arms," he said, was senseless. "To do this apart from and in defiance of innately nationalistic aims spells foredoomed failure."

Kennedy could have spent the rest of his life in Congress with every reason to believe that eventually he would become Speaker of the House. He was easily reelected in '48 and '50 — no one could be found to run against him in the first election, and in the second his margin of victory was the largest in Massachusetts. But the House bored him; each member had too small a share of national responsibility, and he came to regard it as a waste of time. As early as 1950 he decided to run for governor or senator. Every poll predicted that he would lose in either race, but he told you he wouldn't much care. Anything would be better than remaining trapped with political mediocrities, stultifying rules, and the archaic seniority system. The two offices would be at stake in the '52 election. They were then held by the Democratic governor Paul Dever, and the illustrious Republican senator Henry Cabot Lodge. Jack's decision would depend on Dever's. If the governor ran against Lodge for the Senate, Kennedy would go for the statehouse. If Dever wanted to run for reelection, the senatorial campaign would pit Jack against Lodge, now strengthened by his leadership in persuading Eisenhower to run for President. So strong was Lodge that if neither Dever nor Kennedy challenged him, no other opponent would be available.

Mounted on a bedroom wall of the Bowdoin Street apartment was a large map of Massachusetts. Soon it would be peppered with pins showing where Jack had spoken since the last election. Before the state went to the polls again, he intended to make at least one appearance in each of its 39 cities and 312 towns. Studying the map, he told Dave Powers, "You've got to get me some dates here, here, and there. When we've got this map completely covered with pins, and Dever makes up his mind, I'll announce my candidacy." Where, a friend asked, would he speak? The answer: anywhere. At Catholic communion breakfasts and Protestant church socials, for Knights of Columbus, Moose clubs, Elks, Kiwanians, Rotarians, Optimists, Shriners, Holy Name Societies, AMVETS, VFWs, volunteer fire departments — anyone who wanted him could have him. But he could appear only on weekends; during the week he had to work on Capitol Hill. Every Friday night he would fly from Washington to Boston; every Sunday evening he would board the Federal Express at Back Bay Station and sprawl across a Pullman berth to sleep through the trip back.

He depended on friends to drive him and often they became victims of his black humor. Most of the time he was on crutches. He would drive from Capitol Hill to Washington's National Airport with a friend in the passenger's seat. At the airport he would struggle to his feet on the crutches and the friend would slide behind the wheel to drive the car back to Georgetown. When Jack was driving, every ride was memorable. He was always late leaving the Hill, and he would race down Constitution and across the river, violating every courtesy of the road. You particularly remember the time he cut off a green Chevy. The driver barely avoided a collision. You were telling him the man must be furious, when Jack said calmly: "He's on our tail." Jack shook him by taking a shortcut; he was out of the car and you were behind the wheel when the green Chevy reappeared, and screeched to a halt beside you. The man leapt out, livid, and shouted: "Who was driving this car?" Leaning pitiably on his crutches, Jack shook his head, pointed at you, and said mournfully: "He was. Terrible driver." He then hobbled off, grinning, leaving you to explain the inexplicable. Another time, in Massachusetts, you were driving at eighty miles an hour because he was running late, when a motorcycle policeman appeared in the rearview mirror. You stopped, got out, and gave the law your spiel. Eventually, and miraculously, he let you go. A few miles down the road, you were approaching a railroad crossing; its bell was ringing and its red light flashing. Jack said urgently: "Come on, we've got to beat that train." You tried, but were a moment too late. Jack, disgusted, said: "If you hadn't wasted so much time back there talking to that cop, we would've made it."

He could be hard on you. But he was much harder on himself. His schedule was grueling. And no one, he knew, would be electrified by a crippled candidate. Arriving for a speech, he would leave the crutches in the car and, grinding his teeth, enter the hall. When the applause began, he would beam and stride to the rostrum. After the speech, the questions, and the handshaking, he would collapse in the car and close his eyes in pain until he could reach the motel, where he would soak in a hot tub for an hour before bedtime. That is, he soaked if there *was* a hot tub. In those days, before the Massachusetts Turnpike, good motels were few.

By New Year's Day, 1952, the Bowdoin Street map was concealed by a thicket of colored pins. Now he was ready. By Palm Sunday, Dever's private polls had convinced him that he had no chance against Lodge, so he decided to run for a third gubernatorial term. Jack phoned Archbishop Cushing — not yet a cardinal — asking if it would be appropriate to make a political announcement during Holy Week. Cushing enthusiastically endorsed the idea, adding that Kennedy would have his vote. During his weekend appearances, Jack had noted, on three-by-five cards, the names of local enthusiasts who might be useful in the coming campaign. These "secretaries," as he called them, were usually well-groomed young suburban types with impeccable manners. Slowly, as summer waxed and then waned, a Kennedy sticker on your car became a status symbol.

Lists of names, however, do not constitute an organization. Kennedy had needed planners and a structure to win his congressional fight, and in challenging Lodge he was facing Republican managers whose fathers and grandfathers had campaigned for Lodge family candidates. Jack needed a strong manager, and he phoned Bobby. Veteran Democrats, the kind of men Dever was mobilizing, were dumbfounded. Bobby was twenty-six, just out of law school, busy establishing himself as a federal prosecutor in the Department of Justice. He knew nothing of Massachusetts politics. But the ambassador gave Bob his marching orders, and Bob reluctantly agreed. With him he brought Ken O'Donnell. Larry O'Brien was already aboard. Rose and her daughters had held three teas, open to all, in Worcester, Springfield, and Quincy. The teas had proved immensely popular, and Bobby urged them to plan more. By election day they had been hostesses at thirty-five teas attended by between sixty-five and seventy-five thousand women. The Kennedys were going through the state like a corn borer through a field of Golden Bantam, and the statewide pros of '52, like the Eleventh District pros of '46, were baffled. They sat around Kennedy headquarters at 44 Kilby Street in Boston, reminiscing about the grand fights of the past, until Bobby told them to stamp and address envelopes or get out. He himself was undertaking tasks which are rarely the responsibility of a campaign manager. He wanted a Kennedy poster on a building which would be visible to commuters crossing the bridge between north Boston and Charlestown. It was, he was told, inaccessible. "Drive me over, Dave," he said. "I'll put it up." And so he did, swaying on the top of a long ladder while Powers, saying Hail Marys, held the bottom.

Lodge told Arthur Krock that he expected to win by 300,000 votes; Jack, he said, was simply wasting Kennedy money. But in the September primaries, Kennedy drew 75 percent of the vote compared to Dever's 60 percent. Dever suggested that his organization and Kennedy's work together. The ambassador thought it made sense. Bobby discussed it with Jack, O'Donnell, and O'Brien. Their decision was unanimous: no merger. Dever, furious, said the only Kennedy he would deal with would be Joe. Of Bobby he said to his staff: "Keep that young prick out of here."

Lodge's greatest strength was also his greatest weakness. His identification with Eisenhower undoubtedly won him votes, but Lodge was also speaking for Ike in other states, and in his absence Jack was making immense progress. The two senatorial candidates appeared together once, in a debate sponsored by the Waltham chapter of the League of Women Voters. They agreed on virtually every issue. It was a contest between personalities, the suave, aristocratic, condescending WASP and the graceful, witty Irishman. Somehow the grace and the wit gave Kennedy an edge. Viewers who preferred him were hard-pressed for reasons, but they felt committed. One said he was "very classy," another that he "talks so nicely," and a third, a girl, cried: "I believe in anything he believes in."

By November 7, election eve, Jack was exhausted. He had been on the move for eight months, living on cheeseburgers and malteds, and had shaken 750,000 hands. Yet that evening it all seemed to have been in vain. Eisenhower was carrying Massachusetts by 208,800 votes; Dever, the final figures would show, was losing by 14,456. A GOP sweep of all state offices appeared to be certain. Especially this seemed true of Lodge, Ike's man. Five hours after the polls had closed, commentators were still confident that he couldn't fail. At 3:30 A.M., however, one felt the first tremors of a shift. In towns where he had been thought to be weak, Kennedy was holding his own. At 5:00 A.M. stunned Republicans agreed that Jack, swimming against the powerful GOP tide, had won. Kennedy's plurality was 70,737 votes; over a quarter-million people had voted for Ike but cut Lodge to back Jack. It had been a night of almost unbearable suspense for everyone except the new senator-elect. His mastery of Massachusetts politics was now complete. With figures from key precincts he had predicted the outcome shortly before midnight. His staff had been sweating blood then when he said casually: "I wonder what kind of job Eisenhower will give Lodge."

Back in Washington he resumed what Jackie calls "a very spasmodic courtship." Six months passed between two dates; she crossed the Atlantic a second time, to attend the coronation of England's new queen. Now she was an employee of the Washington *Times-Herald*. During her job interview she had been asked if she knew how to use a camera and had replied (untruthfully) that she certainly did. Hired at $42.50 a week, she had hurriedly learned about f-stops, shutter speeds, and ASA numbers. In January 1953, after he had taken his senatorial oath, she snapped Jack's picture. He took her dancing at the Shoreham's Blue Room, to dinner with Bobby and his bride, and to several films, among which their favorites were *Stalag 17*; *Julius Caesar*, with Marlon Brando; *The Robe*, starring Richard Burton; and *From Here to Eternity*. "But," Jackie later told you, "it was still spasmodic, because he spent half of each week in Massachusetts. He'd call me from some oyster bar up there, with a great clinking of coins, to ask me out to the movies the following Wednesday in Washington. He loved Westerns and Civil War pictures. He was not the candy and flowers type, so every now and then he'd give me a book." Among the books were *The Raven*, Marquis James's biography of Sam Houston, and, inevitably, Buchan's *Pilgrim's Way*.

The courtship was not only spasmodic; it was also remarkably casual. He sent her no love letters; indeed, he didn't write at all, except a single postcard from Bermuda, the entire text of which read: "Wish you were here." Unlike Ethel, Jackie was bored by politics. Kennedy brought her to Hyannis Port, strong evidence that his intentions were both honorable and serious. The moment the ambassador laid eyes on her, he decided that Jack had to marry her. A statesman (he no longer thought of his son as a politician) has to have a wife, he confided, and "a Catholic politician has to have a Catholic wife. She should be classy. Jackie probably has more class than any girl we've ever seen around here." But she was apprehensive, dazed by the endless succession of games, sports, and discussions. Later she said, "Just watching them wore me out." And although she was now completely under Jack's spell, his manner sometimes exasperated her. Stewart Alsop, who had also been baffled by it, thought that "if it were not so calm, if it were more strident and pushful, it would be plain arrogance." Occasionally it came close to arrogance. Proposing to Jackie in the spring of 1953, he told her that he had actually decided to marry her a year before. He hadn't been ready then; now he was. She flashed: "How *big* of you!"

It was at about this time that you noticed his way of compartmentalizing his life and wondered if it was deliberate. There were his family, the Irish politicians, newspapermen, writers, artists, intelligentsia unconverted to political piety, several constellations of political friends — moderate, liberal, conservative — and odd figures like Frank Sinatra, whose trivial celebrity gossip amused him. Usually he kept them apart from one another. In the White House, for example, Powers, O'Brien, and O'Donnell were rarely invited to the glittering receptions in the East Room. In some instances acquaintances in one compartment would have, had they met, been extremely hostile to those in another. Jackie didn't really come to know Kenny O'Donnell until after Jack's death. Once during Kennedy's White House years you pointed out that everyone he knew seemed to fit in this nook or that pigeonhole. He acknowledged it, but compared it to a wheel instead, with himself at the hub and others as spokes. "It was instinctive at first," he said. "I had different identities, and this was a useful way of expressing each without compromising the others. I know it's confusing at times, but it is very effective in governing. Franklin Roosevelt did the same thing, you know."

The looming relationship between him and Jackie was known to only a few. Your first hint of it came when he asked you, apropros of nothing: "Do you think there is really much of a problem in marrying a girl twelve years younger than you are?" The answer was obvious; Dave and Jo Powers were separated by twelve years and their marriage was ideal. A few weeks later he dropped you a note; after giving "everything a good deal of thought," he said, he would be "getting married this fall. This means the end of a promising political career as it has been based up to now almost completely on the old sex appeal. . . . As I am both too young and too old for this — will need several long talks on how to conduct myself during the 1st 6 months — based on your actual real life experience." You wondered if Jackie knew what life with a rising politician would be like. Soon she had a couple of inklings. To her chagrin, the announcement of their engagement had to be postponed until after June 13, because the *Saturday Evening Post* would publish an article then on "Jack Kennedy: The Senate's Gay Young Bachelor." She had also flown to Hyannis Port a second time, anticipating a week of sailing with her fiancé. Boarding the boat, she was introduced to another guest, a *Life* photographer. The photographer would accompany them, Jack explained, as though it were the most natural thing in the world, to gather material for a picture essay on their romance, "Life Goes Courting with a U.S. Senator."

It is the bride's family which stages weddings, and Hugh ("Hudi") Auchincloss believed in grandeur. He and Jackie's mother, Janet, had presented her on her eighteenth birthday in 1947 at Hammersmith Farm; the reception had been so elegant that Cholly Knickerbocker anointed her that year's "Queen of Debutantes." Wedding guests were farmed out to Hudi's relatives and friends — you were billeted with Wilmarth "Lefty" Lewis, the Walpole scholar who, having married an Auchincloss, was Jackie's stepuncle. Then Jack's pals looked around to see where the action was. It seemed to be at the Newport Country Club, visible from Hammersmith Farm. Jack was a member, but, too busy for a golf match, he agreed to play a couple of holes, then quit, promising to reappear to pick you up at the eighteenth hole. There seemed to be a certain tension among the caddies when he departed. The explanation came after the last hole. Jack was sarcastic, though highly amused. He said: "I hope you enjoyed your game, because as a result of it there has been an almost total breakdown of relations between the mother of the bride and her dashing prospective son-in-law. It seems that there is an ironclad rule of the club that nonmembers can only play when there is a member present to sanction the match. Now they know that their worst fears are being realized. They are convinced that one of the last strongholds of America's socially elite is being invaded by mongrels without pedigrees." Unchastened, the gang headed for Bailey's Beach, a game of touch, and a swim.

The evening before the wedding Hudi entertained at Newport's Clambake Club. Jack gave the men Brooks Brothers umbrellas; Jackie's bridesmaids received monogrammed silver picture frames. There were the usual toasts: Jack said he was marrying Jackie to get her out of the newspaper business, where she was a threat to his career; Jackie held aloft her Bermuda postcard; Bobby, still terrified of speaking then, stammered through a memorized speech. The most unforgettable event of that dinner was the work of Red Fay. The Redhead, Grand Old Lovable, had served as master of ceremonies at three affairs when his sisters were married. Consulted by Jack, he said that the groom's first toast should be to the bride, and — this was important — "when the glasses are drained, no one should drink out of them again. They must be instantly thrown into the fireplace." That may have been the custom in Red's California circle (it may also have been an act of revenge from a victim of Jack's peculiar sense of humor), but it wasn't in Newport; the goblets at this dinner had been in Hudi's family for generations. His jaw sagged as he saw them shatter. New cut-glass goblets were brought in. Then Jack, inspired, said: "Maybe this isn't the accepted custom, but I want to express my love for this girl a second time." Into the fireplace they went, and Hudi, aghast, excused himself to acquire replacements. It took him a long time. When the third batch arrived, they looked suspiciously like something from Woolworth's.

On Saturday, September 12, 1953, Archbishop Cushing united Jack and Jackie as man and wife in Saint Mary's Church. The bride was startled to see deep scratches on the groom's face; he had been up early for a game of touch. There were six hundred people inside and at least six thousand outside. The couple left the reception for a honeymoon in Acapulco, where, after a two-hour struggle, Jack caught a nine-foot, eight-inch sailfish which, mounted, was hung on the wall of his Senate office and later in the west

THE
PERFECT
COUPLE

Sailing at West Palm Beach, December 1953

*Taking their vows in Saint Mary's
Church in Newport, Rhode Island,
September 12, 1953*

wing of the White House. He had bought Hickory Hill, Justice Robert Jackson's huge red-brick Virginia mansion across the Potomac. Both he and Jackie looked forward to raising a large family. It seemed that nothing could go wrong for them, yet in that first year almost everything did. Jackie suffered a miscarriage; childbearing, her obstetrician said, would be difficult for her. In the Senate her husband faced an issue he couldn't win: the censure of Joe McCarthy. McCarthy had to be humiliated, and Jack knew it, but it would be highly unpopular with his constituents. Nationwide Gallup consistently found that only 29 percent of the population disapproved of the Wisconsin senator, and among the Irish Catholics of Massachusetts the figure was far lower than that. As Dever said at the time, "Joe McCarthy is the only man I know who could beat Archbishop Cushing in a two-man election fight in South Boston." Finally, Kennedy's spinal condition had worsened. He could not move without crutches.

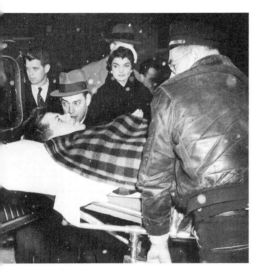

He was sidelined throughout the summer of 1954. His only hope was surgery, to remove a metal plate inserted by naval physicians in 1944, and then fusion of the separated vertebrae. The doctors unanimously advised against surgery. Because of Jack's adrenal insufficiency, after a major operation, shock and infection would be almost inevitable. At best, they said, his chances of survival were fifty-fifty. The patient replied that he accepted the risk. Punching his crutches, he said: "I'd rather be dead than spend the rest of my life on these things." On October 21, at New York's Hospital for Special Surgery, physicians attempted a lumbar spine operation. They failed. As predicted, infection set in. Priests administered the last rites. Then he rallied, and on December 20, lying on a stretcher with Jackie at his side, he was flown to his father's elegant white stucco villa in Palm Beach for Christmas. There he lay by the lovely Grecian pool just off the south patio, looking toward the sea wall planted with tall royal palms, brooding, his mind locked in inner turmoil.

In January, Bobby called Red Fay and asked him to spend ten days with Jack. The Redhead found Jack in great discomfort, forcing himself to read and then memorize passages from Churchill. Grand Old Lovable watched his friend give himself an injection, and, to brighten the moment, said, "Jack, the way you take that jab, it looks like it doesn't even hurt." Before he could dodge, Kennedy reached over and stabbed the needle into Fay's leg. Grand Old Lovable screamed with pain. Jack said flatly: "It feels the same way to me."

In February, he was flown to New York again; again he went under the knife, and this operation was partially successful, though if you visited him in the hospital then, and saw the dressing being changed, you had to stifle a gasp; the hole in his back was so large you could have put your fist in it up to your wrist. Back at the ambassador's house in Palm Beach he was moved into a room just off the patio. Jackie stayed in the next room, day and night, never too far away to hear him call for help. Usually the ambassador was also nearby in his "Bullpen," a solarium surrounded by tall adobe walls, where, stark naked, he swung his big deals over the telephone.

Kennedy had never lost his flair for writing. Throughout his years on Capitol Hill, he had contributed to periodicals ranging from *McCall's* and *Parade* to the *New York Times Magazine* and the *Foreign Policy Bulletin*. His Palm Beach room was packed with cartons of books from the Library of

Congress. All had been sent down, on his instructions, by Ted Sorensen, his administrative assistant. While still in New York recovering from his second operation, Jack had reflected on the career of John Quincy Adams, who had lost his seat in the Senate because he had taken an unpopular stand on a matter of principle. Other politicians had also sacrificed their careers because they would not bow to public opinion. At first Jack thought of writing a magazine article about them, then decided the subject was worth a book. Strapped to a board, unable to sleep for more than an hour or two at a stretch, he read the books Sorensen had sent, studied replies to his letters from Jules Davids, a Georgetown University professor, and James M. Landis, the retired dean of Harvard Law School. Then he started writing, in his loose, widely spaced hand, on heavy white legal-length pages. It went slowly. Frequently he paused to strike out sentences or whole paragraphs and write inserts in the margin. Once a chapter was ready, he dictated the draft to a secretary. If he was too weary to hold a book, Jackie and Dave Powers took turns reading to him. By early May he had a manuscript, and he submitted it to Harper and Brothers. It was accepted after he had written a brief anecdotal opening for each chapter. Allan Nevis told Harper's that he thought it a valuable contribution to American history, and wrote its foreword. Kennedy titled the book *Profiles in Courage*. It was published early in 1956 and dedicated to Jackie.

By March 1955 the first signs of partial recovery had become visible. He could rise from his bed and walk, unsupported by crutches, to a poolside chair fifty feet away. The next day he walked across the lawn, to the beach. Standing there, with the salt water lapping at his bare feet, he smiled broadly. On May 23, he flew to Washington, ignored the crutches and wheelchair at the bottom of the ramp, and rode to the Capitol for a press conference. In the Senate, Lyndon Johnson and William Knowland, the two party leaders in the chamber, greeted him warmly. At his office, room 362 of the Senate Office Building, a large basket of fruit awaited him. The card read: "Welcome Home, Dick Nixon."

He would never be free from pain, though the nature of his illness was widely misunderstood. His adrenal insufficiency led to rumors that he was a victim of Addison's disease. At the Democratic National Convention of 1960 some Johnson supporters spread the word that Kennedy was "diseased," strongly implying that his problem was a social disease. Actually, the victims of Addison's disease are weak and easily fatigued. Kennedy, however, could campaign twenty hours a day, day after day, sometimes working straight through sleepless nights, driving himself harder than the youngest and healthiest members of his team. He did have to take precautions. Because of his incompetent adrenal glands, he took two pills every day at noon. He was required to wear a canvas back brace at all times, and a left shoe with a quarter-inch medical lift. When he sat, the chair should, if possible, be a rocker. At night he had to sleep with a bed board beneath his mattress; if a bed board was unavailable, the mattress would be moved to the floor. He needed three hot baths a day, a rest on a heating pad after lunch, and, later, a rigorous series of calisthenics prescribed by Dr. Hans Kraus of New York. His quickest relief from insupportable pain was a unique treatment devised by Dr. Janet Travell. The doctor drove a long hollow needle into afflicted tissue and flooded it with novocaine, thus relaxing the

muscle. Once, when the physician was visiting Kennedy's home, Jackie asked her if it was possible to give him a shot which would provide complete relief from pain. Yes, Dr. Travell replied; there was such a shot, but it would remove all feeling below the waist. Jack grinned. He said: "We can't have that, can we, Jackie?"

American intellectuals, *hoc genus omne*, have long eluded definition. It may seem unreasonable that a well-read man whom Harvard had graduated with honors, who had studied under Harold Laski, published two distinguished books and articles in learned journals, and who in conversation could lace his arguments with classical allusions would not qualify as a member of the country's intellectual community. Nevertheless, Kennedy was ineligible. One remembers William Faulkner's reply to a student who was puzzled by literary symbolism: "You'll have to ask an intellectual about that. I'm just a writer." Most intellectuals are liberals, and the only postwar politician to win their favor was Adlai Stevenson. Those of us who knew the private Adlai and his conservative instincts cannot doubt that, had he been elected President, intellectual disillusionment with him would have followed within six months at the most.

The intellectuals never had illusions about Kennedy, nor did he about them. Kennedy thought they had been a liability for Stevenson and wanted no part of them. Liberal piety, he believed, could be just as narrow as bigotry. Asked for his political philosophy, he quoted the Greek definition of happiness: "the full use of your powers along lines of happiness." Pressed about whether, were he President, he would be liberal or conservative, he replied: "I would hope to be responsible." Intellectuals remained skeptical. And after he entered the White House they colored him black. C. Wright Mills saw him as a member of "the power elite"; Kennedy, he later wrote, made him "ashamed to be an American." Alfred Kazin thought Kennedy's "shrewd awareness of what intellectuals can do" was "irrelevant to the tragic issues and contributes nothing to their solution"; writers who admired Jack and enjoyed his favor were, Kazin wrote, victims of manipulation. Even before 1960, when the identities of the front-runners became increasingly clear, Eric Sevareid wrote in the Boston *Globe* that no real differences existed between the candidates. "The 'managerial revolution' has come to politics," Sevareid concluded, "and Nixon and Kennedy are its first completely packaged products."

Profiles in Courage did nothing to reassure liberals. One of the politicians Kennedy had singled out for praise, they pointedly noted, was Robert A. Taft, omitting the reason Taft had been included: his unpopular stand against the Nuremberg trials. Kennedy wrote that Taft "was partisan in the sense that Harry Truman was — they both had the happy gift of seeing things in bright shades. It is the politicians who see things in similar shades that have a depressing and worrisome time of it." After the book had been awarded a Pulitzer Prize, Kennedy's critics said that he hadn't written it; the manuscript had been the work of a ghost-writer. As long as these shabby rumors were passed along only at cocktail parties, the author was helpless, but Drew Pearson crossed the libel line when he repeated them as a guest of ABC-TV's "Mike Wallace Show" on December 7, 1957. Jack decided to sue. "I have no choice," he said. "This challenges my ability to write the book, my honesty in signing it, and my integrity in accepting the prize." Establishing the truth proved easy. There was the first draft of the manuscript, written in Jack's hand. Witnesses were plentiful: nurses who had attended the patient in Palm Beach, secretaries who had taken Kennedy's dictation, and such visitors as Red Fay and Dave Powers. Pearson identified the ghost-writer as Ted Sorensen, the senator's legislative aide, who had checked out Jack's reference books at the Library of Congress and sent them down to Florida. ABC's lawyer cross-examined Sorensen and agreed that the senator had written the book, assisted only by researchers and editors — help he had acknowledged in his preface. Sorensen signed a sworn statement confirming this; both ABC and Pearson then apologized and publicly retracted the lies.

The next epigram to sweep the capital was: "Kennedy should show less profile and more courage." The implication that Jack had cowered during his years on the Hill was absurd. He had first made news as a congressman when he attacked the American Legion. Again and again he had ignored parochial appeals from his constituents, putting the national interest first. He had supported the closing of the Murphy General Hospital in Waltham, putting twelve hundred Massachusetts voters out of work. The blue-collar vote is essential to any Democrat; nevertheless, he led the Senate investigation of labor racketeering, furnishing an "outstanding" example, the *New York Times* declared, of "utmost skill in the art of compromise." Nevertheless, unions boycotted, and even picketed, his public appearances. Though he was not a member of Americans for Democratic Action, his legislative record received 80 to 90 ratings from ADA and the *New Republic*. Despite heavy mail urging him to do otherwise, he approved Eisenhower's liberalized international trade program, abolition of the GI Bill loyalty oath, aid to Communist governments in Yugoslavia and Poland, and a U.S. commitment to join Canada in building the Saint Lawrence Seaway. President after President had sought congressional approval of this plan, and all had been thwarted by domestic interests, the hard core of the opposition coming from Massachusetts. The dockers Kennedy had represented in his congressional seat were against the seaway. Over a period of twenty years, not a single congressman or senator from Massachusetts had ever cast a yea vote on the issue. Nevertheless, Jack did so, believing that, though it was a blow to New England, it would bear rich fruit nationally. Boston papers called him "the Suicide Senator."

The prickliest issue to come before the Senate in the 1950s, and the one liberals would throw at him again and again, was McCarthyism. It was traumatic for most senators, and especially so for Kennedy. On December 2, 1954, when the Senate voted 67 to 22 to censure Joe McCarthy, Jack was recorded on Capitol Hill as "absent by leave of the Senate because of illness." In fact, he was not only in the hospital; he was on the critical list. No one accused him of malingering, but such liberals as Eleanor Roosevelt felt he should have recorded his vote later, and spoken out frequently and vehemently on Joe's demagoguery. The record is tangled. Like the rest of the Senate, Kennedy had approved funds for investigation committees, includ-

*Senator Kennedy calls on
Eleanor Roosevelt*

*Old and young Democrats
at a party Advisory Council
meeting in New York*

*JFK was still on crutches
in 1955 at the time of his
private audience with the
pope*

In his Senate office

Committee members and
counsel at the Senate Labor
Committee rackets hearings

Senator Mansfield was
about to call it a strike
when Senator Jackson hit
a single, leaving Senator
Kennedy empty-handed

ing McCarthy's, and on ambiguous measures involving tugs between libertarian rights and the needs of national security, Kennedy had opted for national security. He opposed all appointments McCarthy sought, however, and in August 1954 had prepared a speech calling for McCarthy's censure. Had he been well, he would have delivered it. The question was whether or not he should have released it to the press afterward to put the record straight. He didn't, and at the next Gridiron Dinner, where Washington correspondents roast politicians, costumed reporters sang, to the tune of "Clementine":

> *Where were you, John? Where were you, John?*
> *When the Senate censured Joe?*

McCarthy was a cynical "black Irish" rowdy cast in the Curley mold, but without the Shamrock's redeeming features, and, as such, was an affront to everything Jack represented. But the Kennedy family was involved. Bobby had briefly served on McCarthy's staff — he quit after a fight with Roy Cohn — and the ambassador was one of those primitives who believed Communists had wormed their way into the U.S. government, and that "Tailgunner Joe" knew how to get them out. The ambassador had invited Joe to Hyannis Port for a weekend. It seems improbable now, but McCarthy had a certain rough charm then; even so astute a reporter as Richard H. Rovere acknowledged having left the senator's office after a lengthy interview completely unaware that he had been "switched, conned, and double-shuffled by one of the masters." Still, Joe *had* been a Hyannis Port guest. Ingenuously, perhaps, Jack told friends it would have been "in ill grace" for him to attack McCarthy. Another time he told you: "If I had made a big thing about giving McCarthy an extra kick after he was censured, I would have looked cheap." These are less persuasive than a casual remark later: "Hell, half my voters in Massachusetts look on McCarthy as a hero." His performance, though not courageous, is not discreditable. What is puzzling is the liberal bitterness which followed and never died. Hubert Humphrey had sponsored a bill to outlaw the Communist party, an act of outright servility to McCarthyism. Yet the liberal intellectual community quickly forgave Hubert and then forgot.

In June of 1956 Jack invited you to join him in a drive to Newport, where a mutual friend was getting married. During the trip he seemed preoccupied, and when you commented on it, he explained that he was wrestling with the question of whether or not he should try for the vice-presidential nomination at the Democratic National Convention in August. His father was vehemently against it, arguing that Stevenson would lose, and that if Jack were on the ticket, the defeat would be attributed to anti-Catholicism. Probably for the first time in your life, you agreed with the ambassador. Jack wasn't so sure. He thought this might be the right time to strike.

Actually, the JFK for VP boom was already on, fueled by his friends' enthusiasm. By the time he arrived at Chicago's Conrad Hilton Hotel —

Jackie, pregnant, was staying nearby with the Shrivers — volunteers were passing out Kennedy buttons and banners. The Chicago *Sun-Times* had endorsed him; every convention delegate had received a reprint of its editorial. Many who had served with Jack on Capitol Hill were working on other members of their state delegations. New Hampshire's votes were committed by primary to Estes Kefauver. The rest of New England's delegates, strongly for Jack, had breakfasted with Abe Ribicoff of Connecticut as chairman. Three New England governors were urging Adlai to pick Jack as his running mate. On the advice of party elders, Jack called on Eleanor Roosevelt. It turned out to be bad advice. She dressed him down, before a roomful of delegates, for being soft on McCarthyism.

During the third day of the convention word was passed that Kennedy was no longer under consideration. He called on Stevenson, who asked Jack to nominate him. That seemed to confirm the rumors; by tradition the vice-presidential nod does not go to the nominator of the presidential candidate. Jack told you afterward: "I thought the matter was closed and was not especially unhappy." Stevenson's nomination swiftly followed and Adlai then electrified the convention. He didn't mention Eisenhower, who had been twice stricken by illness during his first term, but no one could doubt the significance of his allusion when he told the delegates that they had a solemn obligation to ponder who would occupy the White House "if the elected President is prevented by a higher will from serving a full term." Having pondered it himself, he had "concluded to depart from the precedents of the past. I have decided that the selection of the vice-presidential nominee should be made through the free process of this convention."

It didn't bring freedom; it brought chaos. The delegates had come to Chicago to choose a presidential candidate. No one had run in vice-presidential primaries, no one had weighed qualifications for the office; they had assumed that here, as in past conventions, the decision would be made by the head of the ticket. As the gavel fell at the next session of the convention, entrants in the vice-presidential sweepstakes were Estes Kefauver, Albert Gore, Robert Wagner, Hubert Humphrey, and John F. Kennedy. Ribicoff put Kennedy's name in nomination with a ringing speech. Florida's George Smathers seconded it. They needed another seconder. Bobby spotted John McCormack, standing ten feet away on the convention floor, and told him Jack would be honored if McCormack would do the job. McCormack was startled. Only a few weeks earlier Kennedy had outmaneuvered him to take over the Massachusetts political machine. He began: "Well, that's nice of him —" and broke off because Bobby was practically carrying him to the rostrum. Jack, watching television from his command post, was dumbfounded to see the man he had just routed at home boosting him before the entire nation.

The first ballot vote gave Kefauver 483½ and Kennedy 304; Gore, Wagner, and Humphrey trailed far behind. A Kennedy trend became clear in the second ballot. New York and New Jersey gave him 126½ new votes. Jack was in the tub soaking his back when Lyndon Johnson tremulously announced that all 56 Texas delegates would go to "that fighting senator who wears the scars of battle . . . John Kennedy of Massachusetts." Kennedy was in first place. Of the 651½ needed to nominate, he had 618 votes, while Kefauver's total was 551½. Ted Sorensen came over and held out his hand.

THE DEMOCRATIC NATIONAL CONVENTION, 1956

Seeking the vice-presidential spot

"Congratulations, Jack. That's it." Kennedy replied, "No, not yet," and began to dress calmly in front of the television.

At this point two factors became crucial. The large electric tote board had been dismantled the previous evening, so the delegates did not realize that Kennedy was within a few votes of victory. The other factor was the convention chairman, the party's canniest politician, "Mr. Sam" — Sam Rayburn of Texas. Mr. Sam looked out across the sea of delegates and saw, amid the pandemonium, a dozen delegations waving their standards, calling for recognition. They wanted to switch votes, but everything depended on which of them the chairman chose first. He knew that South Carolina, Illinois, and Alabama wanted to switch to Kennedy, while Tennessee, Oklahoma, and Minnesota were swinging to Kefauver. McCormack learned that Missouri had decided to change its votes from Gore to put Kefauver over the top. Possibly feeling that he had been both manhandled and exploited by Bobby — as he had been — he yelled from an aisle: "Sam! Sam! Missouri!" Rayburn, himself no Kennedy enthusiast, recognized Missouri, and moments later Kennedy knew it was all over. He slammed his right fist into his left palm and said, "That's it — let's go." Appearing on the platform, grinning broadly, he delivered a witty, generous speech and moved that Kefauver be nominated by acclamation. The delegates roared their approval.

It was at that moment that he became a national political figure, and he had achieved it under ideal circumstances. His generous support of Kefauver had won the admiration of millions, and since he wouldn't be on the ticket, he had nothing to win or lose in November. However, he didn't see that in Chicago. Although only a handful knew it, his defeat rankled. He felt resentful and betrayed. This had been his first race outside heavily Catholic Massachusetts, and he wondered if he had been a victim of bigotry. His feeling that he had been jobbed by certain state bosses was more valid. David Lawrence of Pennsylvania and Robert B. Meyner of New Jersey, who were pledged to him, had turned their coats at the last minute. In each case, the leaders' voices, announcing state votes, had all but been drowned out by the shouts of their furious Kennedy delegates.

Afterward, on a long sail off the Cape, he purged some of his frustration by talking it out. He still felt bitter, but there was not a flicker of self-pity in his flat voice. Instead, he was fiercely sardonic. He casually asked if you had ever thought of giving up writing for politics. "If you do," he said heavily, "be prepared to ride in an overheated limousine in ninety-three-degree heat in Fort Lauderdale, and in an open motorcade in thirty-degree cold in Bellows Falls, Vermont, and in Twin Falls, Idaho. . . . But that's only part of it. Be prepared . . . to hear your record distorted and your public remarks twisted. I could hardly recognize myself [in Chicago] . . . the vicious, reactionary Massachusetts senator who was antifarmer, antilabor, an unreliable Democrat, a slave to the pope, a dying man, and — that most damning indictment of all — my father's son. Finally, if you become a candidate you must remember always to speak at an intellectual level that will be understood by everyone in your audience, regardless of education, IQ, or literacy." That being true, he said, beginning to enjoy himself, "the party picked the perfect man as its vice-presidential nominee. A Texas delegate explained to me that Kefauver's secret is that he makes the most ignorant white man in

Texas feel superior. Don't knock it; it's an art. And a necessary one. Even Stevenson finds it essential to mispronounce the word *elite*." He paused, but wasn't quite ready to abandon the subject. Running before the wind now, he said: "The hell of it is, I love it. Not the fakery, but learning to talk to voters in their own language. Stevenson hates it. He's dying to be President, but he hates campaigning. That's the difference between us, and it's important." Later, relaxing on his father's porch, he said quietly: "Chicago taught me a lot. I know now that you don't get far in public life until you become the total politician. That means you've got to deal, not just with voters, but with the party leaders, too. From now on *I'm* going to be the total politician."

His father appeared in time to hear the end of this, and his smile was broad. "You know what I was just saying to your mother? I asked her had she noticed that you hadn't shed a tear after that nutty race. It's still true: Kennedys don't cry." He added, and this was the first time you heard it, "Don't get mad; get even." Jack nodded. "I've had over twenty-five hundred speaking invitations this week, and I'm going to accept a hundred and forty-four. Did you see that story in the *Herald Trib?*" The New York *Herald Tribune* was a Kennedy bugbear, unswerving in its loyalty to Republican causes. His father nodded; the piece, an account of Kefauver's victory, had begun: "The famous Kennedy luck ran out today." Jack said: "With only about four hours of work and a handful of supporters, I came within thirty-three and a half votes of winning that nomination. If I work hard for four years, I ought to pick up marbles." A few days later, when a fellow senator told him that he would be a cinch for second place in four years, Kennedy said shortly: "I'm not running for the vice-presidency anymore. I'm running for the presidency." At the next Gridiron Club show a character playing Joseph P. Kennedy sang:

> *All of us, why not take all of us?*
> *Fabulous — you can't live without us.*
> *My son Jack heads the procession*
> *Then come Bob, groomed for succession . . .*

Jackie lacked political savvy in those years and the marvel is that she later acquired it. She never adjusted to the Kennedys as Ethel did, but she came much closer than Ted's wife, Joan. And few wives have been tried as Jackie was in 1956. She had gone to Chicago expecting excitement and throughout the week she had been miserable and bored. Mostly she sat in the Shrivers' apartment staring at the television. Twice she had taken a seat in the box reserved for distinguished guests of the convention. She saw the tumult on the floor and understood none of it. Now and then Jack would pass by, but he was so tense, withdrawn, and exhausted — and so clearly busy — that they only exchanged a few words. Being seven months pregnant, she assumed that once the circus was over, she and her husband would have a holiday together. To her dismay — and indignation — he told her that after the final gavel he would fly to the Riviera for a two-week vacation with his father. He suggested she stay with the Auchinclosses in Newport. Jack knew that bearing children was difficult for her. He should have anticipated that she might have trouble, as she did.

Ken and Helen O'Donnell were in Hyannis Port, spending a few days with Bobby and Ethel, when an urgent call came from Janet Auchincloss in Newport. Her daughter had gone into labor prematurely. The baby, a girl, was dead; Jackie was in critical condition. Bobby tried to notify his brother by transatlantic telephone, but Jack had gone sailing and there was no way to reach him until he returned. Bob drove to the hospital and sat by his sister-in-law's bed, day and night, until his brother arrived. Afterward, Jackie would say fondly from time to time, "Bobby's always there when you need him." After the assassination, when Air Force One was returning from Dallas, Bob drove out to Andrews Field and hid in the back of an army truck until the plane touched down. The moment it stopped he leapt out to be by Jackie's side. In that breathless voice of hers she said: "Oh, Bobby. You're always where you're needed."

Once she had recovered enough to travel, Jack brought her home from the hospital and led her to a lounge chair on his father's porch. Then he, Bob, and Ken talked politics. She told a friend: "Politics is sort of my enemy as far as seeing Jack is concerned." There were friends who thought their childless marriage might be headed for the rocks. It was certainly unsteady that autumn. As a political celebrity, he was expected to crisscross the country, speaking for Stevenson, though he was convinced his leader was a loser.

On November 6 Eisenhower buried Stevenson in an awesome landslide, amassing a triumphant margin of nearly ten million votes. Suddenly, for reasons which had nothing to do with the lost election, Senator and Mrs. John F. Kennedy were once more a happy, congenial couple. There were various explanations. He was treated with new respect by the Washington community; they were invited everywhere. Jackie cultivated the wives of her husband's friends, and although her closest friend would always be her sister, Lee, she found her new acquaintances delightful. He had his Pulitzer, was awarded an honorary degree by his college, was elected to Harvard's Board of Overseers, and saw his picture on the cover of *Time*. Reconciled to the prospect of a smaller family than they had planned, Jack and Jackie sold Hickory Hill to Bob and Ethel, whose fifth child had just been born. They moved into a red-brick Federalist house with a pleasant back garden on N Street in Georgetown.

Their greatest gift in 1957 was a baby girl, born on November 27. Jack had never been interested in other people's children, but he became passionately devoted to Caroline, although incessant campaigning frequently left Jackie, in effect, a single parent. She became a familiar Georgetown mother, wearing what were variously called pedal pushers, toreador pants, or Capri pants, pushing her baby in a stroller or playing with her in the little park there. By now she had learned to field reporters' questions. Had her husband surprised her since their marriage? "He's more serious than I thought he'd be." Had she learned to share the Kennedys' enthusiasm for sports? "Well, I'm learning to play golf." That was untrue. She was trying to learn, but her instructor, her husband, was inept. Once she became bogged down in a sand trap. She whacked and whacked, but nothing helped; the ball just dribbled back. "Let me show you," said Jack, striding over confidently. He struck a graceful pose and executed a perfect swing. The ball advanced eight inches and then returned to the same place. "See?" said Jack, handing her the club. "That's the way you do it."

She shared his love of movies, and among those they saw and liked in these years were Fellini's *La Strada*, Mike Todd's *Around the World in Eighty Days*, *The Bridge on the River Kwai*, Billy Wilder's *Witness for the Prosecution*, *Room at the Top*, *Separate Tables*, *Cat on a Hot Tin Roof*, and Hitchcock's *Vertigo*. Jack had given her free rein in redecorating the house; she filled it with eighteenth-century furniture and drawings. He would complain about the price of clothes; she would alter her budget to conceal impulsive buying. She found two expensive rugs, bought them, and then juggled her books so they wouldn't show. Jack loved the rugs. In time he found out what she had done, but was more amused than angry. Millions of couples play the same game. Jackie would have enjoyed playing it forever, but she had hitched her wagon to a star, and the star was ascendant.

His most important step toward the top would be his 1958 campaign for reelection to the Senate. It was assumed, and that was part of his problem. To impress the party's national leadership, he had to roll up a heavy vote. Registered voters who know the outcome before the polls open are likely to stay home. And because Jack was barnstorming the country, supporting Democratic candidates elsewhere, his campaigning in Massachusetts would be limited to seventeen days. His receptions in other states were not always cordial; it was not a good idea, that year, for politicians in any part of the country to speak up for civil rights and integration, but Kennedy had accepted a Mississippi invitation before the school-integration crisis at Little Rock, and refused to back out now. Mississippi's state Republican chairman challenged him to set forth his views on integration. Kennedy did; to his Jackson audience he said: "I have no hesitancy in telling the Republican chairman the same thing I have said in my own city of Boston, that I accept the Supreme Court decision as the supreme law of the land." And that, he pointed out, meant he believed in integrated schools.

With Bobby, Larry, and Kenny in action, supported by Dick Donahue, another Ivy League Irishman, Jack's reelection fight moved into high gear. O'Brien was a scheduling wizard. At the end of a typical day he said proudly: "We ran the senator through fifteen speaking appearances in fifteen cities and towns, from Chelsea to Gloucester, and had him back in bed by eleven o'clock at night." Over one lunch in the back room of a Haverhill restaurant, Jack dictated about twenty-five assignments he wanted completed by the end of the afternoon. Jackie, always perceptive, gave Kenny a quizzical look. "You're always writing things down," she said. "But I never see you looking at the pad after we leave the restaurant. Do you ever do anything about these things he wants you to do?" O'Donnell said: "Never. I wait till he calms down and then I rip these notes off the pad and throw them away." She laughed. Jack didn't. He gave Ken an even look and said: "You son of a bitch. I'll bet that's exactly what you do." Ken replied that someone on

JACQUELINE
BOUVIER
KENNEDY

the team had to act responsibly, and he had a point. Introducing local dignitaries, Jack was capable of the most startling japes. He would say: "Excellency, have you met Congressman Powers?" or, "Mr. Mayor, I'd like to present Ambassador Fay" or, "Mr. Secretary, I think you know General Benjy Bradlee." He was incorrigible. One afternoon near Hammersmith Farm, he was surrounded by nuns, and you could hardly believe your ears when you heard him telling them, in his most earnest voice, "You know, Jackie always wanted to be a nun . . . she went to a convent school and really planned to take the orders."

But, God, he was proud of her! He would predict that when word was passed to the next town that she would be campaigning with him, the crowd would double. It would; sometimes it seemed to redouble. They would work down a main street, she on one sidewalk and he on the other. Every now and then he would glance over and say with mock envy: "Look, she's drawing twice as many as I am. As usual." He made the race sound casual and fun, which it was, but beneath the air of banter and blarney his pros were leaving nothing to chance. That was part of the campaign outsiders never saw. It was grueling; volunteer workers toiled door-to-door, canvassing every town and county, signing up pledges. On election eve Jack quickly toured Boston with a few friends — it was a rainy night; if you had neither raincoat nor umbrella you got soaked — winding up at the G and G Delicatessen on Blue Hill Avenue, a Jewish neighborhood in Dorchester. Jack, Bob, and Ted, too tired to talk, climbed atop a table and sang "Heart of My Heart." As music it was dreadful. They were all off-key. Their voices cracked and broke. They couldn't even hold the melody. But if you were there that night you will never forget it, or fail to remember your excitement when the figures started rolling. They were unbelievable. Nearly two million voters had gone to the polls — a record for an off-year election — and Kennedy won 73.6 percent of the vote, the largest majority won by any senatorial candidate in the United States that year. It accomplished exactly what Jack had wanted. Roscoe Drummond wrote in the *Herald Tribune* that although the national sweep had been Democratic, Kennedy's was the most significant victory. Moreover, Drummond pointed out, Protestant hostility toward Catholic candidates, accepted by generations of politicians as an article of faith, had weakened and perhaps vanished altogether. He pointed to the victory in Minnesota of senator-elect Eugene McCarthy over Edward Thye — "a Catholic defeating a Lutheran in a Protestant state."

For over two years now Jack had gone through the motions of a potential presidential candidate. That made him interesting, but far from unique. With the national conventions twenty months away, seven or eight other men in public life were testing the political climate, hiring pollsters, speaking here and there in hope of winning serious support from men with money and power, kingmakers with crowns to bestow. Most men with symptoms of Potomac fever juggle the idea for a while, contemplate it, and feel its pull growing or diminishing until time and events force their hands. In Kennedy's case it was different. He and his father went over election statistics, studied projections from analysts the ambassador had hired for this one job, and concluded that the time to lunge for the supreme prize of American politics was upon them. Not the announcement; that would be delayed for fourteen months, until the first week of 1960. Meanwhile, Jack would step up his speaking activities and organize his campaign, undertaking a nationwide expansion of his senatorial strategies; making himself available to newspapers, national magazines, and all three television networks; and traveling ceaselessly to talk to local party leaders, entertaining the men and women who would be delegates.

Nixon, whom Eisenhower had rather reluctantly anointed as his successor, would be doing the same thing, but Kennedy had devised a second strategy. In his role as vice-president, Nixon presided over the Senate. He was not, however, allowed to speak there. Senator Kennedy could, and he meant to, often. In the senatorial chamber, the great issues of the 1950s were coming to a head. He intended to take a strong stand on civil rights, a labor "bill of rights," and an end to talk of federal subsidies for parochial and private schools — wasted talk, he said, since the Bill of Rights clearly ruled them out. The most sensitive issue confronting him was what Paul Dever had delicately called "the canonical impediment" — his religion. It was also the least understood. Theodore H. White, the historian of modern elections, writes: "In many of the most important dioceses of the nation it was known in 1960 that if the Catholic church had any silent inclination, it leaned to Richard M. Nixon rather than to John F. Kennedy." Kennedy was simply too liberal for the Roman Catholic hierarchy. He was also irreverent. He said he had asked Cardinal Spellman if the pope really was infallible, and Spellman had replied, "I don't know, but he keeps calling me Spillman." This was an intrafaith matter, however. More than three out of every four Americans were not Catholic. Most of them merely wanted assurances that a Catholic President would owe Rome no allegiance. His vehement opposition to federal support for parochial schools was a move in the right direction, but further steps were necessary. In a formal public statement he declared: "I believe in an America where the separation of church and state is absolute — where no Catholic priest would tell the President how to act, and no Protestant clergyman would tell his parishioners how to vote." He continued in that vein until the Vatican newspaper, *L'Osservatore Romano*, told its readers that the church "had the duty and right" to tell them how to vote, and that it had every intention of doing so. Kennedy read the translation of this. He handed it to a friend and said in a low, slow voice: "Now I understand why Henry the Eighth set up his own church."

Later, he said, he would deal with bigots of all faiths. But he began his quest for national office by holding the first of his two key councils of war in the ambassador's Palm Beach home on April 1, 1959. There was no question of who was in charge. Jack presided, opened the meetings, and gave lengthy presentations, all without notes. It was a virtuoso performance. He provided a complete rundown, from memory, of the political situation in each of the forty-eight states and Puerto Rico, Alaska, and Hawaii. Local politicians were named; identified as friendly, hostile, or on the fence; and rated according to the number of delegates each would control at the convention. Then Jack explained which states and territories had primaries, which of these primaries were binding, which delegations were tied together by the unit rule, which would be ruled by instructions from a state convention, and which were free to vote for whomever they liked. There were revelations, even for those who took pride in their grasp of party politics. Some men looked dazed. He *had* thrown a lot at them. It was part of the

FDR legend that he could do this sort of thing — hand you an outline map of the United States, draw a line across it from any direction, and then tell you, in succession, the names of all the counties through which the line passed. Adlai Stevenson, for all his incomparable gifts, could never have displayed such mastery of American politics. Jack could, and just had. The man beside you leaned over and whispered, "We've not only got the best candidate. We've also got the best campaign manager."

Over the summer Kennedy was changing, deepening; he was given to longer silences, less eager for verbal fencing. At Hyannis Port he was reading; among the books scattered around were *The Organization Man*, *The Last Hurrah* (whose author, Edwin O'Connor, acquired much of his material from Clem Norton, a figure in Jack's first congressional campaign); the new Barth, the latest Camus, an Angus Wilson play; Nevil Shute's *On the Beach*, *Parkinson's Law*, *The Ugly American*, and, looking out of place among all these, two Ian Fleming thrillers, *Diamonds Are Forever* and *From Russia with Love*. But these were diversions. He wanted to talk about politics, and did. While Lyndon Johnson had been slumbering at the LBJ Ranch, the Irish poacher had been stealthily branding animals Lyndon thought were his — Congressman Charles A. Buckley of the Bronx, for example, and Mayor Richard J. Daley of Chicago. "Well," Jack told you, "we all know Lyndon; he's the ultimate paranoid. Now his feelings of persecution are being fully justified. He should be grateful to me."

After a long pause, you asked about Humphrey. He seemed, for once, unsure of himself. The pause lengthened. Finally he said, "That's the real weakness of the system, you know. Hubert should be leading the merry chase. Everyone who knows him, who's even met him, senses how able he is. But he's still a regional figure, and this is an enormous country. He's just not *known* outside Minnesota and the Washington community. And there aren't many ways he can *get* known. He can't afford marketing; that's for the very rich. A press buildup is out; that's mostly for Republicans. High patronage in Washington, especially on the cabinet or ambassadorial level, will work; Ike has done it for Nixon. Lacking all those, a regional leader can only break out on the national scene by showing a lot of muscles in the primaries. Hubert's got heart, and he's got talent. But a lot of us are running this time, and we're mostly well-heeled. I just don't see how he can cut it."

He seemed vulnerable at that moment. You had been waiting to ask one question for a very long time. "Why do you think you can be President?" He stared for a moment, then gave a little lopsided grin and looked out to sea. "Don't you suppose I've asked myself that a thousand times? The thought is intimidating. But then, you know, I look around me at the others in the race, and I say to myself, well, if they think they can do it, why not me? *Why not me?* That's the answer, and I think it's enough."

The second strategy powwow before Jack's announcement of his candidacy was held in Bob's roomy Hyannis Port home on the afternoon of Wednesday, October 28, 1959. The calendar pages were turning swiftly now.

In that year only sixteen states held an open primary. Delegates elsewhere were lined up by barter, patronage, back-scratching, or, now and then, by plain bribery. But these sixteen were clean, and they offered the only route to power for outsiders like Kennedy and Humphrey. If they could not establish popular strength there, the party would turn away. But if one of them built up a head of steam, knocking off every challenger, denying him the nomination would not only be difficult; it would doom the boss-picked nominee at the general election. The country wouldn't elect a man who seemed to have cheated another candidate out of the office. Of the sixteen states, Hubert Humphrey had filed in five, John F. Kennedy in seven. They would first collide on April 5 in Wisconsin.

In Hyannis Port that Wednesday, three days before Halloween, the leaves outside had turned red and yellow and soon they would be gone. The meeting room was expansive, dominated by a large fireplace, and furnished with comfortable lounge chairs, easy chairs, and hassocks, which, when the meeting opened, were occupied by fifteen men and women, including the ambassador; Robert Kennedy; Kenneth O'Donnell; Lawrence O'Brien; Theodore Sorensen; Pierre Salinger; Stephen Smith; Louis Harris, a public-opinion analyst; John Bailey, political boss of Connecticut; and Edward Kennedy. Not seated, but facing the others with his back to the fireplace, dressed in a sports jacket, slacks, and loafers, looking almost a decade younger than his forty-two years, was John Fitzgerald Kennedy, candidate for the presidency of the United States.

Their campaign had been slowly picking up momentum. Ten rooms of office space had been rented in Washington. Earlier in the fall Bob Kennedy had resigned as a Senate committee counsel to manage the campaign. Jack, slipping off his jacket, opened the proceedings. Later his public speaking won wide approval, but he was at his best as a conversationalist, and that was how he spoke to today's group. It was another first-class effort — three hours of political analysis, surveying the entire country without a map or note. His command of detail was overwhelming. During a lull, one member of the meeting murmured, "He can still drive down an avenue in Boston and remember which stores put up his campaign posters ten years ago."

After his sum-up, he invited questions and corrections. On one point there could be no confusion. The nomination had to be won in the primaries. Only when they had demonstrated his popularity could he bargain and broker with the political leaders of the Northeast, who liked him but believed that, as a Catholic, he hadn't a chance. And while he was campaigning in one primary state, commitments, including financial commitments, must be met in the others. Volunteer organizations, contacts with professional politicians, office space, mailing lists, literature — all these had to be kept running at full efficiency. The nomination would be worthless if, after he had won it, he found himself unequipped to face the Republican nominee in the general election. *Every primary has to be won,* he said. *It has to come up seven every time.* An early handicap was that the staff was split on the wisdom of fighting Humphrey in Wisconsin, and that the division would remain for two months, until Kennedy, supported only by his father and Lou Harris, overrode Bobby and the rest and invaded the state. Meanwhile, challenges had to be accepted or refused in states not contemplated in those early planning meetings, among them Maryland, Indiana, Oregon (unavoidable; if you were a contender your name was printed on the ballot whether you liked it or not), West Virginia, Ohio, and California.

All this sounds as complicated now as it seemed at the time. An incumbent President was about to move out of the White House, and the line of prospective tenants was a long one. As it turned out, however, the simplifying force would be the primaries, which in the age of television could provide instant drama and create celebrities overnight. But few foresaw this. Harry Truman dismissed primaries as "eyewash." Political bosses regarded selection of the party's nominee as their right and duty. In the opening months of 1960 those vying for their favor — and scorning the primaries — were Lyndon Johnson, Stuart Symington, and the most beloved of Democrats, Adlai Stevenson. To these must be added a dozen dark horses and favorite sons, each praying that lightning would strike for him. At that time neither Humphrey nor Kennedy was considered a front-runner. Most seasoned observers expected their duel to end with mixed results; it was inconceivable that one of them could win *all* the primaries — and a standoff, it was assumed, would eliminate both.

Ironically, by deciding not to meet Kennedy's primary challenge, his most formidable competitors forfeited the race. No one can predict what the outcome would have been had they elected to slug it out with him. Humphrey was as able a politician as any of them, and Kennedy decked him twice. But a field of rivals would have greatly expanded the struggle, with plots and subplots proliferating on all sides, introducing figures whose significance would tower for a few days and then vanish forever, producing melodramas, minor tragedies, victories which would loom large and be forgotten — all of them confusing, baffling, exasperating, and infuriating the voters. But because Kennedy and Humphrey were the only two Democrats in the field, and because they confronted each other in only two states, the issue was decided there.

They should have crossed foils first in Ohio. Kennedy, however, found a way of locking up the Ohio delegation without spending a moment or a dime there. He did it by playing very rough politics; it wasn't attractive, but a President who can't be hard is vulnerable, and so is his country. Ohio's Governor Mike DiSalle intended to run in the state primary as a favorite son and told Kennedy, "Get a couple of important Protestants to announce for you, and I'll endorse you." Jack didn't believe him. In 1956 DiSalle had been one of the Catholics who fought Kennedy's bid for the vice-presidential nomination. Moreover, DiSalle was a protégé of Truman, and the ex-President was frankly against Kennedy. Jack wanted a public commitment now, and he knew how to twist the governor's arm. Ray Miller, Cleveland's Democratic boss, was spoiling for a fight with DiSalle. Jack sent Bobby and John Bailey to Ohio. Bobby laid it out in stark tones. Either DiSalle endorsed his brother, Bob said, or the Kennedys would back Miller in a showdown. DiSalle capitulated. Jack told no one of this. A week later, every front page in the country reported that the entire Ohio delegation had been pledged to Kennedy. The votes were important, and so was the message. Adlai wouldn't have grasped what had happened; neither, probably, would Humphrey. But Johnson doubtless saw it at once, and so did Daley, Buckley, and Carmine De Sapio of Manhattan. Now they knew that Kennedy was not only charismatic and rich; he also was capable of piracy, and they respected piratical leadership. Of course, he had to be a winner, too.

In September 1959 Kennedy had quit flying commercial airlines and bought a Convair prop plane ("It's cheaper"), christening it the *Caroline*. Now, as it glided toward its first Wisconsin airfield, a disconsolate Kennedy staff looked down on the bleakest of snowscapes. Relieved only by the angular shapes of black leafless trees and sharply etched farmhouses and barns, the white mantle stretched in all directions.

You stepped down the *Caroline*'s metal folding steps, and the wind hit your face, cold as malice. Even the welcoming committee looked miserable. A motorcade carried Kennedy from Eau Claire to Cornell, but when he stopped to greet bystanders, they stared at him, mute and unresponsive. In Cornell's N-Joy Café, a rally awaited him. There were eight people there. He was allowed to address a few high school civics classes. Everyone but Jack was depressed. By the end of the day, he had seen about sixteen hundred people, of whom twelve hundred were too young to vote. Someone said: "Cold people, cold towns, cold people." "This is the toughest," he acknowledged. "But don't knock the kids. When they get home they'll talk to their parents, and parents *do* vote."

Jackie, again pregnant, arrived from Washington, and announced that she had come to do her part. She campaigned, as she did everything else, in her own way. In Kenosha she entered a supermarket, listened to the manager announcing bargains over his public-address system, gave him a warm smile, and asked would he mind if she said a few words. The next voice the incredulous shoppers heard was Jacqueline Kennedy's. "Just keep on shopping while I tell you about my husband, John F. Kennedy." She talked, in her breathy but persuasive way, of his wartime service and his achievements on Capitol Hill. She ended: "He cares deeply about the welfare of his country — please vote for him."

With the exception of the ambassador, all the Kennedys appeared in Wisconsin. Teddy risked his neck but drew a crowd by performing a dangerous stunt on skis. Bobby told Helen Keyes, the daughter of the Kennedys' dentist, to make arrangements for each of his sisters, Jean, Pat, and Eunice, to attend nine house parties a day — 378 in all. Paul Corbin, a Wisconsin volunteer, helped her, as she didn't know a soul in the state. Bit by bit — a druggist here, an undertaker there — she made progress. Over breakfast in Wisconsin Springs, they discovered that their waitress, a Democrat, did not intend to vote for Kennedy. "I can't," she said. "He's a Catholic." Helen asked if she would invite her friends to meet one of the senator's sisters. The waitress said: "Well, I'll ask my father, but aren't Kennedy's sisters Catholics, too?" Corbin pointed at Helen. "This lady is a Baptist and *she's* for Kennedy." Helen, a devout Catholic, silently said the short form of the Act of Contrition. The waitress's father agreed; the party was a success.

Jack had found his own technique for dealing with the religion problem. He would solemnly say: "I think it well that we recall what happened to a great governor when he became a presidential nominee. Despite his

Announcing in the Senate Caucus Room, January 2, 1960

CAMPAIGNING FOR THE PRESIDENTIAL NOMINATION

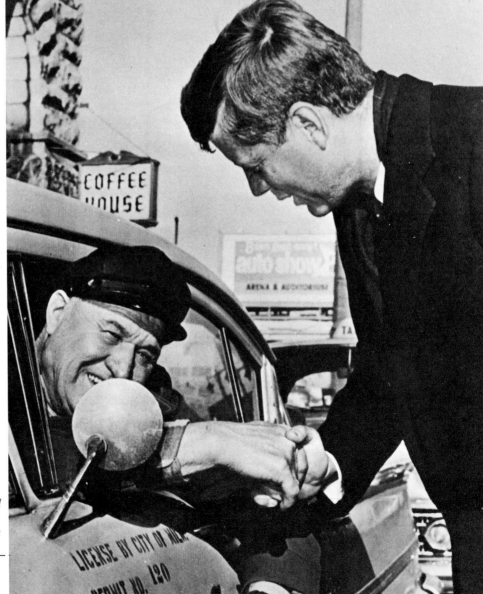

JFK's first presidential campaign handshake, Milwaukee, Wisconsin

The New Hampshire primary

At a United States Steel Company plant

With Jackie at a press conference

Campaigning and winning in the West Virginia primary

Mending fences with Mrs. Roosevelt

The convention

successful record, despite his plainspoken voice, the campaign was a debacle. His views were distorted. He carried fewer votes than any candidate in his party's history. To top it off, he lost his own state that he had served so well." Everyone was waiting for him to name Al Smith. He let them wait. Then: "You all know who he was, and I'm sure you remember his religion — Alfred M. Landon, Protestant." It was a good story and everyone laughed. Nevertheless, on the Sunday before polling day the Milwaukee *Journal* divided the voters into three columns: Republican, Democrat, and Catholic.

The Kennedy press cult was one of the striking phenomena of the 1960s. Kennedy and his people were attractive, colorful, witty, and entertaining. That should have helped him. Instead, in Wisconsin it hurt. Political reporters were so fascinated by him that they assumed the state's voters felt the same way. What had begun as an uphill battle — a young challenger with an unpopular religion struggling against a popular senator from the state next door — became, in the eyes of the press, a Kennedy walkaway. Approaching May 10 — primary day — forecasts of his victory rose almost hourly. It was an inversion of Jack's underdoggery. Anything short of an overwhelming triumph would be interpreted as a Kennedy failure.

And that was what happened. Jack won more popular votes than any candidate in the history of Wisconsin's primaries, carrying six congressional districts and two-thirds of the delegate votes. O'Brien, O'Donnell, Powers, and Sorensen were elated. The senator was not. He had been watching the television commentators in silence, sipping a bowl of chicken-noodle soup, ignoring the whoops around him. Eunice sensed his mood. "What does it mean, Jack?" she asked. In a low, bitter voice he replied: "It means that we have to do it all over again. We have to go through every one and win every one of them, all the way to the convention." He, alone among them, understood the implications of the vote breakdown as it would be interpreted by the East Coast bosses who controlled the delegates he needed. He had won 56 percent of the popular vote, but he had lost all four Protestant districts, had carried one of mixed religions by a hair, and had rolled up all of his popular majority from heavily Catholic areas. It had been his great hope to strangle the religion issue here. He had failed, and now he had to tackle it on a far more ominous battleground — West Virginia, deeply religious and 95 percent Protestant. It looked like a trap.

And there was no way out. Humphrey should have quit. Since he could not carry Wisconsin, a state next to his own, he could not be relied upon to take the Middle West, his home ground. As a presidential contender, he was finished. He should have withdrawn in West Virginia. That was not just the Kennedys' view; it was the opinion of Hubert's political allies. But Humphrey was a statesman of vision who could become a great President, and he knew it. Although he had been warned to expect a devastating primary defeat, he had come through a tight race with his head held high. Moreover, he argued with some justice that Wisconsin's crossover rule — which permitted members of one party to vote in the other party's primary — meant that Kennedy's figures had been inflated by Catholic Republicans. So reporters who called at his hotel room were told. "You can quote me as being encouraged and exhilarated. . . ." Humphrey was still a candidate.

To the Kennedys it was obvious that Johnson, Symington, and Stevenson's backers wanted to use Hubert as a pawn, hoping he could stop Kennedy on the national convention's first ballot in July and give them room for maneuver. But Jack's men were still confident — indeed, overconfident. Bobby, Larry, and Ken flew to Charleston, West Virginia, where Bob McDonough, a seasoned pol, had been organizing the state for over a year. A Harris poll, taken four months before the Wisconsin primary, indicated that Kennedy could destroy Humphrey in West Virginia, 70 to 30 percent. As the newcomers entered the room in the Kanawha Hotel where McDonough's key workers were meeting, they were surprised to note that everyone was silent and unsmiling. "Well," Bobby said cordially. "What are our problems?" A man jumped up and yelled: "He's a Catholic. That's our goddamned problem!" Suddenly the entire room erupted. Men were shouting that West Virginians would never vote for a Catholic, whatever the race, for President or dogcatcher. Bobby stared at them. These people had been working for Kennedy for months, and no one had told them that their candidate was a Catholic. He checked the Harris poll, which had been the source of so much optimism. Harris had made the same omission. Here in West Virginia, Bobby now realized, religion was more than a key issue; it was *the* issue. Virtually every West Virginian either had a television set or knew someone with one. Network commentators, covering the Wisconsin primary, had stressed the religion issue and specified that Senator Kennedy was a member of the Roman Catholic faith. As a result, the latest Harris figures here were Humphrey 60, Kennedy 40. As though he didn't know, Jack asked the pollsters to identify the reason for the switch. Respondents were sought for follow-up interviews; the replies were as anticipated: "But no one in West Virginia knew you were a Catholic in December. Now they know." "A man's religion shouldn't have anything to do with it. But . . ."

West Virginians admired heroes, so radio and TV spots were prepared showing Jack being decorated. Jack would call Humphrey a "front man" for politicians who wouldn't face him now, here, on West Virginia soil. He asked crowds: "If Johnson and the other candidates want your vote in November, why don't they have enough respect for you to come here and ask for your support in the primary?" In a state which had long felt slighted, the response was encouraging. He visited their villages in the mountain hollows, went into the impoverished mining areas, and had himself lowered into a mine. The desolation, the bleakness, and the hunger touched him more than anything else in the entire campaign. Still blackened with soot, he stepped up to a microphone and said ringingly: "President Eisenhower should take Vice-President Nixon by the hand and lead him into these homes in McDowell County and Mingo County and Logan County so he can see how the families of West Virginia are trying to live." He shook every hand stretched toward him, and spoke until, having lost his voice, he signaled Teddy to substitute for him. (Teddy made a rousing, impassioned speech, and so prolonged was the cheering that Jack stepped up to the mike to croak that his brother was not old enough to meet the constitutional age minimum for the presidency.)

In Logan and Mingo and McDowell and Slab Fork, Kennedy's touchers were not shrill high school girls. They were old women, older than he would ever live to be, deformed by years of cruel labor, and they reached out with trembling fingers to brush his sleeve or jacket. He had a special way with them. He would lean over, smiling tenderly, and let his cheek glide against theirs. In that intimate moment he would say softly, so softly that you had to be right there to hear it: "Thank you, dear. Thank you."

After Eleanor Roosevelt came to understand Jack's record on Mc-Carthyism, reconciliation swiftly followed, and she became one of his most ardent admirers. She told a friend: "I don't think anyone in our politics since Franklin has had the same vital relationship with crowds. Franklin would sometimes begin a campaign weary and apathetic. But in the course of the campaign he would draw strength and vitality from his audiences and would end in better shape than he started. I feel that Senator Kennedy is much the same — that his intelligence and courage elicit emotions from his crowds which flow back to him and sustain and strengthen him."

In West Virginia, Kennedy's greatest asset was the wholehearted support of Franklin D. Roosevelt, Jr. In ramshackle huts clinging precariously to the steep-pitched hills above the mines photographs of FDR, now discolored and curling with age, occupied the place of honor. And now here was his son, looking remarkably like him at that age, soliciting for Kennedy. (A closely guarded secret: young FDR had been recruited by the ambassador. Moreover, at the ambassador's suggestion, letters urging West Virginians to vote for Jack, and signed by young Frank Roosevelt, were shipped to Hyde Park and mailed with that famous postmark.) Frank gave everything he had, speaking of Jack with enthusiasm and admiration, and he too bore a swollen, empurpled, bloody hand on primary day. "Do you know why I'm here in West Virginia today?" he would ask rhetorically. "Because Jack Kennedy and I fought side by side in the Pacific. He was on the PT boats and I was on the destroyers." This was a remarkable version of the Pacific war, and one day Frank followed it with an extraordinary distortion of history. Holding up two fingers pressed tightly together, he declared: "My daddy and Jack Kennedy's daddy were just like that!"

The Harris polls continued to report that religion dominated the campaign. Kennedy's advisers were split on the issue. Sorensen and the rest of the Washington staff urged him not to raise the question in public; it was too explosive. Kennedy's West Virginians disagreed completely. Their neighbors and friends didn't hate Catholics; they feared them. Silence would only feed and strengthen that fear. Louis Harris, shuffling a sheaf of poll reports, said he was in complete agreement. On April 25, two weeks before the polling day, Kennedy assembled his staff to tell them he would attack, breaking the silence about his religious faith and encouraging discussion of it. He was prepared to answer all charges, questions, accusations, and insinuations — and without consulting clerical authorities. "Let's face it," he said. "It's the most important and the biggest issue in this campaign. Hubert can't talk about it, although it hasn't escaped my notice that he uses 'Give Us That Oldtime Religion' as his theme song. So when I talk about it, I'll be the only candidate talking about the most important issue that all the voters are thinking about."

The next day, a Tuesday, passed quietly. On Wednesday he was speaking at a noon rally on Main Street in Morgantown, telling a small crowd which appeared indifferent that the need for change in the federal government was urgent, when he paused. His voice changed, picking up a cutting edge, and a friend, standing off to one side, suddenly realized he was ringing changes on a talk he had given in Boston fourteen years earlier. Then he had been defending himself against charges that he was a carpetbagger. Here in Morgantown he had a different purpose. "Nobody asked me if I was a Catholic when I joined the United States Navy." The crowd stared at him. It was a time of many social taboos which have since vanished, and one of them was that you never discussed your religion with anyone except your priest or preacher or members of your family. So the people of Morgantown's Main Street gaped. Politicians didn't *say* things like that. But Jack was saying them, and he was picking up momentum. He asked: "Did forty million Americans lose their right to run for the presidency on the day they were baptized as Catholics?" Then: "Nobody asked my brother if he was a Catholic or a Protestant before he climbed into an American bomber plane to fly his last mission." Jack switched to another, more conventional topic. A few feet to your right one man murmured to another: "Pretty good talker, I'd say."

He never said whether or not he had planned to make those remarks, but among those who knew him the later consensus was that he had acted on a sudden impulse. As the crowd drifted away and he slid into the car, he said: "How did it go?" Still shaken, all his friend could manage was: "Very good. Keep it up." But you could see he was proud. It had been on his mind a long time, and he'd taken the plunge and found the water fine. Beginning at the next stop and continuing through the ten days that followed he would slip in feisty lines such as: "I refuse to believe that I was denied the right to be President on the day I was baptized." Attendance at his talks rose sharply. People listened attentively. They didn't ask questions about religion, though he had worked out possible answers and was ready for anything.

Thus far, he was still on the stump. Newspapers rarely carry the remarks candidates make on street corners, and while what he was saying was undoubtedly passed along by word of mouth, only a minority had actually heard and seen him. That situation altered on Sunday, May 8, two days before the election. Kennedy appeared on a half-hour paid telecast with Frank Roosevelt. There was no script. Roosevelt asked questions and Kennedy replied extemporaneously. The religion question, the whole point of the program, was raised by Roosevelt after they had been on the air three or four minutes and could be sure the families out there had poured their coffee, settled down, and were tuned in. Kennedy's answer lasted at least ten minutes — nearly half the broadcast. He reviewed the long struggle between church and state and the monumental decision to separate the two. Then, looking directly into the camera, he said:

> . . . so when any man stands on the steps of the Capitol and takes the oath of office of President, he is swearing to support the separation of church and state; he puts one hand on the Bible and raises the other hand to God as he takes the oath. And if he breaks his oath, he is not only committing a crime against the Constitution, for which Congress can impeach him

— and should impeach him — but he is committing a sin against God.

At that point Kennedy raised his hand from an imaginary Bible, and, repeating himself softly, said: "A sin against God, for he has sworn on the Bible."

Theodore H. White described this as "the finest TV broadcast I have ever heard any political candidate make." It turned the tide of voter opinion, now running strong. Harris's pollsters, stationed all over the state, were checking and rechecking certain streets in key communities at calculated intervals on a day-to-day basis in heavily populated Kanawha County. "You could see them switch," Harris said. On Monday, the day after the broadcast — which was the day before the election — Harris found, for the first time in the campaign, a narrow Kennedy lead. In the election on Tuesday, Kennedy took the county 52 to 48 percent.

During the final days of the campaign the most thwarted, provoked, and aggravated politician in the United States was Hubert Horatio Humphrey. His entire life had been a testament to tolerance and charity. He would rather have cut his throat than accept a vote from a bigot. Yet once Kennedy had laid the case of anti-Catholic prejudice before the voters, Hubert's position was hopeless. The issue now was tolerance versus intolerance. Neither candidate was responsible for that; it was the bigotry that had done it. But its implications for Hubert were appalling. A West Virginian determined to demonstrate his tolerance, if only to himself, almost *had* to vote for Kennedy.

Humphrey had, of course, been urged to avoid this primary, but he had done nothing to deserve the humiliations which were now visited upon him. Before leaving Wisconsin he had seventeen thousand dollars in debts. Saturday, three days before the West Virginia vote, TV producers threatened to cancel his Sunday evening performance unless they received cash in advance. Hubert, haggard after only four hours' sleep, wearily wrote out a check. Nor was that the end of his mortification. He was buying time for a telethon. Viewers phone in questions; the candidate answers. But it works only if the candidate has a staff which screens the calls. Humphrey couldn't afford a staff. The result was bedlam. Two reasonable calls came in; he fielded them well. Then the raspy voice of a demented woman came on the air: "You git out! You git out of West Virginia, Mr. Humphrey! You can't stand the Republicans gitting ahead of you!" Finally a technician cleared the line, but the madwoman was succeeded by a series of exhibitionists who couldn't resist the opportunity to hear their voices on television. The fiasco continued until a male voice, resonant with authority, intoned: "Clear the wires, please, this is an emergency!" Hubert, at his wit's end, tried to explain that this was not an ordinary telephone call and that they were on the air. The man with the emergency quit, leaving time for one more caller. He spoke gruffly, and seemed to be under the ludicrous impression that Hubert Humphrey was on the payroll of a mining boss. Had Humphrey been endowed with Kennedy's gift for irony, his anguish might have been mitigated. But he lacked Jack's temperament, and his pain was deepened by cruel, undeserved laughter.

Tuesday dawned bleak and drizzly, and Kennedy awoke with an overwhelming premonition of defeat. Harris was wrong, he thought. He could feel it. He told Bobby that he was going home — he didn't want to see the others — and before noon the *Caroline* put him back in Washington. He suggested that Jackie invite Ben and Tony Bradlee to dinner. Later the four of them could take in a movie. The Bradlees arrived with a bottle of champagne. "One way or another we'll crack it open this evening," Jack said. Before leaving for the film, he called Bobby at Charleston's Kanawha Hotel. The polls had closed at 8:00 P.M., but no returns were in. "O.K.," Jack said to the others. "Let's go to the pictures."

In the Kanawha, Bob waited for the first figures. But Humphrey and Kennedy were only two of the names on the ballot. Over a hundred other races were involved, and to the town clerks and gamekeepers whose jobs were at stake, the figures for those races eclipsed everything else. Then the results from the top of the ballot started coming in: early precincts in the eastern panhandle, where people lived their whole lives without laying eyes on a Catholic, were voting heavily for Kennedy. By 9:45 Kennedy was taking Humphrey, 60 to 40 percent. Suburbs, factory towns, hill slopes, pocket villages; there were no exceptions. A half hour later another deluge of returns arrived. The same pattern was emerging in the cities. By 10:00 P.M. it began to look like a statewide sweep.

Well before midnight Humphrey decided to concede. Prolonging the agony was pointless. From his room in the Ruffner Hotel he sent out the appropriate telegrams and phoned generous supporters. His graceful telegram of congratulation did not reach Kennedy headquarters until 1:00 A.M. Bobby muttered: "God, poor Hubert. Wisconsin, and now this. He works and works and spends and spends and loses and loses." Since Jack was in Washington, Bob acted as he always did in such circumstances. If his brother was supposed to do something and couldn't, Bob did it for him. He walked through Charleston's rainy streets bareheaded — he seldom even noticed the weather — to express his personal appreciation for Hubert's telegram. Humphrey said he wanted to greet Jack on his return. He intended to be a good loser; that was important to him. On Capitol Street they stepped into Humphrey headquarters. Jimmy Wofford, a folksinger who had accompanied Hubert throughout the campaign, was strumming his guitar — old Depression songs, songs of the New Deal, of Humphrey's youth, of a poorer but infinitely more generous America. Humphrey's eyes were bright with tears as he started to read a statement to his staff. He didn't finish; Jimmy started sobbing. Hubert patted his shoulder and said, "Aw, Jimmy." Bobby came over to put his arm around Humphrey. He led them up to the Kanawha, and he, too, was crying. You remember Bobby Kennedy. Everybody used the same word to describe him. The word was *ruthless*.

Senator Kennedy and his party had piled into his car and headed for the Trans-Lux to see *Suddenly Last Summer*. Unfortunately they were too late to get in, so they walked across New York Avenue to the Plaza, which showed X-rated movies. Pornography was less outrageous then than it later became, but *Private Property* was nasty enough, starring one Katie Manx as a horny housewife who spread-eagled for every milkman, newsboy, and iceman who could identify a woman in heat. Halfway through the movie someone wondered if this sordid little valentine was on the Catholic index of forbidden films. It was. The man who would presently become the first Catholic President, whose piety had entranced West Virginians two evenings before, was watching a dirty movie.

He wasn't enjoying it. Ordinarily he found sex fascinating. Gossip about film stars or congressmen always found him an eager audience; almost any fetching girl who happened to roll by had his undivided attention. Under other circumstances he would have enjoyed Katie Manx's romps in various improbable positions, but tonight his thoughts were in Charleston. He began to suspect that he had written himself off too quickly. Every twenty minutes he would slip out to the lobby, call Bobby, return to whisper, "*Nothing definite yet*," and slump in his seat, flicking a fingernail against his teeth. Eventually the last handyman pleasured Ms. Manx for the last time, and the Kennedys and Bradlees headed for N Street.

As he opened the door of his N Street house, the phone was ringing. It was Bobby. Jack had won; had, in fact, rolled up a stunning majority. After war whoops and a call to the ambassador, the Bradlees fetched their bottle of champagne from the refrigerator. A phone call alerted the crew of the *Caroline* for immediate departure. The Bradlees were invited; so were Steve and Jean Smith. At the Kanawha airport the press wanted a statement. Jack said, "I think we have now buried the religious issue once and for all." Apparently he had completely forgotten Jackie. At the Kanawha Hotel, as the merriment mounted and 3:00 A.M. approached, she slipped out, crept into the car, and sat there alone and disconsolate, waiting for the return trip to Washington. As Jack headed for the door a reporter asked where he was going. He said gaily: "I have to study up on the problems of Maryland tonight. I'm campaigning there tomorrow — the primary is on Friday." He left by the wrong door, and had to hunt for Jackie. Along the way he passed Hubert Humphrey's press bus parked outside the Ruffner. Under the windshield wiper a cop had slipped a ticket for illegal parking.

Sitting with Jack in the leafy backyard of his Georgetown house, watching him work out various combinations of figures, you asked him if he really felt insecure about the convention. "*Every* politician feels insecure," he said. Showing you a list of candidates and their estimated votes, he asked with a faint smile, "Which is the threat?" You instantly replied: "Johnson." Jack said: "*Wrong*. He has no power base outside the South. In this town people think he's a national figure, but except in the District the man on the street has never heard of him. His great mistake was not entering at least one northern primary. He can twist senators' arms because he's got power there; patronage. But congressional power isn't national power. Most voters have a low opinion of Congress. It would take an act of God to put Lyndon in the White House. No, the one who worries me — not much, but some — is the man with an international reputation, presidential stature, and a worshipful following." Suddenly you had nothing to say. Stevenson had been your idol; at one point he had also been your friend. Jack knew that. His voice dropped a register. "Remember, *I* was a Stevenson man. I put his name in nomination. But he's not the man he was. . . . Can you even imagine what happens to you if you run for the presidency and lose? And then do it again? Nobody can judge such a man, but Stevenson has changed. The old Adlai would never even have thought of the coy game he's playing now."

Certainly Stevenson's position appeared to be curious. Everybody, it seemed, wanted to know whether he was or was not a candidate this year. Adlai had said he would not seek the nomination, he would not help anyone else, he would not try to stop anyone. If the party called on him to serve in any capacity, he would accept the call and feel profoundly honored. You said: "He wants a draft." Jack said: "No, he thinks he wants one. What he wants is the nomination, like the rest of us, and like the rest of us he'll do anything that he thinks will work." You were doubtful then, but later, in Los Angeles, you heard Jack ask Adlai to put his name in nomination, to do for him what he had done for Adlai four years earlier. Stevenson's reply, which made no sense, was a sad, "No, it wouldn't be fair to Lyndon." As you left, Jack said with a bitterness rare for him, "Fair to Johnson? He's got a short memory. He forgets that I was for him in fifty-six, when Johnson and Rayburn were both against him." Later you told Dave Powers the story. Why, you wondered, had Stevenson done it? To Dave, the born politician, there was no mystery. "It's obvious," he said. "The prick's a candidate."

After Wisconsin and West Virginia, one would think Kennedy had earned a long rest. But in politics it is the losers who rest. The next seven weeks were to test his stamina. He visited, and often revisited, eleven states, appearing before state conventions and state committee meetings, talking late into the night with governors and party leaders, and bargaining with professional politicians who, in the arithmetic of conventions, count more heavily than the delegates chosen in expensive, lengthy, wearing, enervating primaries.

On June 27 Kennedy addressed his last state convention in Montana, and he had 550 solid, certified votes. Nothing could deny him any of those. Beyond that lay inviting but uncertain territories. Minnesota, Kansas, and Iowa, representing 78 votes, were supporting favorite sons who would eventually have to be abandoned. The balance was held by three states: New Jersey, Pennsylvania, and California. Among them they could commit 203 votes, far more than Kennedy needed. Actually, his position was far stronger than his figures suggested. He was deliberately underplaying his hand. Many delegates had pledged themselves to him in secret; to declare now would subject them to harassment and threats. And many others who were prepared to declare for him now stayed silent at his request. His rivals still nursed the hope that if they could get past the first ballot, his support would begin to crumble. He wanted them to cherish that illusion, because he held another card whose very existence was unsuspected by any but his most trusted aides. Governor John M. Patterson of Alabama was prepared to deliver his entire delegation to Kennedy on the first ballot. Jack asked him to withhold some delegates in the beginning. Alabama always opened the roll call. Should a second ballot be necessary, Patterson could announce new Kennedy strength in his delegation, giving Jack's candidacy a psychological boost at a critical moment.

Almost a week before the convention opened, Bobby arrived in Los Angeles with his vanguard and established a base in the Biltmore Hotel's room 8315 — actually a four-room suite. As the days passed and the excitement mounted, the feeling of confidence in 8315 became a kind of intoxicant. It was under these circumstances that Jack's team saw Lyndon Johnson hold a special press conference on July 5, five days before the convention's opening gavel. Kennedy men disliked Johnson; they thought him a hypocritical, unprincipled opportunist of illiberal views. He announced with his pious solemnity that he had searched his soul, found himself capable of serving his country as President, and was, from this moment, available. Kennedy headquarters rocked with laughter. Johnson was claiming 502½ votes; the majority, 385 delegates, came from the South and border states, but he said he had scattered backers in the Northeast and — this was new — 80 solid votes in the West and mountain states. In this suite there were files on each of the 4,509 delegates and alternates. After a few minutes of checking, chuckles were heard, and as notes were compared the mirth grew. As best they could tell, the delegates Johnson thought he had recruited were all hidden Kennedy votes — Jack's second-ballot reserve.

As the *Caroline* touched down at the Los Angeles airport you saw three thousand people appear out of nowhere, bearing down on the aircraft. Bands were playing, banners waving, and girls shrieking. The crowd carried Kennedy along; he was helpless, their prisoner. He finally found his feet in front of newsmen and TV cameras and gave them a brief flash of wit. The *New York Times* had run an editorial calling him the best of the candidates. He said, gravely: "I expect to be one of those who can truthfully say, I got my job through the *New York Times*."

His family, friends, and staff were scattered all over Los Angeles. The Biltmore suite was the nerve center. The key people, veterans of Wisconsin and West Virginia, had arrived the day before. Bobby, Larry, Ken, and Pierre Salinger — Salinger was now handling Kennedy's press relations — were based in the suite. The candidate, however, needed seclusion. Suite 9333 was reserved for him, but he didn't even want to be in the hotel. A week earlier he had sent Dave Powers to L.A. to find a hideaway. Its location would be known only to Bobby and Jack's secretary, Evelyn Lincoln. Dave found an apartment building at 522 North Rossmore Boulevard owned by Jack Haley, the actor, who agreed to rent Kennedy the penthouse, including two television sets for watching action on the convention floor. Beneath

Kennedy would be the apartment of William Gargan, another actor. Haley and Gargan were sworn to secrecy. Here Jack would be only a ten-minute drive from the convention site, the Los Angeles Memorial Sports Arena. Four telephone lines were installed, including one for nightly talks between Jack and Jackie, whose pregnancy kept her in Hyannis Port. Jack's parents had moved into Marion Davies's Beverly Hills villa. During the early sessions Jack planned to watch convention coverage on a television set beside the pool there; after dining with his mother and father, he would return to his hideaway. It was a sound plan, and it worked until Wednesday, the third day of the convention, when Kennedy was briefly at the Biltmore. Pierre was begging Dave to give him the hideaway address, arguing that once Jack had been nominated, photographers and cameramen would need pictures of it. Dave refused; Jack wanted to return to North Rossmore and pick up his swimming trunks. Once he had joined his parents, the hideaway could be disclosed. It went back and forth. Finally Jack intervened: "Oh, for God's sake, give him the address." Dave did, and Pierre rushed off happily. At that moment Frank Roosevelt appeared and dragged Jack off to a party of delegates, delaying his departure for fifteen minutes. By the time he and Dave reached the hideaway, the street was cluttered with television equipment, and a crowd of spectators had gathered. Jack glared at Dave, who had done everything in his power to prevent precisely this, only to be overruled by Kennedy. "Well," Jack said, "this is one hell of a hideaway, isn't it?" Leaving unseen was a real problem. Carrying their swimming trunks, the next President of the United States and his closest aide stealthily descended a fire escape on the back of the building, climbed over a back fence into a neighbor's garden, and made their way to the Davies villa. There they swam and then watched Orville Freeman nominate Kennedy.

The ambassador, proud of his son, at times almost unable to contain his love for him, reaching out and touching him on his shoulder, was also a source of tactical political advice. For example, Joe predicted that Robert Meyner of New Jersey, by refusing to commit himself to Kennedy now, was committing political suicide. "You'll win on the first ballot," he told his son, "and he'll be left high and dry." That was the voice of the political street fighter, his entire attention concentrated on the immediate objective, the nomination. His son was looking beyond the convention, to the coming campaign. He needed a united party. Unfortunately some of the older leaders seemed more interested in savaging him than beating Nixon. Harry Truman had opened the attack in a televised press conference, asking Kennedy: "Senator, are you certain that you are quite ready for the country, or that the country is ready for you in the role of President?" Harry clearly preferred more mature Democrats, naming Johnson (whom Kennedy suspected of stage-managing Truman's performance), Symington, Meyner, and Chester Bowles. (Stevenson was unmentioned.) Truman raised other arguments, but age was the real issue. The transfer of power from one generation to another cannot be painless. The four chieftains in suite 8315 were Bobby, thirty-four; Ken, thirty-six; Pierre, thirty-five; and Larry, the old man on the Kennedy team, forty-three. Worse, Ted Sorensen, Kennedy's chief adviser in Washington, was only thirty-two. When Johnson had growled that he wouldn't "be pushed around by a forty-three-year-old boy," he meant Jack. Eisenhower felt the same; he always referred to Kennedy as "that boy." This

The Democratic presidential candidate at a rally in New York City

convention, James Reston wrote in the *Times*, would be remembered as "the assembly that witnessed the Changing of the Guard."

Charges by a former President of Kennedy's own party could not be ignored. Truman's idea of an open convention, Kennedy said in his sharp rebuttal, seemed to be one "that studies all the candidates, reviews their records, and then takes his advice." To call him inexperienced, he added, was downright absurd. His fourteen years on Capitol Hill meant that he was more seasoned in national public life than any twentieth-century President when elected to office, and that included Woodrow Wilson, Franklin Roosevelt — and Harry Truman. The White House, said Kennedy, needed precisely what he offered: "strength and health and vigor."

Monday evening there was a respite from factional bloodletting. At the Democratic convention dinner the speaker was the junior senator from Massachusetts. He reviewed the recent record of the Republican President, and it was a highly successful speech, largely because, in the two months between the West Virginia primary and tonight's gathering, Dwight Eisenhower had been lurching from one disaster to another. The Russians shot down the U-2, the United States government offered a plausible explanation, and then Moscow produced the American pilot and incontestable evidence that the U.S. account had been a mesh of outright lies. Ike flew to Paris for a summit conference, which collapsed when Nikita Khrushchev called the American President a "hypocrite" and a "liar." Rioters in Korea toppled the regime of Syngman Rhee. Castro seized all U.S. property in his country and formed an alliance with the Soviet Union. Disarmament talks with the Soviet Union, which had once seemed promising, broke down completely and were abandoned. In Africa, the newly independent Congo Republic quickly dissolved into chaos, culminating in civil war and inexplicable massacres. The President, bedeviled by black "sit-ins" on Greensboro, North Carolina, luncheon stools, had looked forward to his long-awaited visit to Japan. The trip was called off when the Japanese premier withdrew his invitation on the ground that, after three weeks of anti-American demonstrations by students and militant leftists, he could not guarantee the President's safety.

It was a good year to be united against a Republican nominee. But despite Kennedy's commanding lead, Johnson toured state delegations during the day before the balloting with a naked plea to "Stop Kennedy." He cited his record, telling them he was entitled to and expected their support. This was LBJ the majority leader; if you didn't vote his way, he'd stick it in you and break it off. But these were not senators. Johnson attacked Kennedy's liberal credentials and then, reaching back to Exodus 20:5, visited the sins of the father upon his child, painting the sins blacker than they had been, declaring that Joe Kennedy had been, not only an appeaser, but one who "thought Hitler was right." Finally, and desperately, the rumors about Jack's "disease" were being spread.

Kennedy's physicians — Janet Travell and E. J. Cohen — testified to his fitness. Johnson threw up his hands. Of *course* he believed the medical testimony, and he couldn't imagine who could have been responsible for such a despicable tale. (O'Donnell wanted to suggest publicly that LBJ ask his closest political allies, John B. Connally, Jr., and India Edwards, the Democratic National Committeewoman, who had proposed a "health test" for all nominees and who reportedly had insinuated that Senator Kennedy's "disease" was social, but Jack vetoed that; in November he would want Texas's twenty-five electoral votes in his column.) Sam Rayburn nominated Lyndon. Then Gene McCarthy, the freshman senator from Minnesota, rose to nominate Governor Adlai Ewing Stevenson of Illinois, and the convention erupted. All day events had been building toward this moment. Stevenson was not merely admired, he was deeply beloved — tears misted over the eyes of men and women who had fought with him in '52 and '56, upon his own Saint Crispin's days.

Eleanor Roosevelt was there — she had been a figure at conventions for over forty years — but she knew a lost cause when she saw it. McCarthy, however, was a believer, brought back through some time warp from the summer of '52. Kennedy, with characteristic objectivity, observed that McCarthy's was quite simply the finest speech of the convention. When it ended the demonstration began. The galleries and the bays outside the hall were packed with Stevenson enthusiasts, and they came rocketing down the aisles. Yelling, wriggling, chanting, snake-dancing, they congested the floor as gold balloons drifted overhead and popped. Paper banners streaming in every direction read WE WANT STEVENSON. The chanters picked it up, and state standards bobbed up and down. Kenny calmly told you: "All these people running around mean nothing. They can't cast a half-vote among them." The ambassador, watching Marion Davies's poolside TV, was briefly alarmed. Jack phoned Bobby for the latest vote rundown. Bob said that the demonstration, though well organized, had influenced no votes. Indeed, Stevenson's delegation count had dropped sharply. Hanging up, Jack said, "Don't worry, Dad, Stevenson has everything but delegates."

Jack reached his apartment just in time for the first ballot. He had a cardboard tally sheet. Alabama had been called. The chairman of the delegation was replying: "Alabama casts twenty votes for Johnson, three and a half for Kennedy, and —" In an instant, the screen darkened, the voice faded, and every light in the apartment went out. "God Almighty!" Jack cried. A kitchen match was struck, the blown fuse replaced, and as the power returned Jack heard Arizona delivering him seventeen votes. Then a second fuse blew and they were again in darkness, Kennedy reciting his entire vocabulary of profanity. Followed by his small entourage, he stumbled down to the Gargan apartment, where Bill and his wife were quietly following the roll call. Jack said: "Do you mind, Bill? Both of our sets blew out." At that moment California reported three more Kennedy votes than Jack had expected, and Abe Ribicoff delivered all twenty-one Connecticut votes. The word from upstairs was that the lights were on again. Evelyn Lincoln, distraught, was convinced her electric typewriter was to blame, but no; it was a new air-conditioning unit Jack had rented for his bedroom. He called downstairs: "Bill, leave the door open. We may be back."

As the balloting resumed, he marked the delegate commitments on his sheet. His total had reached 750 — only 11 more would put him over the top. Wyoming was next on the roll. As Jack peered at the screen he saw his younger brother crouching, the Wyoming delegation gathered around him. Teddy's grin had never been broader. Jack said quietly: "This may be it." And it was. The state's delegation went for him in one block, and that made him the Democratic presidential nominee of 1960. Everyone crowded around, gripping his hand, and as he thanked them he said: "Get Jackie at the Cape."

After a brief talk with Jackie, he hurried to the sports arena, where he would make a short appearance before the convention. He was approaching it on foot when he saw Bobby, and the brothers stopped for several minutes of discussion, with everyone else there stepping back to a respectful distance. Jack finally turned away, and seeing a line of party leaders standing quietly to one side, he shook hands and thanked each — Bailey, Ribicoff, Soapy Williams, Bill Green, DiSalle, Averell Harriman, Dick Daley, David Lawrence. A band was playing "Toora-Loora-Loora" and then, as he entered the hall and mounted the platform, "Happy Days Are Here Again." The delegates cheered hoarsely as he stood there smiling, flanked by his mother and his sisters. He spoke briefly, expressing his gratitude, and then rode back to North Rossmore.

On reaching the apartment Kennedy told Dave he was too tired for a celebration, but he was hungry. Dave fried him two eggs, then Jack prepared for bed. Meanwhile, his staff, with Bobby as chairman, was discussing the vice-presidency. Everyone there was under the impression that their leader was considering only two senators: Symington of Missouri and Henry M. Jackson of Washington. Johnson's name had not been raised. Only a few weeks ago Kennedy had said that if he could not be President, Johnson was the best-qualified alternative. But hard words had been spoken this week, and the big Texan was anathema to the men who had worked so hard for the Kennedy triumph, not to mention the liberal bosses who had delivered their delegations and perhaps a majority of those who had backed Kennedy in the primaries. Moreover, Johnson had said that under no circumstances would he swap his position as Senate majority leader for the empty office of the vice-presidency. Reading congratulatory telegrams while Dave fried eggs, Kennedy was therefore startled to find that the warmest and most graceful had come from the candidate who had run second in the balloting. "LBJ," it read, "now means Let's Back Jack."

Before slipping between the sheets, Kennedy tried to phone Johnson, but LBJ had left instructions that he was not to be disturbed. Jack then dictated a telegram to him, asking for a 10:00 A.M. meeting. Dave thought: *My God, he's going to offer it to Lyndon Johnson.* Powers's dismay was matched by Lady Bird's. Jack, not trusting Western Union, phoned at 8:30 the next morning and told her he would like to call on her husband. She woke Lyndon and blurted out: "Honey, I know he's going to offer you the vice-presidency, and I hope you won't take it." Lyndon phoned Sam Rayburn, who said much the same thing.

Then the Texans started thinking. No matter who became President, the post of Senate majority leader would be only a shadow of its greatness under Eisenhower. The vice-presidency would free Johnson of his sectarian role and his Texas constituency. Finally — and for Rayburn this was conclusive — they had to consider the man the Republicans were about to nominate. Sam Rayburn couldn't even bring himself to speak Nixon's name. "Lyndon," he said, "you've got to go on that ticket." What, LBJ asked, had changed his mind? Mr. Sam said, "That other fellow called me a traitor, and I don't want a man who calls me a traitor to be President of the United States."

Kennedy's men took it much, much harder. After Jack had phoned Lyndon, he called the Biltmore suite and told Bobby his decision. Bob was shocked. Salinger and O'Donnell were outraged. Bobby recovered quickly, however, and said they needed Texas to win in November. Dave told you, "If Jack wanted to give it to Eleanor Roosevelt, Bobby probably would have said all right." Kenny's rage mounted as he thought of the anti-Johnson pledges they had given to labor and civil rights leaders. Jack arrived in the suite, took one look at him, and said, "We'd better talk alone in the bathroom." He was in his toughest mood, but O'Donnell was entitled to an explanation. In the first place, Jack said, Johnson hadn't accepted his offer and probably wouldn't. But: "I'm forty-three years old, and the healthiest candidate. I'm not going to die in office. So the vice-presidency doesn't mean anything." It could swing southern states into the Democratic column in November, however, and if Kennedy won without Johnson "I wouldn't be able to live with Lyndon as the leader of a small majority in the Senate. Did it ever occur to you that if Lyndon becomes vice-president, I'll have Mike Mansfield in the Senate, somebody I can trust and depend on?"

O'Donnell began to cool down. Elsewhere in the suite, however, the mood remained ugly. Walter Reuther, Arthur Goldberg, and George Meany, according to those who had seen them, were apoplectic. To them LBJ was anti-union, a Republican in Democratic clothing. Doubtless it had been a difficult decision for Kennedy, and whether or not he really hoped Lyndon would decline will never be known. It was one of the subjects he did not discuss. His commitment to him couldn't have been absolute, however, because he gave him a chance to withdraw. The excuse was the possibility of a floor fight. Johnson replied that there was nothing he loved more than a good floor fight, and that was that; LBJ was aboard for good.

Meanwhile, the tide had turned in the Kennedy suite. DiSalle, Bailey, Ribicoff, and Lawrence were milling around Jack, congratulating him for strengthening the ticket. The liberals were still muttering about the "sellout," until Alex Rose called David Dubinsky, labor's elder statesman. After phoning, he turned to Reuther and reported: "He said Kennedy is making a smart move! He said picking Johnson is a political masterstroke!" Johnson's nomination went through smoothly, and on Friday night John F. Kennedy delivered his acceptance speech to eighty thousand spectators in the Los Angeles coliseum, with another thirty-five million Americans watching on television, declaring that "we stand on the edge of a New Frontier."

Great experiences are thought to change people, and those who know them look for evidence of it. Kennedy's whole life had been a process of change — indeed, one of his most remarkable traits was his capacity for growth — but as far as you could tell, he was the same man after his nomination — with one interesting exception. He had always been generous

toward his political opponents. He sympathized with the men he defeated. In his Senate office he had warned his staff that he wanted to hear no ugly remarks about politicians who differed with him; anti-Ike jokes were banned. But after Los Angeles it became increasingly clear that he scorned Richard Nixon. His contempt for him began when newspapers quoted Nixon as having made a tactless remark in Hawaii. Kennedy laughed and said he hoped that was the beginning of a trend. Then he began reading Nixon's campaign speeches. He thought them appalling; why, he asked, was the man talking down to people? His remarks grew sharper: "I can't stand the way he puts everything in Tricia's mouth. He's a cheap bastard; that's all there is to it." Nixon's habit of opening his speeches with "Pat and I" disgusted Jack. When Harold Macmillan later disclosed that Eisenhower had told him Nixon would never be invited to Camp David, saying, "I wouldn't have him on the place," Kennedy was immensely amused. He insisted that he was not among those who made a fetish of hating Nixon, yet said he considered him "beyond saving," and at various times called him "sick"; "sick, sick"; and, on at least one occasion, "sick, sick, sick." Most politicians disparage their opponents, particularly when the race is heated. These remarks are remembered because in Kennedy's case they were unique.

Kennedy had conceived his strategy. He would appeal to the young, the blue-collars, and the liberals. His two great bases were the Democratic South — holding it would be Johnson's task — and the industrial regions. The Kennedy campaign would concentrate on nine big states: Massachusetts, California, New York, Texas, New Jersey, Illinois, Ohio, Michigan, and Pennsylvania. If carried, they would give him 237 of the 269 electoral votes needed to put him in the White House. His techniques included the mass registration of seven million unregistered voters (nearly three out of every four new registrants were now Democrats), the articulation of ideas from his Ivy League brain trust, and the innovative political tactics of Irish pols, led by O'Donnell, O'Brien, and, of course, Robert Kennedy.

Nixon was briefly handicapped by bad luck. In Greensboro, North Carolina, he struck his right kneecap on a car door. The injury did not heal; it became infected. Unless he remained in Walter Reed Hospital for two weeks of intensive treatment, he was told, the cartilage would be destroyed. Thus, he lay on his back from August 29 to September 9 with his leg in traction, wretched at the thought of the lost time. (While he was out of action, Kennedy did not refer to him once.) Jack intended to run as hard and as far as he could as long as he could, but the Republican nominee believed that a campaign had high and low tides, and that to ignore them was to risk boring, and therefore alienating, the electorate. His object was to "peak" the campaign — bring it to a climax — on election day. Like his opponent he planned to zero in on key states: New York, California, Michigan, Texas, Pennsylvania, Ohio, and Illinois. He also promised to appear in each of the other forty-three — a pledge he later regretted. He had no brain trust; now, as always, he was a loner, a solitary, brooding introvert. While the theme of Kennedy's drive was that American prestige was slipping and

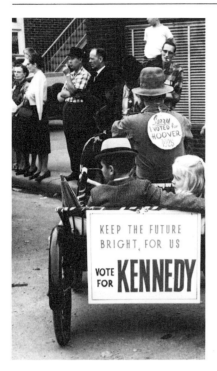

Americans must move forward — "Let's get this country moving again" was the slogan, contributed by Walt Rostow — the Republican standard-bearer preached the virtues of free enterprise, individual responsibility, inflexible anticommunism, and a continuance of the peace and prosperity which had marked the Eisenhower years. Nixon's built-in advantages were support from big business, greater experience, his strong middle-class roots, and Eisenhower's incumbency. But Ike dealt Nixon the worst blow of the campaign. During a press conference he was asked: "What major decisions of your administration has the vice-president participated in?" The President's almost unbelievable reply was, "If you give me a week, I might think of one."

After Nixon's nomination, the Republican had taken a slight lead in Gallup's polls, but by late August the two candidates were running neck and neck, and there was never a time during the campaign when either nominee could feel secure. Two events in the race were grievous for Nixon: Kennedy's confrontation with religious bigotry and the television debates. West Virginia had demonstrated that while Kennedy's faith could cost him votes if the issue were ignored, once the silence was broken he could gain. Nixon had therefore instructed his staff to refrain from discussing Kennedy's religion. Unfortunately, he could not restrain Dr. Norman Vincent Peale, perhaps the most famous Protestant clergyman in the country and a Nixon friend. Peale led a group of Protestants in issuing a provocative statement; they expressed doubt that any Roman Catholic President could free himself from the influence of the Vatican. Nixon couldn't attack Peale, and his muteness was interpreted as agreement with him. Kennedy, meanwhile, had been offered an incomparable opportunity. The Greater Houston Ministerial Association had invited him to appear before them and defend the right of a Catholic to become President. Nixon had also been invited, but had instantly declined. Kennedy accepted.

The issue had been inflamed by Dr. Daniel Poling, a Philadelphia clergyman who had also run for office as a Republican. Poling charged that Kennedy, as a young congressman, had refused to attend a fund-raising dinner honoring the four chaplains who went down with the SS *Dorchester* in World War II. Kennedy had indeed declined, because he had been asked to come as a "spokesman" for the Roman Catholic church. He could appear as a congressman, as a navy veteran, or as a private citizen, he said, but he had no authority to represent his church. Johnson and Rayburn had advised him to give Houston a miss, but Jack was adamant. He was told that he could make an opening statement, that questions would follow, and the event would be televised.

Assembled that evening were three hundred ministers and three hundred spectators. Kennedy was tense and nervous, but as usual it showed only in his hands. On the air he was sharp, forceful, precise, and immediately in command. The real issues in this presidential race, he told them, were not his religion, or Nixon's, or anyone else's. They were hungry children, elderly Americans who couldn't afford their doctors' bills, disgraceful slums, inadequate schools, and inept U.S. foreign policies. "These," he said, "are the real issues. But because I am a Catholic, the real issues in this campaign have been obscured. So it is apparently necessary for me to state once again — not what kind of church I believe in, for that should be important only to me — but what kind of America I believe in." He restated the position he had taken in West Virginia. The questions were obvious and vaguely stated; Kennedy handled them concisely and with ease. Dr. Poling's grievance was served up to him, and he knocked it out of the ball park — how could he possibly have agreed to attend as a "spokesman for my Roman Catholic faith"? In a nearby hotel room, Dave Powers was watching the TV screen with Sam Rayburn. In Los Angeles, Rayburn's support of Kennedy had been tepid. Now he was shouting: "By God, look at him — and listen to him! He's eating 'em blood raw!" A few days later, in Austin and then in Dallas, Rayburn told crowds that Kennedy was "the greatest northern Democrat since Franklin D. Roosevelt."

As the calls came in and the telegrams piled up, Jack became euphoric. Houston was exactly the tonic he needed for the first debate against Nixon, now two weeks away. In the past decade the number of American families owning televisions had increased eightfold. Awaiting the event, in living rooms all over the nation, would be some seventy million people. There were to be four debates, but the first was expected to be the most important. It was, by far. It drew the largest audience and it was a Kennedy triumph. The result was dismaying for Nixon and came as a surprise. He was an assured, skillful debater. Watching Kennedy's televised acceptance speech at the end of the Democratic convention, and unaware of his rival's fatigue, he had thought the Democratic nominee spoke too rapidly, with a voice which was too high-pitched, of concepts which were too complicated for the average American. That was why Nixon accepted the challenge of the debates.

At the end of this first one, you felt that in words and ideas it was a standoff. But that in itself was a Kennedy victory. Until then Nixon had been the more famous of the two, holding, as he did, the higher office. But here they had stood toe to toe, and Kennedy had held his own. More important — this shouldn't have mattered, but it mattered immensely — he had *looked* better. People who heard them on radio that evening thought they did equally well, but the larger television audience saw the senator as tanned and fit while Nixon had lost five pounds in Walter Reed. He was haggard, and he wore a shirt collar too large for him. He slouched, his expression was dour, and his complexion was pasty, a consequence of coating his face with makeup designed to hide afternoon beard growth. Another factor may have been Jack's declining respect for his adversary. It seemed devastating, and obvious to any viewer. Nixon would be making an important point and the camera would switch to Kennedy, whose amused, faintly disdainful expression would break the thread of the Republican's argument. At the end of that first debate, Nixon drew Jack aside for several minutes of earnest conversation. Afterward, you asked Jack what that had been all about. "Nothing," he said crisply. "Absolutely nothing. The weather for a while, and then how hard it was to sleep during a campaign. But all the time he was keeping an eye on the photographers. If he saw one about to snap the shutter, he would look firm and jab his finger on my chest, as though setting me straight on some big foreign policy issue. Nice fellow." Later he asked: "Do you think the people realize I'm the only man standing between Nixon and the White House?"

Sometimes there were crowds; sometimes there weren't

Gallup's next poll showed Kennedy moving ahead decisively. Nixon regained his lost weight, looked as fit as Jack, and scored more points in the subsequent debates, all to no avail; millions had seen as much as they wanted, and their minds were made up. After the last debate and before Eisenhower intervened, creating an entirely new campaign, Gallup's findings were Kennedy 51 percent, Nixon 45; 4 percent were undecided.

In retrospect what you remember most about Jack's presidential campaign was its high good humor. In one speech Kennedy said: "Campaign contributions will not be regarded as a substitute for training and experience for diplomatic positions." A few days later he added: "Ever since I made that statement I have not received a single cent from my father." At times Jack played with his humorless opponent, using him as his straight man. Nixon called him "another Truman." Kennedy shot back: "I have no hesitation in returning the compliment. I consider him another Dewey." Republicans said (not for the first time) that Joe Kennedy was going to bribe voters. "My father," Jack said, "told me not to buy one more vote than is necessary. He said he's damned if he's going to pay for a landslide." He almost seemed to welcome hecklers. At New York University he dedicated his closing remarks to a group of Young Republican jeerers: "all you young Nixonites — all eight of you." One of them shouted something about their candidate standing up to Khrushchev in the "kitchen debates." Jack said: "Mr. Nixon may be very experienced in kitchen debates, but so are a great many other married men I know."

Eisenhower made his move on Halloween, eight days before the election, and a tremendous surge toward the Republican nominee came within a hairbreadth of carrying the popular vote. The great mystery is why Ike waited so long. There are several answers. Four years earlier Eisenhower had offered his vice-president a cabinet post, Defense or State, arguing that he could use such a base to strengthen his position for the '60 election, but Nixon was offended; he thought Ike was trying to get rid of him. At the Republican National Convention in Chicago, Ike left after his own speech and did not stay to see Nixon nominated. Again, Nixon was hurt, while Eisenhower was under the impression that he had helped him by leaving him the whole stage. Kennedy's attacks on Ike's record stung, and Ike, eager to stump now, awaited an appeal from Nixon. Nixon expected Ike to volunteer. Finally, a low-level White House aide heard a low-level vice-presidential aide mention that Nixon was in desperate need of the President's help. As soon as Eisenhower heard that, he started packing.

He drew tremendous crowds, lacing into Kennedy and eliciting roars of approval. As Theodore H. White wrote: "Eisenhower has . . . a magic in American politics that is peculiarly his: he makes people happy." Ike was positive that the few U.S. problems still unsolved would vanish tomorrow, and his audiences believed him. Jack had been taking a very different line. Typically he began: "I don't run for the office of the presidency to tell you what you want to hear. I run for the office of President because in a dangerous time we need to be told what we must do if we are going to maintain our freedom." Then he would speak of chaos in Africa, the collapse of

American foreign policy, our stagnant economy, our bored, drifting youth; when Jack laid it out like that, you felt challenged. We were perhaps the last liberal patriots to stride down the campaign trail. This was our country, and it was on the wrong track, and we were going to set it right.

To others, however — those who shrink from challenges — Kennedy's message must have sounded like a litany of despair. His own confidence was shaken; he had intended to arouse the people, but perhaps he had merely frightened them. In this mood he arrived in San Francisco. Surrounded by a mob, he was moving across the lobby of the Palace Hotel when he saw a friend and made a familiar gesture which meant: see me upstairs. It was 1946 in Boston's Bellevue all over again. There was Jack, soaking in a hot tub. He began with mock hospitality: "Sit down, be my guest." Then the mask fell away. Speaking in an entirely different key, he said: "Last week Dick Nixon hit the panic button and started Ike speaking. With every word he utters I can feel the votes leaving me. I tell you, he's knocking our block off." Softly, almost to himself, he said, "If the election was tomorrow I'd win easily, but six days from now it's up for grabs."

So anxiety arrived, an uninvited guest. Yet fear eludes memory; the feeling simply cannot be recaptured. Other recollections flood back, a montage of sights and sounds: Kennedy's mounting disgust for Nixon's way of flinging his arms high in the air . . . Jack's own gestures, the chopping right hand used to stress points . . . Nixon's denunciation of Truman's profanity, vowing never to sully the presidency by using blasphemy in the White House . . . Kennedy's teenaged "runners," "touchers," "leapers," and "screamers" during his motorcades . . . Nixon promising that his administration would never allow Red China into the UN . . . the enthusiasm on college campuses when Kennedy spoke of the years ahead, "the challenging, revolutionary sixties" . . . Nixon favoring a resumption of atom-bomb tests and charging that his opponent's criticisms were "running America down and giving us an inferiority complex."

Abruptly the end approached and Kennedy was going home. The *Caroline* landed at Bridgeport, Connecticut, at midnight and you joined the motorcade near Waterbury, where, on both sides of the road for nearly thirty miles, cheering New Englanders, wearing coats over their pajamas, waved torches and flashlights and red lights, and fire engines were lined up outside every firehouse, sirens screaming, bells ringing, and Kennedy, after reaching his hotel room at 3:00 A.M., appeared on the balcony, urging people to go to bed, but the forty thousand people stayed outside, cheering until dawn. Monday you reached Lewiston, Maine, at 1:30 A.M. It was cold; the streets were silent, empty. Suddenly the motorcade entered a park, and over twenty thousand people switched on their flashlights; when they recognized Jack the roaring began, a roar of joy, and here you were in a freezing factory town in the middle of the night, feeling a warmth and exultation to cherish in the years left to you.

The last day began in Providence, Rhode Island, and the procession swung through Massachusetts, Connecticut, Vermont, and New Hampshire, ending in the North End of Boston, where he had first campaigned fourteen years earlier. He was scheduled to address a mass meeting in the Boston Garden, but the streets were so jammed he was late; then he had to struggle again to reach Faneuil Hall. There, where the Sons of Liberty had gathered 190 years earlier to plot the Boston Tea Party, he made his farewell television talk to the nation. After it, on the fourteenth floor of the Statler Hilton, he chatted with a couple of old friends over a chicken sandwich and a glass of milk. In the past week he had never had as much as four hours of sleep in one night. Tomorrow, you thought, he can sleep late. But no; he wanted to be called at 7:30. Jackie would be arriving from Hyannis Port to vote with him. He was nervous about that. She was in the eighth month of her pregnancy, enthusiastic crowds were unpredictable, and, well, he wanted to *be* there.

On that bright day, 68,832,818 Americans went to the polls, among them Mr. and Mrs. John F. Kennedy of 122 Bowdoin Street, Boston, who cast their ballots in the Third Precinct of the Sixth Ward at 8:43 A.M. The crowd Jack had predicted was there, but his wife was unjostled. However, the bite in the air brought him a new worry: she might catch cold. Therefore, the top of their convertible was brought up before the drive to the airport, where they boarded the *Caroline* for Hyannis Port.

The whole clan had gathered at Bobby's house to await the first returns. Kennedy carried Connecticut by 100,000 votes. His sisters were yelping with joy, assuming that that meant much more than it did. The ambassador's friend Morton Downey, the tenor, was passing sandwiches and crooning "Did Your Mother Come from Ireland?" and upstairs Lou Harris sat with a slide rule and reams of paper, checking his calculations against those of the networks' computers. "It's Lou against the Machine," Jack said with a chuckle, lighting up a Havana Royal panatela. Presently he, Jackie, and Bill Walton left to dine at Jack's house, and when they rejoined the others, no one was cheering. He was losing in Ohio, Wisconsin, Kentucky, Tennessee, and the farm belt west of the Mississippi, and running behind expectations in Michigan and Illinois. Everyone was visibly distressed — except the nominee. He retained his sense of humor. Lyndon called from Texas, and Kennedy grinned as he hung up. He reported LBJ's comment: "I see we won in Pennsylvania, but what happened to you in Ohio?"

Ahead of them lay what Jackie later called "the longest night in history." Slowly a pattern emerged. Nixon had lost, but Kennedy, though ahead in electoral votes, had not won. The outcome seemed to hinge on four states: California, Illinois, Minnesota, and Michigan. Any two of them would give Kennedy the presidency; if he failed to take two, the election would be thrown into the House of Representatives. Jack yawned, rose, and prepared to leave. A friend asked where he was going. He said, "To bed. The votes are all in; I can't change any of them now." As he slept, the battles seesawed. Jack lost California but won Illinois, Michigan, and Minnesota. He awoke to find that he had 303 electoral votes as against Nixon's 219. He was President-elect. The Secret Service had moved in at 5:45 A.M., and your most vivid memory of that day is the horror on the agents' faces as they

A heroic welcome at the Boston Garden

watched the fiercest touch game in the Kennedys' ferocious history, with the man they were sworn to protect being assailed on all sides by members of his own family.

In retrospect, the next ten weeks are tenuous, like the pause between innings, or periods, or halves of a sport. One series of great events was finished; another could not start until the players had changed uniforms. This feeling of transience was heightened by Jack's mobility; he was interviewing prospective cabinet members and announcing appointments in Palm Beach, at the Carlyle Hotel in New York City, and on the doorstep of his Georgetown home. He had said he wanted a "ministry of talent." But finding the talent was harder than he had expected. "For the past four years," he said privately, "I spent so much time getting to know people who could help me get elected President that I didn't have any time to get to know people who could help me, after I was elected, to be a good President." He had decided to appoint Arthur Schlesinger, not to write the history of his administration — Jack intended to do that himself — but because he knew Arthur would write his own account anyway, and would do a better job if he could watch it unfold as a special assistant in the White House rather than as a reader of *Time* and the *New York Times*. Schlesinger would not, however, be permitted to bring any "wild-eyed ADA types" with him, and neither would the Irishmen be allowed to "pack the administration with the Knights of Columbus." All members of his team were busy studying a heavy green volume describing twelve hundred jobs which a President could fill without consulting Congress. Jack said places would be found for all, and he assured them: "Don't worry. I've seen the FBI files, and we've all done something."

One by one the appointees were chosen. Jack's talks with his father led him to Dean Rusk for secretary of state and Robert McNamara for secretary of defense. He wanted Robert Lovett; Lovett declined but recommended McGeorge Bundy, dean of Harvard College, who became a special assistant in national security and foreign affairs. Orville Freeman was designated secretary of agriculture. (A reporter asked him why he had been chosen; he replied: "I think it has something to do with the fact that Harvard doesn't have a school of agriculture.") Adlai Stevenson would be ambassador to the UN. And the attorney general would be Robert F. Kennedy. Bobby fought this. He knew it would touch off an uproar; already the *New York Times* had warned the President-elect against giving his brother a major appointment. Jack was unimpressed. The fact that they were brothers was irrelevant, he said: "I want the best men I can get, and they don't come any better than Bobby." The ambassador intervened and persuaded his reluctant brother to accept. It was characteristic of the Kennedys that, once the matter was settled, Jack taunted his brother. Asked how he planned to make the announcement, he said he would wait until two o'clock some morning, open the door, look up and down N street, and, if there was no one there, whisper, "It's Bobby." Afterward, replying to a question about the propriety

The President-elect returns to his family in Hyannis Port

of his choice, he said publicly, "I don't see anything wrong with providing him with a little legal experience before he goes out to practice law." That was too much for his brother, who protested. Jack told him he'd have to learn to laugh at himself. "But you weren't laughing at yourself," Bobby pointed out. "You were laughing at *me.*"

After a quiet Thanksgiving in Georgetown with his wife and daughter, Jack boarded the *Caroline* that evening for Palm Beach, and he was discussing subcabinet appointments when the pilot received an urgent message. Jackie's baby hadn't been expected for another two weeks; nevertheless, she had gone into labor and was now in the hospital, about to undergo cesarean surgery. Jack was upset; he said remorsefully, "I'm never there when she needs me." Landing in Florida, he returned immediately on a faster plane, sitting in the pilot's cabin wearing earphones and tensely awaiting word from Washington. It came at 1:17 A.M. He was now the father of John F. Kennedy, Jr. Both Jackie and the baby were fine. Kennedy mopped his brow with a handkerchief, and for the next two weeks he stayed in Georgetown, visiting the hospital three times a day and taking Caroline for walks and pony rides. Once Jackie and John were ready to leave the hospital, they all flew down to Palm Beach, where she spent the weeks before the inaugural resting in the sun.

Kennedy and Eisenhower met formally in early December. To Ike, Jack had been not only "that boy" but also a "young whippersnapper." Kennedy boned up for their talk as he had crammed for his first debate with Nixon. Clark Clifford accompanied him to the White House, where Eisenhower and General Wilton B. Persons awaited them. President and President-elect spent an hour and a quarter together and then reappeared walking arm in arm. Later Persons called Clifford to tell him that Ike had been "overwhelmed by Senator Kennedy, his understanding of the world problems, the depth of his questions, his grasp of the issues, and the keenness of his mind."

On November 18, Kennedy had learned that the CIA was equipping and training anti-Castro Cubans for a return to their homeland. Helping them, Ike told him, was "the policy of this government"; he hoped that "this effort" would be "continued and accelerated." On the last day of the departing administration, the outgoing and incoming Presidents met again, and Eisenhower said his deepest concern was Laos. Standing at a map of Southeast Asia, he said: "This is one of the problems I'm leaving you that I'm not happy about. We may have to fight." Later, when Kennedy had settled into the White House, he told an aide wonderingly: "You know, Ike never briefed me about Vietnam."

The N Street home had been sold, and like any family preparing to move into a new house, the Kennedys were attending to countless details, some of them peculiar to their new address. Jack wanted top hats worn at the inaugural, he wanted Marian Anderson to sing the national anthem and Robert Frost to write an inaugural poem, and he wanted the Fitzgerald family Bible for the oath. He would be grateful, he said with mock sarcasm, if some way could be found to prevent his daughter from upstaging him during press conferences. At the last one she had teetered into the room wearing her mother's shoes. He was told that the problem couldn't arise again, at least not here. During the two remaining days of the transition he and his daughter would not be living under the same roof. Jackie, back from Florida and in a whirlwind of preparations, was evicting him from his home — "kicking him out," as Evelyn Lincoln explained it in a call to Bill Walton, "because everything has to be moved to the White House, and they'll be down to the last shreds of furniture, and there isn't any place for him." Where, Walton asked, would he go? Evelyn said: "He's decided to come to you," and hung up. At 4:15 P.M. on January 19, twenty hours before his inaugural, the President-elect was working in a tiny corner office in Walton's home. He was conferring with Arthur Goldberg, who would be his secretary of labor, when he glanced out the window. Enormous snowflakes had just started to billow down, and it didn't look as though they would stop for a long time.

HIMSELF

Softly through the long blue winter twilight the snow sifted down in great powdery layers, and by 8:00 P.M., when the President-elect and his wife arrived to attend a concert in Constitution Hall, the District of Columbia lay frozen under a thickening white coverlet. All over the city, long black limousines, carrying distinguished passengers to heralded events, were snarled in a mammoth traffic jam. Somewhere around the Lincoln Memorial was a motorcade from Hickory Hill, led by the attorney general designate and his wife, Ethel, and followed by the cars of all the Kennedy friends who had been unable to find accommodations elsewhere. Bobby's procession was headed for the armory, where Frank Sinatra and Peter Lawford were anxiously awaiting the audience for the "gala entertainment" they had been rehearsing for weeks. Abruptly they heard a sidewalk crowd chanting, "It's Bobby Kennedy! It's Bobby Kennedy!" as policemen moved in, making room for the Hickory Hill motorcade.

Still the snow fell, speckling the pink faces of soldiers using flame-throwers to melt the caked ice around the inauguration stands on the east side of the Capitol, deepening in Washington's many squares and circles, stitching the eaves of the Executive Office Building and the federal triangle complex with the same shimmering thread. Open fires were lit along the Mall in an attempt to keep it clear for traffic, but the flames had to be kept too low to help much, for the snow was accompanied by a wind that howled in from the Potomac and the Tidal Basin, sending the hard white silt scudding before its raw gusts. As if by the touch of a Merlin, the President-elect's limousine and its Secret Service backup car broke free of the jam and sped on while every other automobile was at a standstill. Voices from dim figures on sidewalks begged him to put on the light, "So we can see Jackie," and he complied, not to please them, but to work; he was still editing his inaugural address. Earlier he had read Jefferson's and wryly told Walton: "Better than mine." At Walter Lippmann's suggestion he had changed "those nations who would make themselves our enemy" to ". . . make themselves our adversary." One final alteration remained: "ask what you will do" for your country became "ask what you can do."

At midnight he called on Joseph Alsop, then continued on to inaugural balls until 3:45 A.M., when Jackie admitted him back into his own house. At daybreak the snow had stopped, but the temperature was twenty degrees and the winds punishing. Jack went to mass alone — delighting his mother, who, though he could not see her, was sitting in another part of the church. At 10:40 A.M. Sam Rayburn and Senator John Sparkman arrived at N Street in the presidential bubble-top Lincoln to pick up the Kennedys. The Eisenhowers awaited them in the Red Room at the White House. Ike put on his top hat, and his wife, laughing, said: "He looks just like Paddy the Irishman." On Capitol Hill the waiting crowd was huge, and they were shivering; they saw Kennedy and cheered, hoping to hear his speech soon. These hopes receded as Cardinal Cushing honked his way through an invocation which seemed endless. The new administration appeared to be opening in disarray. As His Eminence ended, smoke began to curl up from a short circuit in the wires under the lectern. Momentarily the horrified chief of the Secret Service envisaged the whole stand going up in flames. Three times he was on the point of ordering an evacuation and checked himself. Then the smoke cleared, only to be succeeded by another setback. Rising to read his poem, Robert Frost was blinded by the sun glaring on the snow, so he recited another from memory. At last Chief Justice Earl Warren administered the oath. It was 12:51 P.M. Kennedy had been President almost an hour. He turned to face the crowd, and one sensed a lifting feeling on all sides. Hatless and coatless, his breath frosting on the air, the vigorous new chief executive set the tone of a new era: "Let the word go forth from this time and place, to friend and foe alike, that the torch has been passed to a new generation of Americans . . . tempered by war, disciplined by a hard and bitter peace, proud of our ancient heritage."

Fewer than half of America's voters had cast their ballots for Kennedy in November, but voter sentiment fluctuates, not just during campaigns but continually. He entered office determined to broaden his support in the country. After the election he had read Richard E. Neustadt's *Presidential Power*, which concludes that the public's opinion of a chief executive "takes shape for most constituents no later than the time they first perceive him as being President (a different thing from seeing him as a candidate)." Kennedy was determined that the first time Americans saw him as President he would be at the post and pulling away. Although tomorrow was a Saturday, he told his staff it would be a workday, and after a good night's sleep in the Lincoln bed, he himself was in the Oval Office before eight o'clock, accompanied by a few old friends. He experimented with the eight buttons on his telephone console, punching those which would summon Evelyn and Ken, whose offices were adjacent to his own. He also pushed what Ike had called the panic button; within moments a helicopter was fluttering down on the south lawn outside. It all seemed unreal. Jack asked Red Fay, "Paul" — this was subtle, their relationship had been altered — "do you think this is adequate?" The Redhead replied: "I feel any minute now that some guy is going to stick his head through one of those doors and say: 'All right, you guys — out of here.'"

Throughout that day and in the weeks that followed, the new President vibrated with energy. He would pace corridors while dictating rapidly, read on his feet, dart out for brisk constitutionals, and return in a fast walk

that was almost a sprint, restlessly snapping his fingers. Of a typical day James Reston wrote in the *New York Times*, "He did everything today except shinny up the Washington Monument." "When you see the President," a senator remarked, "you have to get in your car and drive like blazes back to the Capitol to beat his memo commenting on what you told him." The presidency, Kennedy had said, was "the vital center of action." That fitted his temperament; so he was both following his instincts and buffing his reputation when he held the first live, televised presidential press conferences, organized the Peace Corps, reorganized the White House staff, and delivered an unprecedented number of speeches. Jackie was asked why he was so hyperactive. "Because he wants to know it all," she said. But he had another motive. He wanted, to the greatest possible degree, the undivided attention of his countrymen. And he was getting it. Newspapermen and television commentators reported the progress of the new administration almost breathlessly. The televised news conferences were immensely popular. Remembering his first debate with Nixon, Jack became the first President to recognize and exploit the possibilities of TV.

His hustling accelerated; he was determined to expand his all-important base. The people he needed were watching him, and he wanted to be sure they liked what they saw. The hatless, coatless vigor helped, except in the hatting industry, which saw its sales plummet. Nice Al Webb, a PT veteran and hatter executive, arrived with two hats custom-made for Jack and Red Fay. In the Oval Office, Nice Al removed the hats from their boxes as though they were fragile Stradivarii. Jack and the Redhead tried them on. Nice Al stood back to observe the effect. He said unconvincingly, "You both look great." Jack and Red looked at each other and burst out laughing. "Al," said the President, "are you willing to destroy the beloved image of our country's leader just to save the hat industry?" Crestfallen, Nice Al retreated. To make a permanent record of the occasion, Cecil Stoughton, the White House photographer, was summoned to the office. His photograph of the President and Red survives. In it they look like a couple of house detectives.

But to the country, the bareheaded Kennedy was looking more and more like a President. Americans approve of self-starters. It was reassuring to learn that Ike's successor was very much in charge. The first televised sessions with the White House press corps were, of course, crucial. One of them — the third — was watched by some 65 million people in 21.5 million homes. Marshall McLuhan acclaimed him as a virtuoso. And presently the wisdom of the Neustadt approach was reflected in studies by opinion samplers. Kennedy's racing start had converted an enormous segment of the electorate, millions of Nixon voters who had changed their minds. And, Gallup reported, the number of Americans who approved of the way Kennedy was doing his job was growing steadily.

Jackie's emergence as a national celebrity was more languid. She hated the goldfish-bowl aspect of living in the White House, the tourists who lurked outside the grounds, the shouts of encouragement from boys watching her on the White House tennis court, and the amateur photographers with telephoto lenses who snapped pictures of her children in their play area. But she genuinely loved the mansion, and devoted herself to a restoration of its former majesty. Pierre Salinger found her charming but intractably negative when he approached her for public appearances. Then CBS suggested that she show and tell about the mansion's new decor, and to Pierre's delight, this time she said yes. Millions of Americans saw her for the first time, and they saw her at her best, knowledgeable about antiques, classic designs, interior decoration, and the subtle use of color. She would never abandon her struggle for privacy — less for herself than for Caroline and young John — but after that program she was not only a household name but also a household image. It was at this time that French towns began vying for the honor of being the home of her ancestors. Like Jack in his early campaigns, she was everything parents wanted their children to be, and since she still looked as though she were in her twenties, their daughters shared that yearning.

"Presidents, like great French restaurants, have an ambiance all their own," Douglass Cater has observed. The Kennedy image was forming, an amalgam of, among other things, Jack's glamour and vitality, Jackie's cameo beauty, Caroline's Kate Greenaway appeal (who could resist a little girl who, when asked for a request by the leader of the Marine Band, replied, "Old MacDonald Had a Farm"?), little John's first toddling, the elegant rhetoric of the presidential speeches, the football on the attorney general's desk, and the new idealism. These people loved America with zest, knew how to court her, and how to shield her when she had been won.

Looking back on their first weeks in power, Bob Kennedy would say, almost wistfully, "Those were the days when we thought we were succeeding because of the stories on how hard everybody was working." Certainly the press and television coverage was massive. TV specials, syndicated newspaper stories, and magazine articles dwelt on "The First Hundred Days," as though they were comparable to the opening months of FDR's presidency. Less than two weeks after Kennedy had been sworn in, a group of celebrated authors and photographers began work on a book, *Let Us Begin*, to be published on his hundredth day in power. It was ready for the presses when a dramatic event made drastic revisions necessary. The event was one of U.S. history's most farcical incidents, which took its name from Cuba's Bahía de Cochinos, the Bay of Pigs. This was the scheme Eisenhower had mentioned to Kennedy on November 18. Cuba was to be invaded by fourteen hundred anti-Castro Cuban exiles — "La Brigada," as they were grandly called. The Central Intelligence Agency had planned the attack, the Joint Chiefs of Staff had endorsed it, and Kennedy gave it the green light — thus committing the gravest blunder of his career. The exiles were poorly trained and inadequately armed. Their maps were out-of-date. Castro's troops outnumbered them 143 to 1. After less than three days of stumbling about, the survivors were rounded up, humiliated at a show trial in Havana's Sports Palace, and led off to prison. John Fischer wrote in *Harper's* magazine that while Kennedy "was still trying to move in the furniture, in effect, he found the roof falling in and the doors blowing off." Later, Americans learned that the CIA planners believed that the President, once he realized that American prestige had been committed, would intervene with U.S. air cover, ships, and infantrymen. Nixon would have done it; he said so in the November 1964 *Reader's Digest*. His instincts at the time, he wrote, were to "find a proper legal cover and . . . go in."

The new President refused his flank. He saw where military intervention would lead: occupation by unpopular troops who would become targets for terrorists and resistance fighters, leading to hostages, reprisals, and endless, hopeless bloodshed. Therefore he blew the whistle on the adventure and made a public statement accepting all blame for the disaster. Actually, of course, Eisenhower was responsible for a large part of it. He had ordered the training of the insurrectionists, had incorporated their plot into United States policy, and had urged Kennedy to carry it forward. When the new President had asked for the Pentagon's opinion, the Joint Chiefs had unanimously predicted that the insurgents would be successful. Only then was the CIA given a green light, and its incompetence had led to disaster. The episode crippled JFK's prestige just as his administration was finding its feet. America's allies in Western Europe were appalled. As evidence of the catastrophe mounted, the President, alone with his wife, broke down and wept. Later he told you that he could see but two consolations for the blunder. The first was that he had lost all illusions about the Joint Chiefs' infallibility. Their future opinions would be received skeptically, subjected to ruthless scrutiny, and weighed against the judgment of experienced civilians. The second consolation arrived on May 3, two weeks after the calamity. Kennedy was remarking on the difference between the British and American forms of democracy. Had he been prime minister in England, he said, his government would have fallen and he would have been evicted from his home. At that point Evelyn arrived with an advance copy of the latest Gallup poll. The figures showed an unprecedented 83 percent of the American people behind him. He tossed it aside and sighed. "It's just like Eisenhower," he said. "The worse I do, the more popular I get."

The White House is very white. Under a roving moon its painted sandstone walls gleam through Andrew Jackson's beloved magnolias with a haunting ghostcandle glow, and the barbered lawn lies quiet as a park, and sometimes, when the light shifts, the mansion seems to recede. Partly this is a trick of landscaping, partly it is us. So much intrudes, Americans take their presidency personally, deeply, and solemnly. Thus, mythbound, you lurk behind the old black fence on Pennsylvania Avenue, squinting at the floodlit north facade. The haze of sentiment grows denser. You can scarcely believe that the place is inhabited.

It is, because the White House is also a house. If Jack took you on one of those tours which gave him so much pleasure in the closing weeks of that winter, you left with some grasp of what life there must be like. During the day, he couldn't use the magnificent rooms downstairs, because they were on display to the public. Evening entertainment was frequent, however; the President played host at about ten parties a year for as many as 2,000 guests and countless smaller affairs for 150. Jackie introduced many dinner parties that were really small — for ten or eight or six, including one memorable one for Igor Stravinsky's seventy-fifth birthday. The householder's employer charged no rent and paid for most of the entertaining, but each year the tenant from Massachusetts found himself digging deeper into his own pocket.

The grounds are lovely and expansive, but if any member of the First Family leaves the grounds, men carrying guns come along. They have no choice; it is the law. Inside, below the east terrace, there is a private theater which would show any movie ever made and some the public wouldn't see for months. In those days there was also a swimming pool, always kept at ninety degrees — uncomfortable for most people, but welcome to a man with a bad back. The telephone system was, quite simply, the best in the world. There were two switchboards, one operated by women on the fourth floor of the Executive Office Building next door, and the other, in the EOB basement, manned by signalmen in the White House Communications Agency. In those days the mansion's telephone number was NAtional 8-1414. Of course, if you dialed it, Jack didn't answer personally, but if you knew the name of an aide, you were put straight through. The switchboard could find anybody in the world, including people in airplanes. Once the operators were asked to find a man whose Cape Cod number was unlisted. They located him in California — visiting a friend whose number was also unlisted. The obverse of this was that when the President was wanted, there was no place to hide. He rarely ate a meal or slept through a night without interruptions.

As Jack once put it, "I have a nice home, the office is close by, and the pay is good." The office was, in fact, only fifty yards away. The posts of Secret Service agents were everywhere. If the President turned toward an elevator, it opened, and other agents were alerted to his approach. If presidential duties required travel anywhere in the world, at any time, one of his helicopters took him to Andrews Air Force Base, where Air Force One, a luxurious converted Boeing 707, would be ready to take off the instant he arrived.

The mansion has two low wings, east and west, housing the offices of presidential aides. The east wing stretches out to East Executive Avenue, across the street from the Treasury Building. Tourists enter through the East Avenue gate. West Executive Avenue, on the other side of the White House, has been closed since 1942, when an agent in the Secret Service (SS to White House regulars) pointed out that a sniper there could draw a bead on FDR. The power is concentrated in the west wing, because, ever since Theodore Roosevelt built it, the President's office has been there. O'Donnell, O'Brien, Sorensen — men of that rank worked in offices above, below, and around Kennedy's Oval Office. In the west wing basement Mac Bundy presided over the War Room. The east wing was home to Dave Powers, Arthur Schlesinger, the military aides, and the First Lady's social secretary — the second tier of aides. The lowest tier was housed in the EOB, formerly the State, War, and Navy Building, across West Executive Avenue (now used for parking). Vice-President Johnson's office was over there. LBJ was assigned a single parking space. He did have one enviable perk, however. He and Bob Kennedy were the only two men permitted to enter the Oval Office from the rose garden. Once you have seen that office, you begin to understand why men will put themselves through torment if they have the faintest chance of possessing it for four years. Thirty-five feet long and slightly over twenty-five feet wide, it is tranquil, luminous, and soundproof. Light floods it from its great French windows, nearly twelve feet high; the gloomiest day seldom seems cheerless here. In winter, when the trees are

The White House and its new resident

bare, you can see the Lincoln Memorial and the bone-white Washington Monument, with its winking red light to warn approaching aircraft. The great seal of the President of the United States was, in Kennedy's day, woven into the thick wall-to-wall gray carpeting and molded into the ceiling above. Under Eisenhower the walls had been painted a bleak shade of green. Kennedy had them repainted off-white. It was now the office of a navy man, with framed pictures of tall ships and, over the mantel, a model of the *Constitution*. Two couches stood on either side of the fireplace, with one of Jack's Northern Porch rocking chairs between them. His desk, a gift from Queen Victoria, had been fashioned from the timber of a British warship; Jackie had found it in a dank storeroom, and it now stood flanked by the Stars and Stripes on one side, and on the other side by the presidential flag. On the desk top were works of scrimshaw, finely engraved whales' teeth; leather-bound copies of Kennedy's books; and the fragment of coconut on which, in 1943, he had chiseled the message which eventually brought rescue to him and his men: *Native knows posit he can pilot 11 alive need small boat Kennedy.*

If you weren't LBJ or Bobby, and wanted to see the President, you could reach the Oval Office through O'Donnell's office or Evelyn's. (There was also the main door, but it was rarely used. Its purpose was to let the staff know whether or not the President was inside. If it was closed, he was; if open, he wasn't.) Kenny was appointments secretary, and he took his job very seriously. If you wanted to see the President, he felt, you had to go through him. But Ken's careful schedules were always being gutted by people who, knowing Evelyn to be a soft touch, would take that route. So heavy did the traffic through her office become that Jack, at Ken's insistence, ordered that her door to the Oval Office be closed at all times. Two days later he rang for Ken and pointed at Evelyn's door. In it was a newly bored peephole. Kennedy said, "We can't win."

Actually, of course, he could have solved the problem with one stony look at her, but he liked a certain amount of chaos around him, believing that the more sources of information he had, the better he could govern. For him the really private part of "the property," as he called 1600 Pennsylvania Avenue, was the First Family's apartment on the second floor of the mansion. During Kennedy's years, over a million people filed through the first-floor state rooms under the illusion that they were looking at the President's lodging, when all they saw was a well-appointed museum. However, when an SS agent found your White House pass to be correct, and had phoned ahead for confirmation, you entered a concealed elevator, rose to the second floor above ground level, and emerged into what were obviously quarters *en famille*. Here the tone was quite different. These rooms were closed to outsiders; none of them was seen on Jackie's TV show. Not everyone would feel comfortable in them, because they were so precisely upper-class. The last tenants had been comfortably middle-class. Their tastes had run to the music of Fred Waring and Lawrence Welk, to huge color television sets and war trophies. Now the only martial note among the furnishings was a photograph of the First Lady's father wearing a World War I second lieutenant's uniform, and even he gazed out from his frame with a genteel, East Egg urbanity.

The new look was subdued elegance. Achieving it was no mean

accomplishment. The mansion had changed enormously since the days when John G. Nicolay called it "a dirty, rickety concern," yet it could scarcely be called a triumph of design. Ceilings were lofty dust catchers, rooms were chopped up, doors opened inconveniently. Stepping from the elevator you found yourself in a small vestibule which debouched into a huge hall. This passage ran east and west, bisecting the entire floor like a concourse and creating something of a traffic problem. The President's oval room, or study (as distinguished from his oval west wing office), opened on it from the south, and so — directly across from the elevator — did his bedroom. The children slept along the north side. The western end of the corridor had been converted into a family sitting room, which led to the First Lady's bedroom and the dining room.

The effect could easily have been that of a refurbished New York elevator flat. It wasn't, because the great, barnlike corridor had been toned down by an ingenious use of color, *objets d'art*, and graceful furniture. Slip-covered French chairs were grouped invitingly on off-white rugs. Lovely chandeliers sparkled overhead. American paintings by George Catlin, Maurice Prendergast, Winslow Homer, and John Singer Sargent hung on tinted walls, and below them were handsomely mounted vases and sculptures, a Louis Quinze desk, and a spinet. The most vivid hues, however, came from book jackets. Altogether there were several thousand volumes, rising in tiers: graceful books on art, squat histories, a multivolume encyclopedia, Churchill's World War II memoirs; *Disturber of the Peace*, a biography of H. L. Mencken; a few modern novels — Nevil Shute's *On the Beach*, Giuseppe di Lampedusa's *Leopard* — and a battered, jacketless copy of *Profiles in Courage*, which seemed a shabby orphan here, because everything else was tidy and quietly expensive. The hi-fi–FM–TV console in the west sitting room was long, low, masked. The portable bar there was stocked with Beefeater gin and Ballantine scotch. White matchbooks bore the inscription *The President's House*, and the spine of a buckram scrapbook the simple legend *Caroline*.

The door to the oval room would open, and Kennedy would put his head out. Over his shoulder you could see a member of the subcabinet and guessed, from his expression, that he was being subjected to that staccato cross-examination of which Jack was such a master. The rest of the First Family was in Newport; Ken had said the President wanted to talk about India. Jack suggested you mix yourself a drink. A servant appeared and drew flowered drapes across the broad west window, masking the rose garden. Eastward, moonbeams freckled the old green roof of the Treasury; within, tiny points of light twinkled on the hall spinet, on a picture of Lee Radziwill, on a framed snapshot of young Jacqueline Bouvier with her father and on another of Caroline romping with hers.

The oval-room door opened again. "Come in, Bill. Bring your drink."

Jack's valet awakened him at 7:30 A.M. and the President breakfasted in bed, propped up, on orange juice, two soft-boiled eggs, toast, and coffee laced with cream and sugar. While eating he read newspapers at his amazing

The new administration was in constant motion: ". . . we thought we were succeeding because of . . . how hard everybody was working."
— *RFK*

clip; on some mornings Bundy or Ted Clifton, the President's military aide, would come over with the three-thousand-word Intelligence Check List. George Thomas would have his hot tub drawn by now, and he would rise and ease himself into it. Clifton or Bundy would have left with any instructions for action. Jack would stay in the tub for twenty minutes to a half hour, reading more newspapers, scribbling orders, or signing documents — which frequently emerged moist — on his tub board. By nine o'clock he was on his way to the office, with Caroline tagging along. He would meet appointments and study documents until 1:00 or 1:15. Usually a business lunch would follow; if he happened to be free he would cross to the mansion for a visit with Jackie and Caroline. To their surprise and delight, Jack was seeing more of his wife and children than had ever been possible in the past. Now, for the first time, they were deeply wed in their love.

During the middle of the day he also swam in the pool, built with public donations as therapy for FDR. Jack disliked swimming alone; if you were with him you would breaststroke alongside, and so converse. His father had commissioned a mural for the pool's four walls, a re-creation of a Saint Croix harbor in the Virgin Islands which gave a swimmer the illusion that he was in a lagoon. If you swam after dark, lights twinkled around the harbor, and a moon and stars hung overhead. Leaving the pool, Jack would enter the White House gym, adjoining it, for Dr. Kraus's exercises. One of three navy chief pharmacist's mates, all trained for this specific task, would supervise him. After the swim, exercises, and lunch, he always entered his bedroom and napped for forty-five minutes or an hour. Another short bath followed and then a return to the office. He would often work until 8:00 P.M. or even later, and since he never knew when he would finish, invitations to dine with him often arrived on very short notice. Time permitting, a movie would be shown. In the beginning Jack watched from a series of comfortable chairs, but none was satisfactory, and then a bed was installed. He was more easily bored by dull films now, and even if the movie was good, as often as not he would be called away — why, of course, he never said. On a pleasant evening a guest might be invited upstairs. Jackie would play records — "Alley Cat" and bossa novas, typically — or try to persuade "Bunny" — always in vain — to do his imitation of Noël Coward. In her absence he and a friend would dine upstairs. The White House kitchen staff, before quitting for the day, would have left broiled chicken or lamb chops on a hot plate on the second floor. Then Jack would suggest television or, on a fair evening, sitting on the Truman balcony, talking, Jack puffing on a cigar and you sipping Heineken's from the bottle. At around 11:00 P.M. he would slip into the Brooks Brothers sleeping jacket he preferred to pajamas, kneel by his bed to mumble the Lord's Prayer, and then say sleepily, "Good night, pal. Will you please put out the light?"

After the inaugural he attempted, in his words, "to carry on the life I had led." On his first Sunday as President, he was being driven across town when he asked the Secret Service driver to cruise past his old Georgetown house. As the car entered N street he turned to you and said in exasperation, "Look at all those newspapers piled up all over the front step. I told them and *told* them to cancel deliveries out here. Probably some of my Republican neighbors are already spreading the story. 'How can he run the country when he can't organize his own home?'" Before anyone else in the limousine could intervene, he was out of it, picking up the old papers and tossing them into the backseat. Presidents don't do that sort of thing, and after a while Jack stopped it. In Georgetown that Sunday he had still been running for office.

One evening he and a friend slipped out the mansion's northwest gate and slipped into a neighborhood movie to see *Spartacus*, but thereafter the Secret Service begged him to watch films at home. Perhaps his most successful sortie was his Gettysburg trip. In midweek he called and alerted you to be ready for a Saturday drive to the battlefield. He and his other passengers arrived in a Mercury with the top down. It soon became obvious that he had boned up on the battle and intended to act as a guide. Unfortunately it did not quite work out that way. If he could forget his office, his guests could not. At first he was unrecognized. Everyone in the party was dressed informally, there was no SS, and the car was not the kind you would associate with a President. But there were many tourists at Gettysburg that day. People would glance at him again and again until they finally grasped the enormous fact. They were, quite simply, looking at the President of the United States. Back in the Mercury you felt that loss of anonymity which he lived with all the time now.

In the beginning the new First Family had thought they could go visiting like any other Washington couple. Their first host was to be Rowland Evans, Jr., then a correspondent for the New York *Herald Tribune*. The morning of the party an Evans neighbor opened his front door and found his sidewalk encased in ice. Ice, however, was rapidly disappearing from the Evans walk; a small army of District employees was chipping away the last slivers. The neighbor huffily asked why the special treatment. He was told, and since he, like Evans, was a member of the working press, the Kennedys' dream of a quiet evening was destroyed. The fact was that they were no longer the people they had been. Over four hundred letters arrived at the White House inquiring why the President always seemed to be a few steps ahead of his wife. "Jackie," he once replied lightly, "will just have to walk faster." Actually, she wasn't allowed to. The President outranks everyone, including ladies. Early in his White House years he tried to hold a door for Eleanor Roosevelt. She hung back. She said: "No, you go first. You are the President." He laughed and said: "I keep forgetting." Mrs. Roosevelt said gently: "But you must never forget."

The Know-Nothing party disappeared from American politics in 1856, but its legacy of anti-intellectualism has endured, like some low but indestructible form of animal life. It had fanned the flames of McCarthyism, and its embers flared anew as the country's primitives learned about the new First Family's life-style. Most voters approved of Jack's conduct of the presidency, but it is doubtful that many understood, or had even heard of, the illustrious cultural figures who followed Robert Frost into the presidential presence. Here again Kennedy was breaking new political ground. The tra-

The swearing-in ceremony of the cabinet

*The White House was
the center of action*

The Oval Office

President John F. Kennedy

THE ART OF
PERSUASION

Conducting a press conference

Addressing Congress

ditional appeal to the common man had been to appear commoner than he was; it was exemplified by Oklahoma's "Alfalfa Bill" Murray, a cultivated man who, when campaigning at home, made a point of unfastening his fly before each public appearance and pulling a few inches of shirttail through the opening. There were still a few Alfalfa Bill protégés in Washington, and they were struck dumb by this young new President who sent White House invitations, week after week, to people their preceptor would have regarded as social deviates — artists, poets, musicians, scientists, and scholars. In the Kennedy years, a White House banquet was dazzling. Usually guests sat at the long horseshoe-shaped banquet table, but sometimes it was replaced by a cluster of little tables. Background music, usually from the air force's Strolling Strings, accompanied the food and wine and fell silent for the toasts, which by custom were brief and witty. Arising, the company would find fires burning in the redecorated Blue, Green, and Red Room fireplaces, and flowers filling every niche. They then entered the East Room for entertainment by a ballet troupe, opera stars, Stravinsky, Isaac Stern, Pablo Casals, or a Shakespeare company — the first to appear in the White House since the Taft administration in 1910.

The Kennedys' most brilliant social event was staged, not in the mansion, but on the lawn of Mount Vernon, the first President's estate, with its sweeping view of the Potomac. It was this President's way of repaying a very special diplomatic debt. During his negotiation with Khrushchev which led to a Laotian cease-fire, Kennedy, knowing the Kremlin would be inattentive to his arguments — even if they served its own best interests — had desperately searched for allies. Most countries, including NATO nations, had agreed with de Gaulle's announcement that he wanted no part of any military movements in that part of the world. The President believed that an end to the fighting would also serve Russian interests — the Chinese were another matter, but in the early 1960s Mao was not prepared to defy Moscow — and Khrushchev, reaching the same conclusion, put the Kremlin's massive pressure to bear on the Laotian Communists, forcing an armistice and then a coalition government. Britain had supported Kennedy, and the Philippines and Thailand had offered to send token troops, but what had tipped the balance had been an offer from Pakistan's President Mohammed Ayub Khan to dispatch five thousand soldiers — his army's elite. When it was all over Jack told his staff, "Anything Ayub wants from me from now on, he can have."

A few months later Ayub announced that he would be visiting Washington with his daughter. American diplomats reported that the tough old Pakistani leader would appreciate a red carpet — the wider and thicker, the better. Jack asked Jackie to take over. It was like asking Busby Berkeley to stage a chorus show with an open-ended budget. The production — that is the right word for it — began when a motorcade of presidential limousines, bearing 138 guests, drew up at Anacostia's Pier One. Escorted by officers in dress whites, they were piped aboard four vessels: a converted Peter Tare, the *Patrick J.*, the *Honey Fitz*, and the *Sequoia*. Jack and Ayub were to be on the *Honey Fitz*; Jackie and Ayub's daughter, on the *Sequoia*. The rest of the passengers, Washington's elite in those long-ago days, included Bob and Ethel, Sam Rayburn, Lyndon and Lady Bird, FDR Jr., the Douglas Dillons, the McNamaras, the Mansfields, the Everett Dirksens, the Symingtons, and Mrs. Nicholas Longworth, with whom you enjoyed a lively conversation on the *Patrick J.* The flotilla moved down the river at eleven knots, the mood lightened by a trio playing on each boat, until, at Mount Vernon, traditional honors were paid: bells tolling and passengers standing on the decks facing the old mansion. Ashore, you entered one of a line of black Cadillacs that carried guests up the hill — lining both sides of the road were marines in dress blues, their rifles at present arms — and dined by candlelight under a huge tent. The First Lady had left nothing to chance; for three days cropdusters had sprayed four square miles, annihilating every last chigger, tick, and mosquito. The meal was a triumph of René Verdon, Jackie's handpicked chef: avocado and crabmeat mimosa, *poulet chasseur avec couronne de riz clamant*, *framboises à la crème Chantilly*, and *petits fours secs*. Glutted and gorged, you crossed the lawn to accomplish digestion, light up a Corona Corona, and empty far too many of the goblets of champagne available on tempting trays borne by passing waiters, while listening to the National Symphony Orchestra play Gershwin's *American in Paris* and Mozart's *allegro con spirito* from Symphony No. 35 in D Major. As the party reboarded the boats, aides offered the ladies jackets and sweaters, although most of these were soon doffed as, accompanied by more music, the overfed, somewhat drunken, and entirely euphoric guests danced their way back to Pier One. Next morning, reaching for the aspirin bottle, you wondered what Jack would have done if Ayub had offered him a reinforced division.

Here one must distinguish between the President's taste and his First Lady's. Jacqueline Bouvier was taught hers; she came from a milieu familiar to any reader of the novels of Scott Fitzgerald, whose daughter Scottie was among Jackie's friends. It was a world of sprawling estates with swimming pools, badminton courts, and stables, where little girls played under the eye of governesses and were taught to dance with little boys wearing Eton jackets and white gloves. She was as partial to French food as to French furniture and French wine. She also found Jack a French tailor. As President he wore the clothes she felt were appropriate and the PT-boat tie clasp we all bore — and some still bear — as a badge of loyalty. Probably Jackie was also responsible for those presidential harangues about your shirts, which, he insisted, were not only unstylish but appeared to be soiled; didn't you change them at least four times daily? Once, in the middle of a serious discussion, he said abruptly: "I don't think Bobby is very well-dressed, do you? Why, he still wears those button-down shirts. They went out five years ago. The only people I know who still wear them are Chester [Bowles] and Adlai." But Jack had his own taste. He hadn't learned at his mother's knee. There were just certain manners which he thought were sensible and dignified, and he combined them with an intuitive grasp of what was done and what wasn't. At a Hyannis Port summer party a stranger, who, it became obvious, had never met a senator, kept referring to "Dick" Russell. The President was vexed. Afterward, he said heatedly, "In the many years I've known him I've never called him anything but *Senator* Russell." Evelyn Lincoln worked for him for over ten years. He never addressed her other than as "Mrs. Lincoln."

During the '60 fight he refused to flap his arms around his head like

IN CELEBRATION
OF THE ARTS

With the Vienna Boys' Choir (far left and left, above), Igor Stravinsky (left, below), Pablo Casals (right, below)

Nixon and Eisenhower. It was a cheap circus gesture, in the worst of taste; he would quit politics first. And while campaigning was rough, a politician ought to leave his wife out of it. While his opponent was trotting out Pat, Julie, and Tricia as though they were a troupe of performers, Kennedy used the phrase "Jackie and I" just once, and afterward he was embarrassed. If a candidate lost an election he ought to come out, face the cameras, and gracefully concede. Nixon hadn't done it in '60. Instead, he had sent Herb Klein out to read a cold, brief statement. You remarked that he should have appeared himself, if only to thank the thousands of Republican volunteers who had worked their hearts out for him, and were still watching TV. Jack agreed. He said: "He went out the way he came in — no class." Excellence was always in the best of taste, and he pursued it to the end. Traditionally, the President always tossed out the first ball for the Washington Senators' season opener. He hated the second-rate, even in himself, and so, one day in early April, 1961, there was Jack, in the rose garden between appointments, pitching several balls around. Asked why, he said rather sheepishly, "I want to be sure I do it right." A doctor told him he could deepen and strengthen his voice if he spent a half hour barking every morning. Coming into his bedroom you heard this extraordinary sound and looked inquiringly at Dave Powers. Dave explained. He said: "It surprised the shit out of me when I came in. I thought we had a fucking seal in the White House."

Jack's taste was surest in judging writers, and they knew this. After his inaugural address, E. B. White of the *New Yorker*, who had watched it in a Maine farmhouse, wrote him: "One of the excitements of American citizenship is a man's feeling of identity with his elected President. I never had this feeling hit me so hard as on January 20, 1961, when, watching on television . . . I first saw the lectern take fire, then so much more — thanks to your brave words. I promise that whenever I can manage I'll blow my little draft of air on the beloved flame." Thornton Wilder said Kennedy had awakened "a whole new world of surprised self-respect" in the arts. Lewis Mumford described him as "the first American President to give art, literature, and music a place of dignity and honor in our national life."

Like most of the rest of us he was fond of the songs that had been popular when he was young, dating girls, and dancing. Sitting on the Truman balcony during those summer evenings, he would slip old 78s from the 1930s and 1940s onto his stereo — "Body and Soul," "Stardust," "Beyond the Blue Horizon," "Stormy Weather," "Deep Purple," "My Reverie," "Love Walked In," "My Romance," and "The Very Thought of You." *My Fair Lady* had been his favorite musical until *Camelot* opened, a few weeks before his inaugural, in New York's Majestic Theatre. He had his own stereo in his bedroom, and he liked to drift off while listening to the songs he loved most. His favorite came at the very end of the *Camelot* record, when King Arthur knights a lad on the eve of the king's last battle and tells him:

> *Don't let it be forgot*
> *That once there was a spot*
> *For one brief shining moment*
> *That was known as Camelot.*

Shamelot," said the politicized intellectuals after he was dead. They had never understood him, or he them, though he had tried harder. It was in his character; his instinctive approach to a problem was cool, impersonal, analytical. They had blamed him for the Bay of Pigs, which was fair enough; he had blamed himself. But they were neither angry nor disappointed — they were exultant. "What gets me," he told you, knitting his brow and shaking his head, "is that all these people seem to want me to fail. I don't understand that. If I don't succeed, there may not be another President." They didn't care; if he came to grief, it would prove them right, and the vindication of one's judgment, for some men, has absolute precedence. Jack wondered aloud: "What do they want me to do? Why don't they put it on paper?" Some did; the *Reporter* did. But in Georgetown, cocktail talk was easier, if more irresponsible, and as you made the rounds of these parties, you reached a curious conclusion. A yearning for the past has long been attributed to the necromancy of conservative Republicans, to those who pine for a vanished America — for celluloid collars, flypaper, whalebone corsets, harvest-home suppers, and the benevolent paternalism of the Cleveland Business Men's Marching Club. By the early 1960s, however, that longing had been matched by a liberal hankering for the Great Depression, childhood of a generation, when New Deal liberalism was a flaming cause and Fala was alive, wagging his little tail.

In the Kennedy years the idioms of the New Left had not yet entered America's street language. The Radical Right, on the other hand, had made great progress. The John Birch Society, whose mirror image the Students for a Democratic Society would become, had been flourishing for four years. In a rare lapse of political judgment, the Kennedy brothers had increased its fame and heightened its profile by denouncing it, the attorney general calling it "ridiculous" and the President warning that it was an inept adversary of communism. Its head, Robert Welch, a retired candy manufacturer who liked to be called "The Founder," seemed to enjoy the publicity and was doubtless aware that it helped recruit new Birchers. Welch was strange, and he had even stranger allies. Under the Right umbrella were gathered such groups as the Reverend Billy James Hargis's Christian Crusade and Dr. Fred Schwartz's Christian Anti-Communism Crusade. C. D. Jackson, publisher of *Life*, bore reluctant witness to the power of Dr. Fred's crusade. After an issue of his magazine had treated Schwartz with contempt, advertisers' protests forced Jackson to appear before a Schwartz rally in the Hollywood Bowl and eat crow: "I believe we were wrong, and I am profoundly sorry. It's a great privilege to be here tonight and align *Life* magazine with . . . Dr. Schwartz and the rest of these implacable fighters against communism."

Only once did a member of a lunatic fringe come close to triggering Jack's temper, and then, with a spasm of his fist, he suppressed it. During a White House luncheon for newspaper publishers, E. M. "Ted" Dealey of the Dallas *Morning News*, a bloated man with green-tinted spectacles, embarrassed his fellow guests by telling his host: "We need a man on horseback to lead this nation, and many people in Texas and the Southwest think you are riding Caroline's tricycle." Kennedy flushed; using his daughter's name

Aboard Air Force One

to make a crude point was inexcusable. He replied icily that he "didn't get elected President by arriving at soft judgments," and that as President he had to weigh all proposed solutions and find one which would "assure the survival and success of one hundred eighty million Americans." The editor of Dallas's evening paper, the *Times-Herald*, wrote Kennedy, assuring him that Dealey did not speak for all Texans. The President replied: "I'm sure the people of Dallas are glad when afternoon comes."

A popular novel at the time was Fletcher Knebel's *Seven Days in May*, an account of a high-brass attempt to take over the U.S. government. You asked Kennedy if he was familiar with it. He nodded; "Fletch gave me a copy. I read it the other evening." You probed. Was such a coup possible? Did the Pentagon have general and flag officers who could do that? Jack grinned. He replied: "I know a couple who might wish they could." You persisted; this was important. He looked thoughtful for a long moment. Very quietly he said: "It's possible. We could have a military takeover in this country. But the conditions would have to be just right. If, for example, we had a young President, and he had a Bay of Pigs, there would be a certain uneasiness. Maybe the Pentagon would do a little criticizing behind his back, but this would be written off as the usual military dissatisfaction with civilian control. Then if there were another Bay of Pigs, the reaction of the country would be, 'Is he too young and inexperienced?' The military would almost feel that it was their patriotic obligation to stand ready to preserve the integrity of the nation, though God knows just what segment of democracy they would be defending if they overthrew the elected establishment." He paused, as if bracing himself. He said slowly, "If there were a third Bay of Pigs, it could happen." After another pause he said in his hardest voice: "But it won't happen on my watch."

But Jack's chief concern in the wake of the Cuban fiasco was not extremists, or Pentagon intrigue. His first concern was the Kremlin. If possible, he must persuade the Soviet leadership not to interpret his abandonment of La Brigada as a sign of weakness. The day after the landing had failed he had adopted a fighting stance. He was going to let Castro go this time, he said, but he wanted the world to know that "our restraint is not inexhaustible." The United States was ready to act, "alone if necessary," to "safeguard its security," and he warned Moscow that "should that time ever come, we do not intend to be lectured on intervention by those whose character was stamped for all time on the bloody streets of Budapest."

Among the thoughtful readers of the reports from Cuba was Nikita Sergeevich Khrushchev. The first secretary of the Communist party's Central Committee, or, if you were speaking to him, the Chairman President, was unimpressed by cold-war oratory, having delivered a lot of it himself. Khrushchev saw exactly what Kennedy did not want him to see: a new President, youthful and vulnerable, who had just stumbled badly. James Reston later wrote that Khrushchev "would have understood if Kennedy had left Castro alone or destroyed him; but when Kennedy was rash enough to strike at Cuba but not bold enough to finish the job, Khrushchev decided he was dealing with an inexperienced young leader who could be intimidated and blackmailed." To the despot in the Kremlin, this seemed to be a good time to pounce.

In March 1961, diplomats of the United States and the Soviet Union had scheduled a June meeting between the American President and the Soviet Chairman, to be held in Vienna. On May 12 — three weeks after the Bay of Pigs, a decent interval — the Chairman wrote that the invitation was still open. Jack seriously thought of suggesting a postponement. At this time every advantage was on the other side. Yet that, he decided, would be interpreted as a further sign of weakness. Better the summit, he said, than the brink. But Khrushchev believed that bolshevism's hour had struck. And his confidence was not unjustified. The first year of the Kennedy presidency was also the year — unmatched before or since — in which the Soviets could feel that communism was the wave of the future. Stalin's death, the end of the Korean War, and a slackening in the arms race had swept away the handicaps of the past. Russia's rate of industrial growth was markedly higher than America's. Soviet technicians were exultant; they had built the hydrogen bomb and passed the Americans in the development of intercontinental ballistic missiles.

Two months before, Communist leaders from eighty-one countries had convened, fired by the hope that Communist partisans in the emerging, underdeveloped nations in the Third World might succeed in hoisting the red flag on every continent. World wars were out of the question, the Chairman said; they raised the specter of nuclear holocaust. But "wars of liberation or popular uprisings" were different. "What is the attitude of the Marxists toward such uprisings?" he asked, and then answered: "A most favorable attitude." He identified Cuba, Vietnam, and Algeria as examples of peoples marching "in the van" of "liberation," and he announced a "multiplying of the forces of the national-liberation movement" in the Latin American countries "enslaved by American imperialism." Throughout the twentieth century, and perhaps beyond, the USSR would provide "unlimited support" to peoples fighting for freedom in "just wars." This would be communism's new guiding light. It was, in fact, the starting gun for the irregular warfare which, in the years since the Chairman's speech, has flickered and flared all over the globe.

Khrushchev had goals; he also had a list of problems. There was Southeast Asia. There was the demand, by the Red Army and Soviet physicists, that nuclear trials, suspended over two years ago, be resumed; they now had twenty-, thirty-, fifty-, and even hundred-megaton weapons and were eager to try them out. At the top of the list was the only vital issue, the one which overrode all the others. Khrushchev had variously described it as a "bone stuck in the throat," a "cancerous tumor requiring a surgical operation," and a "Sarajevo" likely to lead toward another world war. The bone, or tumor, or Sarajevo, was the divided city of Berlin. To the Russians, the presence of the West in the former German capital was unbearable, and had been for fifteen years. Ike had made certain concessions. He had agreed that Berlin, as now constituted, was "abnormal." He had offered to negotiate the size of the Western garrison there and the extent to which the city would be used as a base for West German propaganda and intelligence activities. Now, as they shaped the Vienna agenda, Khrushchev began stalking Kennedy over the same point. In his wars-of-liberation speech the Chairman had come down hard on Berlin. He had openly threatened the untested President. If "the imperialists" refused to consider "the true situation," he had said, the Soviet Union would "take firm measures" and "sign a peace treaty with the German Democratic Republic before the end of the year." The Chairman had made it clear that such an agreement would include guarantees that any "violation" of East Germany's frontiers would be considered "an act of aggression against all members of the Warsaw Pact" — meaning that Britain, France, and the United States would either have to evacuate all their troops and civilians from West Berlin or go to war.

Did he mean it? Averell Harriman, America's most experienced Kremlinologist, believed the Chairman would try to frighten Kennedy, to stare him down. The best response, he said, would be to turn him aside. It should be done gently, and Kennedy mustn't overestimate his adversary. Khrushchev would be nervous, too. His only other trip to the West had failed. And he had never forgotten his lowly origins. Kennedy, in his farewell words to the nation before departing for Europe, said: "I go to see Mr. Khrushchev in Vienna. I go as the leader of the greatest revolutionary country on earth." Some people, he said, regarded the United States as a "fixed society," but "that is not my view." Yet he knew that on the central question, the future of Berlin, he could not afford flexibility.

Actually, there was no such plane as Air Force One. The President possessed four identical Boeing 707s bearing the tail numbers 26000, 86970, 86971, and 86972 — each powered by identical Pratt and Whitney jets, each an expensive dream of an aircraft — a hundred tons of gleaming machinery, exquisite appointments, and air-conditioned, soundproof cabins, including an elegant office and a luxurious bedroom to which the President and the First Lady could retire if they wanted to be alone. Kennedy could authorize his vice-president or members of his cabinet to use any ship in the fleet, but only the one in which he rode would bear the presidential seal and the Air Force One designation. There was another difference: the driver was always his personal pilot, Colonel James Swindal, a rakish Alabamian, with a Terry-and-the-Pirates profile. Later, Raymond Loewy would design, under presidential supervision, a particular 707 with a blue motif, and that plane would take JFK to Texas and back in November 1963, but the plane the Kennedys boarded on May 30, 1961, bore a scarlet nose and scarlet engine pods. Whenever you were invited aboard the presidential aircraft you liked to sit in the cockpit with Jim Swindal. It was a pleasure just to watch the man in motion. He always moved gracefully, economically, and purposefully, watching the red glow of the instrument panel, his fingers delicately turning his small black trim-tab wheel clockwise, climbing through turbulence to the clear smooth stream at thirty-five thousand feet.

It was astonishing to realize that the Russian delegation wasn't even leaving the ground. In travel, as in everything else, they followed different stars. Nikita and Nina Khrushchev had left home three days ago; they were riding in a private railroad car and would spend a week reaching Vienna.

The American way seemed infinitely preferable. Jack and Jackie had slipped between the sheets before Swindal had reached the Atlantic coast. After seven hours of sleep they would land at Orly Airport, where Parisians, led by the towering figure of Charles de Gaulle, would greet them. The President didn't know it, but his wife intended to give the French a memory to treasure. Eleven years earlier she had been an obscure student at the Sorbonne. Now she was returning in triumph with two truckloads of luggage, a blinding array of jewels, and entrée to select Paris circles which, last time, had been closed to her.

The French have not always been successful at governing themselves, but as impresarios staging ceremonial state visits they have never been surpassed. As Air Force One appeared in the distance, veiled by a sunlit spring mist, Frenchwomen in blue smocks gave the seventy-five yards of red carpeting a final sweep. Soldiers of the Garde Républicaine stood immobile, red plumes riffled by a soft zephyr, their knee-high black boots gleaming, their sword points upright. Beside them was President de Gaulle, also erect, in a double-breasted gray suit. Swindal made a perfect landing, taxied up, and flicked a switch. The Pratt and Whitney jets hissed into silence. The aft door opened, revealing the presidential seal; Jack ducked into view, Jackie just visible behind him. She was beaming and wearing a pale blue pillbox hat. Her husband nervously fingered his tie. This was an important moment for him. Most other world leaders were old enough to be his father. Two of them, Chiang Kai-shek and Konrad Adenauer, had been almost openly pro-Nixon. He had to be impressive; he had their friendship, but he needed their respect.

Drums rolled, then fell silent. The Kennedys descended the ramp and were greeted by *le grand Charles*, who, for once, condescended to speak a few words of English, asking: "Did you have a good aerial voyage?" Jack assured him it had been fine and de Gaulle said, "Ah, that's good." De Gaulle led the Kennedys to a waiting Citroën and the motorcade began. Somewhere in the distance a 101-gun salute was thundering. Their destination was the Quai d'Orsay, ten miles away, and the spectators were dense. De Gaulle was clearly elated that over a million of his countrymen had turned out to welcome his guests. For the Kennedys, the high point of the procession came when they reached the Boul' Mich' and entered the Latin Quarter. In tribute to Jack, a crowd of American students had gathered there. They held aloft a Harvard banner and chanted, "Kenne-*un*, Kenne-*deux*, Kenne-*trois* . . . Kenne-*dix!*" — a locomotive cheer that puzzled the natives but was instantly recognizable to anyone who had ever watched a college football game in the United States.

At the Quai d'Orsay, one palatial apartment had been set aside for the President and another for the First Lady. Kennedy's was the Chambre du Roi, the King's Chamber. The moment the door closed behind him he headed straight for the Louis Seize bedroom, stripping as he went; he had injured his lower lumbar vertebrae at a tree-planting ceremony in Ottawa a few weeks earlier, and for him the long ride from Orly had been a nightmare of agony. A friend ran ahead to fill the bathtub while he gave himself a novocaine injection. The tub was exotic — huge, and completely gold-plated — and Jack sank into it with a grateful moan. He couldn't soak now; he was due at the Elysée Palace for lunch and his first formal talk with de

Gaulle. But throughout his Paris visit he spent every available moment there, with hot water up to his chin.

At the Elysée, trumpets greeted Kennedy, quickly followed by de Gaulle, who led him to a second-floor office. On certain issues they agreed to disagree. *Le grand Charles* said France would never again send troops to Laos, Cambodia, or Vietnam; Southeast Asia was "a bad place to fight." The key issue for both presidents, of course, was Kennedy's imminent confrontation with Khrushchev. Like Harriman, de Gaulle believed that the Chairman was a dissembler, and he advised Kennedy to ignore the attempts to intimidate him. "He will tell you," the French president predicted, "that he is going to sign a separate peace treaty in six months, breaking our Potsdam agreement and driving us out of Berlin. He has been saying that for three years. When the six months are up, he postpones the treaty for another six months, and then another six months. He'll never sign that treaty because Russia does not want a war."

If the United States, Britain, and France withdrew from West Berlin, it would be a sellout. They would be violating the Potsdam treaty and betraying West Germany, now their ally. Of course, allied troops with conventional weapons couldn't defend the city against Red Army attackers for more than a few hours. Only nuclear weapons could turn the tide. Khrushchev knows that, de Gaulle told Kennedy, and don't let him forget it. Hold fast (*tenir ferme*) and convince the Chairman that you're planning a new airlift. He will back off then. The French leader said that he himself had told Khrushchev that while Berlin's location in the Soviet zone was too bad, still, there it was, and its future status could only be determined within a framework of worldwide disarmament.

The talks between Kennedy and de Gaulle — nearly eight hours of intimate conversation spread over three days — appeared to be conducted in the spirit of statesmanship at its very best. The American President was euphoric. You found that curious at the time and still do. The president of France was at odds with his transatlantic allies on several major bedrock issues: his country's role in NATO, British participation in the Common Market, how to approach emerging nations, and whether or not France really needed a nuclear deterrent. Harriman told you de Gaulle would get worse, and Averell, as usual, was right. Nevertheless, Kennedy told you afterward that the French president was always civil, reasonable, and willing to weigh the arguments of those who disagreed with him. De Gaulle's manner, at the beginning of their first conversation, had been avuncular. At the end of the last of them he remarked that the American President was responsible, able, and — the greatest Gaullist accolade — *"un homme sérieux."* Later Jack showed you the translation of a letter de Gaulle had sent him earlier, urging him not to negotiate with Khrushchev at all. The coda began, "Upon what field should you meet?" An eloquent march of metaphors followed, demonstrating that in the writer's judgment there was no appropriate field. Jack read the translation with great zest. "Isn't it beautiful?" he said at the end. Confused, you asked, "You agree with it?" "Oh, no," Jack

Pablo Casals at the White House

OVERLEAF: *JFK inspects the Berlin Wall*

FOLLOWING OVERLEAF: *Halloween at the White House, October 1963*

*Family gathering at
Hyannis Port, September
1962*

As father and son

OVERLEAF: *Heads of state pay their respects to a fallen leader*

said. "But what a marvelous style!" Actually, his enthusiasm was inspired, not by style in a language he couldn't even read, but by his hero worship of a World War II leader. It couldn't last, and it didn't.

Meanwhile, Jackie, never *sérieuse* yet always stylish, was taking Paris by storm. In her apartment, the Chambre de la Reine, awaiting her instructions, she had found Europe's most celebrated cosmetician, Nathalie, and Alexandre, the eminent Parisian hairdresser. Jackie selected for her first evening appearance a slim white-and-rose straw-laced gown and a fourteenth-century coiffure. Ready at last, she made her sortie. The moment she appeared on the Quai d'Orsay steps, a thousand cameras flashed like a blinding sheet of lightning. French reporters cried: *"Charmante! Ravissante!"* Her waiting husband stared at her. "Well," he finally said, "I'm dazzled." That evening she had an inkling of what Jack went through when campaigning. She shook a thousand hands. Her glove was stained. She was exhausted. Nevertheless, she was still graceful and erect, and her smile was radiant. The French told one another, *"Elle est plus reine que les reines"* — she was more queenly than the queens.

The next day she had her own motorcade. André Malraux, France's minister of culture, had organized it. Jackie and Mme de Gaulle were in the first car, followed by Citroëns carrying Jackie's sister, Lee; Eunice Shriver; Rose Kennedy; and a retinue of Parisiennes renowned for their beauty, their talents, or the influence of their husbands. The First Lady was ceremoniously awarded a wristwatch from the Paris Municipal Council. She visited the country estate of the Empress Josephine, Malmaison, and lunched at Mme de Pompadour's retreat. Her French was as flawless and free of accent as it was fluent. Crowds of the French gathered wherever she went, most of them just staring. They marveled at her grace and beauteousness and, shrugging, told one another: *"Parce qu'elle a du sang français"* — she's French; what else did you expect? But her real quarry was Charles de Gaulle. At luncheon, seated next to him, she opened an animated conversation, in perfect idiomatic French, about tangled French historical questions — the dynastic complications of the end of the Bourbon line, the Duc d'Angoulême, the afflictions which beset Louis XVI — until the French president leaned across the table and told the American President that his wife knew more French history than most Frenchwomen. Creating that impression had, of course, been her intention. Later Jack proudly told you that it was as though Mme de Gaulle had asked him about the private life of Henry Clay. There was one difficulty. If de Gaulle and others decided that the President's wife was an aberration, an exception to the rule, her triumph would be personal and therefore useless to the American cause. The problem was solved by a stroke of good luck. Mac Bundy, sitting near de Gaulle, somehow attracted the French president's attention. Slight, with his sandy crew cut, Mac never looked his age. Certainly no one would have guessed that he had been appointed dean of the Harvard faculty nearly ten years earlier. The French president peered down on him and inquired haughtily, *"Qui est ce jeune homme?"* Jackie identified him as a Harvard man, now of the President's National Security Council staff. Speaking slowly, using the limited vocabulary of a French I student, de Gaulle asked Bundy a simple question about Harvard. Mac smiled and responded in a stream of French that would have been thought brilliant had it come from a sophisticated Frenchman.

At a farewell luncheon for the press, Jack said: "I do not think it altogether inappropriate to introduce myself to this audience. I am the man who accompanied Jacqueline Kennedy to Paris, and I have enjoyed it." As they said their farewells, de Gaulle addressed Kennedy as *"mon ami"* and said: "I now have more confidence in your country." Jack was grateful for that — and aware of Jackie's responsibility for it — because in Vienna there would be none of the support allies give one another. Before his inauguration he had been introduced to the "bagman." In reality there were five such men, all army warrant officers. The "bag," or "football," or "satchel," was a thirty-pound metal suitcase with an intricate combination lock. Within were the codes that would launch a nuclear attack. Kennedy usually ignored the satchel man on duty, and no wonder. The bag's presence was a constant reminder that the President was one of two men who could, on a few minutes' notice, destroy Western civilization. Now, in Vienna, he was going to meet the other man.

Heavy rain was falling when Swindal touched down at Vienna's Schwechat Airport. Everyone on the plane groaned in unison. This visit had seemed jinxed from the start. Even before they left the United States vexing problems had arisen. The Austrians, the Russians, and the U.S. State Department had insisted that the President lay a wreath at Vienna's Tomb of the Unknown Soldier. Absolutely not, said Kennedy. The possibilities of political entrapment were too great. O'Donnell called his man in Vienna with Jack's final decision. Ken said: "The Unknown Soldier is probably a Nazi, but you tell them that while Khrushchev is laying a wreath on his grave, President Kennedy will be at Saint Stefan's Cathedral praying for his soul."

The American embassy compound was depressing: gray stucco, with an unsightly brown trim, surrounded by barbed wire, Austrian guards, and husky, snarling police dogs. The President's Russian guest was punctual: at 12:45 a four-door black Chaika crunched up the drive and Khrushchev's stubby legs appeared at an opened door, followed by Khrushchev himself. Kennedy hurried out, smiled, shook his hand, and welcomed him. The Chairman was wearing a neat gray suit with two star-shaped medals on his jacket. He came up to Kennedy's nose. He was grinning broadly, while the President wore a faint, fixed smile which suddenly disappeared; he turned away from the cameras, thrust his hands in his pockets, and looked Khrushchev over from head to toe. Everyone stopped talking. The President didn't look unpleasant; those who knew him realized that in taking the Chairman's measure he was merely satisfying his insatiable curiosity. Later you asked Jack if Khrushchev was different from what he had expected. "Not at all," he replied. He thought him a blend of "surface conviviality and internal rage."

The schedule looked bleak. Lunch on this first day would be at the American embassy, with the President as host. That evening the Austrian government was entertaining its distinguished guests at a banquet, followed by an after-dinner ballet at the glittering Schönbrunn Palace. Tomorrow's lunch would be at the Soviet embassy, with Khrushchev presiding. The first lunch was Jackie's only chance to beguile him, and she did her best. Once, when he was reciting the number of Ukrainian teachers per capita now, and comparing it with the figure under the czars, she said softly, "Oh, Mr. Chairman, don't bore me with statistics." He laughed, and told her that the Russian space dog Strelka had just been delivered of a litter of puppies. She said, how nice, how cute — something like that.

Her lubricating charm was absent in the first Kennedy-Khrushchev meeting. The Chairman, despite his roly-poly figure, was more impressive here. There was a kind of brutal energy about him; his eyes darted and flashed; he gave the impression that he would be quick to note a slight, and deeply offended by it. The ice was broken, insofar as it was broken at all, by strained small talk. Khrushchev asked Kennedy's opinion of Andrei Gromyko. Jack said, "My wife thinks he has a nice smile. Why do you ask?" "Well," said Khrushchev, "a lot of people think that Gromyko looks like Nixon." Slowly the talk became more serious, the Chairman's manner became blustery, and a certain coarseness crept into his voice. Kennedy sat and listened, awaiting an opening. "We admit our mistakes," he said at last. "Do you ever admit you are wrong?" Yes, Khrushchev replied, he had admitted all of Stalin's mistakes. Challenged on his support for "wars of liberation," he answered that they were the consequence of historical inevitability. Kennedy didn't believe that Marxism passed the test of historical inevitability, and he cited case after case in which Communist minorities were trying to overthrow regimes which were supported by the people in free elections. But Khrushchev wasn't going to give an inch. If he couldn't think of an answer, he sat mute. No one knew when something was going to trigger his rage. Kennedy referred to the danger of miscalculation setting off a nuclear war. Khrushchev, in the President's words, "went berserk. He started yelling, 'Miscalculation! Miscalculation! Miscalculation!' All I ever hear from your people and your correspondents and your friends in Europe and everyplace else is that damned word, 'miscalculation'! You ought to take that word and bury it in cold storage and never use it again! I'm sick of it!" Everyone squirmed, then adjourned for lunch. There the President reached over and touched one of the Chairman's medals. He asked: "What's that for?" Taken aback, Khrushchev said proudly: "That's the Lenin Peace Prize." Kennedy said softly: "I hope they let you keep it."

Jack said later that those meetings with the Russian were the "hardest work in the world." As they sat apart with the interpreter and the hours passed, with Khrushchev's rigidity becoming increasingly apparent, Kennedy felt a growing uneasiness. In the past, when suffering or tragedy might have been at stake, he had conferred with men whose outlook was completely different from his own. Yet eventually something was acceptable to both sides, some compromise was worked out, some consensus was reached. But in these talks, he said afterward, he could find no "area of accommodation." Jack would point out the enormous consequences should something go wrong — millions of American corpses, millions of Soviet corpses. Actually, Khrushchev shared this concern — it was the source of his hidden but growing rift with the Chinese — but here he refused to acknowledge that any concessions, any adjustments, even the smallest, could in any way contribute to the prevention of a holocaust. And while the President was grappling with that, the Chairman would once more declare that he was going to sign the peace treaty with East Germany.

Kennedy, after taking a deep breath, thanked him for his frankness and replied that he would answer with equal candor. The allies were not in Berlin on anyone's sufferance. They had fought their way there. At Potsdam the Soviet Union, recognizing that fact, had signed a treaty giving them the legal status of occupying powers. The allies had subsequently made official, binding pledges, based on that treaty. If the United States accepted expulsion from Berlin, its future commitments would be regarded with contempt. Therefore America rejected the Russian ultimatum. Khrushchev's reply was typical. Kennedy, he said, was invoking national security as an excuse for remaining in Berlin. Maybe Kennedy's next move would be to occupy Moscow also, because that, too, would improve the U.S. strategic position. The President said sharply that the Americans did not want to go anywhere; they were only determined to stay where they were.

After two days of this the conference ended as scheduled, with the luncheon at the Russian embassy. Kennedy, brooding, poking at his food, was reminded that it was time to leave. "No!" he barked. "We're not going on time. I'm not going until I know more." He drew Khrushchev aside for one more review of the Berlin situation. The Chairman remained implacable. In December he would sign the East German treaty. Having done that, he would recognize no continuing American rights in West Berlin. If the United States chose to go to war over this, "that is your problem." Kennedy said tautly: "It is you, not I, who wants to force a change." Khrushchev shrugged. His decision, he repeated, was final. Kennedy snapped, "It's going to be a cold winter," spun on his heel, and strode away.

By the time Air Force One had returned to Andrews Field and Khrushchev was back in the Kremlin, the whole world knew of Russia's ultimatum. The Chairman had increased his military budget by 3.114 billion rubles and delivered a series of bellicose speeches. Jack said privately: "I've got two problems. First, to figure out why he did it, and in such a hostile way. And second, to figure out what we can do about it. I think the first part is pretty easy to explain. Obviously he did it because of the Bay of Pigs. I think he thought anyone so callow as to get into a mess like that was dumb, and anybody who got into it and then couldn't see it through had no guts. So he just beat hell out of me. So I've got a terrible problem. If he thinks I'm inexperienced and have no guts, until we remove those ideas we won't get anywhere with him. So we have to act."

He acted by matching Khrushchev's jump in military spending, calling up reserves, and tripling draft calls. To reassure Berliners he sent his vice-president and General Lucius Clay, the hero of the 1948 Berlin airlift, to Germany's old capital. He was reluctant to make an atomic bluff; it might be called. His chief fear, he told you, was that the Chairman "wants to rub my nose in the dirt," in which case "it's over." At the same time, he mused over the discrepancy between the dispute and the sacrifice that might follow. He did not want to lead his people to death "at midnight in some flaming

With Khrushchev in Vienna

At a state dinner with de Gaulle

With Indira Gandhi (far left, above), the Shah of Iran (far left, below), Kwame Nkrumah (left, above), Archbishop Makarios (left, below), Golda Meir (above)

With J. Edgar Hoover

With Dwight Eisenhower

With Harry Truman

With Billy Graham

town" at "some disputed barricade" if the town was only half a town and the barricade manned by Vopos (East Berlin policemen). He said: "All wars start from stupidity. God knows I'm not an isolationist, but it seems particularly stupid to risk killing a million Americans over an argument about access rights on an autobahn in the Soviet zone of Germany, or because the Germans want Germany reunified. If I'm going to threaten Russia with a nuclear war, it will have to be for much bigger and more important reasons than that. Before I back Khrushchev against a wall and put him to a final test, the freedom of all of Western Europe will have to be at stake."

Meanwhile, Berlin was in an uproar. During July, 30,444 refugees flowed into the Western part of the city. In the first ten days of August another 16,500 crossed. On August 12 alone 4,000 were counted, among them a very high proportion of physicians, technicians, and skilled workers — the very people necessary for the Five-Year Program of East Germany's leader, the veteran Communist Walter Ulbricht. Ulbricht, desperate, decided to act. At 12:30 A.M. on August 13, sirens screamed down the dark and deserted streets of East Berlin as squat tanks — T-34s and T-54s — led East German military convoys to the twenty-five-mile border separating the Western part of the city from the East. Trucks of steel-helmeted Vopos took up positions in major intersections. Troops unloaded lumber, barbed wire, concrete posts, stone blocks, and picks and shovels. Four hours later, at sunrise, the beginning of a wall was visible. Four days later it was virtually complete, imprisoning the Germans who remained in East Berlin.

Allied surprise seemed total. The President was away from Washington. He was still trying to sort out what had happened when, on September 1, Khrushchev gave the screw another turn. He resumed nuclear warhead testing. Over the next months the Soviets detonated thirty major devices, nearly all of them in the atmosphere. The Russians thus became responsible for more radioactive poison in the air than the Americans, British, and French combined. Kennedy authorized a resumption of U.S. tests, though he specified that all must be underground, where they would create no fallout. It was now September 8, the peak of the crisis. The wall was complete, a structure of brick and jagged cement zigzagging through the heart of Berlin. All but one of the crossing points had been closed to the allies.

Ten days later, when Jack was about to leave Hyannis Port for Washington, he was handed a grim note: Dag Hammarskjöld had been killed in a Congolese plane crash (which has never been satisfactorily explained). War had not seemed so close since V-J Day. But Kennedy had learned one thing at Vienna. Consistency was not a Russian virtue. Neither was logic. The Chairman had said that, of course, he admitted his mistakes — Stalin's mistakes. This was wildly irrational, unless intended as subtle humor, and on one point everyone who knew him agrees: Khrushchev's lack of subtlety was total. Similarly, his tantrum over *miscalculation* had made no sense whatever. Kennedy concluded that the Soviets, indifferent to world opinion, would not hesitate to reverse themselves. Here they were, on the verge of mobilizing for war, and here came the Soviet ambassador and two of his men, calling at the White House bearing a nervous, white, fluffy puppy. The ambassador presented a letter from Khrushchev. It was a source of pleasure for himself and his wife, he said, "to fulfill Mrs. Kennedy's wish and to send you and your family little 'Pushinka,' a direct offspring of the well-known cosmos traveler 'Strelka,' which made a trip in the cosmic ship on August 19, 1960, and successfully returned to earth." Kennedy stared at the dog and then at Jackie, who put her hand to her mouth and whispered, "I was only trying to make conversation . . ."

At the end of the letter Khrushchev expressed "on behalf of Nina Petrovna and myself our best wishes to you, your wife, and all your family." That was not the language of a man who was preparing to launch hydrogen bombs which would hammer Washington into the earth like a hot white saucer. The next Russian move was a call by Andrei Gromyko, at 1600 Pennsylvania Avenue, for a talk. ("It looks like a thaw," Kennedy told a friend.) Actually, Gromyko had little new to say. Jack listened, smoking a cigar and making no concessions. Gromyko suggested making West Berlin an international zone, with joint Western and Communist policemen. Kennedy shook his head. "You're offering us an apple for an orchard," he said. "We don't do that in this country."

Nevertheless, the call was significant; if nothing else, it was symbolic. Khrushchev had begun to back away from the brink. To the Belgian diplomat Paul-Henri Spaak, he said, "I realize that contrary to what I had hoped the Western powers will not sign the peace treaty. . . . I'm not trying to put you in an impossible situation; I know very well that you can't let yourself be stepped on." The bone in the throat, it seemed, wasn't really unbearable. "You know," he continued to the Belgian, "Berlin is not such a big problem for me. What are two million people among a billion Communists!" Nor was there any hurry now. He had given Kennedy an ultimatum — "by the end of the year" — but to Spaak he said, "I'm not bound by any deadline." Speaking to the Communist Party Congress, he declared on October 17, "The Western powers are showing some understanding of the situation and are inclined to seek a solution to the German problem and the issue of West Berlin." He concluded: "If that is so, we shall not insist on signing a peace treaty absolutely before December 31, 1961."

Kennedy's successful resolution of the Berlin crisis regained the ground he had lost at the Bay of Pigs, and that was a relief, not only in the United States, but throughout Europe. However, the "popular uprisings" in underdeveloped countries could not be solved by showdowns. Ironically, Kennedy's attempts to counter such insurgency led to a mighty U.S. military establishment, to charges that the United States was an aggressor, and, ultimately, to disaster in Vietnam. Talking about Khrushchev, Jack told you, "Why, that son of a bitch won't pay any attention to words. He has to see you move." That, he explained, was why he had ordered a crash buildup of conventional forces. To avoid nuclear annihilation in a world war, he was prepared to intervene — not with American troops, but with arms, funds, and military advisers — in dirty little wars. The paradox, shedding blood for a greater peace, was put simply by McNamara. He said: "We shall have to deal with the problems of 'wars of liberation.' You cannot carry out a land-reform program if the local peasant leaders are being systematically murdered."

Kennedy's observation that Communist insurgents flourish where there is no middle class — where the rich live in idle splendor while the peasants starve — was hardly original. Yet, almost alone in his administration, he believed that the greatest peril to the security of the United States lay below the Rio Grande. After his graduation from Harvard, during a long trip through South America, he had been shocked by the plight of the poor and the callousness of their wealthy rulers. As a senator he had called for the building of close relationships with Latin America, arguing that the United States, with 6 percent of the world's inhabitants, could not continue to consume 50 percent of its resources forever. Like all such measures it had been killed by the United Fruit Company lobby. As President he could ignore lobbies, however, and on March 13, 1961, he had assembled the Latin American diplomatic corps in the East Room, inviting them to join a new Alliance for Progress (Alianza para el Progreso). The Alliance would work toward regional markets, national planning, commodity stabilization, and programs in education, technical training, and research, all based on the proposition that "to complete the revolution of the Americas . . . political freedom must accompany material progress . . . *progreso sí, tiranía no!*" The applause was prolonged; the ambassadors were clearly moved, though many, aware of the entrenched power in their home capitals, were skeptical and, in private, even cynical.

Five months later the Alianza was formally organized in Punta del Este, Uruguay. Each year Kennedy flew south to meet the delegates. Jackie, in her Castillian Spanish, would speak to those in the hall and, equally important, to the crowd outside. The President always came down hard on the need for reform; that was his stick, and unless they responded to it, the economic carrot would remain beyond their reach. To persuade any who doubted the popularity of his position among the masses, a presidential motorcade would proceed to his meetings with political leaders through the packed streets while the cheering crowds, inundating the presidential limousine with blizzards of pink confetti, chanted in unison, "Viva Kennedy! Viva Kennedy!" In light of the situation twenty years later, when an American of different views occupied the White House, it is interesting to read Kennedy's remarks, on his last trip south, to the assembled presidents of Central America at the University of Costa Rica. He declared that everyone in the hemisphere had a "right to social justice," meaning "land for the landless, and education for those who are denied education . . . [and the end of] ancient institutions which perpetuate privilege." On his return from Costa Rica, you asked him why Nixon had failed so miserably in Latin America four years earlier. Furious mobs had attacked Nixon and his wife in Lima and Caracas, shouting, *"Muera Nixon!"* ("Death to Nixon!"); he and Pat had been lucky to escape with their lives, and Eisenhower's dispatch of warships and marines had embarrassed and humiliated his vice-president. Jack replied that he thought his inaugural address, in its appeal to the new generation, had meant more to Latin Americans than to anyone else. And after he had tamed Big Steel, his popularity down there soared. Nixon's trip, on the other hand, had been badly prepared — "Nixon represented the wrong party in FDR terms, and anyway Nixon is Nixon." Kennedy's concern about Central and South America continued to the end of his life. In his last months he repeated his conviction: "I regard Latin America as the most critical area in the world today." After he had gone no one picked up his fallen Alianza standard. The time bomb was still ticking away south of the border, but he was no longer there to hear it.

It was a cherished Kennedy maxim that victories, if not exploited, are wasted. His greatest triumph, which ended the most fearsome dilemma of his White House years and opened a new path to peace, was his resolution of the Cuban missile crisis of October 1962, a challenge which, at the time, seemed beyond the skills of all statesmen. The climax and outcome demonstrated to Americans, and to the world beyond, the new maturity of the Kennedy administration. Had Kennedy and his men failed, the United States would have emerged humiliated and impotent, and their children would be a lesser generation today, living in a lesser land.

Eighteen months had passed since Kennedy's first, botched, encounter with Castro's regime. Kennedy, his aides, and his cabinet were a seasoned, resourceful team. The Cuban challenge — it is so remembered, though the real challengers were in Moscow — began, for Jack, at eight o'clock on the morning of Tuesday, October 16, 1962, when Mac Bundy entered the President's bedroom — Jack was reading a morning newspaper — and said: "Mr. President, there is now hard photographic evidence, which you will see a little later, that the Russians have offensive missiles in Cuba."

It had been clear since late August that something unusual was going on down there. Over five thousand Russians were on the island. The possibility that they were installing offensive nuclear missiles had been raised but dismissed; the Soviets had never put missiles in other countries, not even the Eastern European satellites bound to them by the Warsaw Pact. Oddly, Henry Brandon of the London *Times*, who was in Havana then, knew all about them. He assumed Washington did, too. But Washington didn't. The administration's hierarchy first learned of them when U-2 turbojets, which could fly ten miles high and photograph a newspaper so clearly that you could read its headlines, brought back irrefutable evidence of missile sites in advanced stages of construction, with transporters, erectors, and launchers. Once they had been completed, the missile bases would be able to fire an initial salvo of forty nuclear warheads at first-strike targets in the United States as far west as Montana.

The President moved swiftly, ordering a sharp increase in U-2 overflights and the formation of an advisory team comprising twenty-one senior government officials. The team was designated the Executive Committee of the National Security Council, or simply the Ex Comm. Bob Kennedy, a member of it, described Ex Comm's mood that first day as one of "shocked incredulity." To keep the Russians from knowing what he knew, the President proceeded with his schedule, including a speech in Chicago, while the Ex Comm examined new evidence, gathered the nation's military strength, and weighed options. By Thursday, October 18, the U.S. intelligence community estimated that the weapons now in Cuba, if fired, would kill eighty million Americans within a few minutes. The Ex Comm was leaning toward a massive strike by U.S. warplanes, possibly followed by an invasion of the

THE CUBAN
MISSILE CRISIS

McGeorge Bundy, JFK, Paul Nitze (obscured by JFK), Maxwell Taylor, and Robert McNamara confer

Cuban squadron leader Tomás Cruz, one of the liberated Bay of Pigs prisoners, embraces JFK

Meeting of the Executive Committee of the National Security Council, October 29, 1962

island. Robert McNamara suggested a naval blockade, though under another name, since a blockade constitutes an act of war. A legal adviser from the State Department suggested calling it a "quarantine," and Bob Kennedy agreed. On Saturday he phoned his brother at the Sheraton Blackstone Hotel in Chicago. Ex Comm, he told him, was ready with a plan. Pierre Salinger was instructed to announce that the President had caught cold and was returning to Washington. Air Force One reached Andrews Field at 1:37 P.M. and Bobby was there to meet it.

By Monday morning, the navy had deployed 180 ships in the Caribbean. The B-52 bomber force was in the air, fully loaded with atomic weapons. The First Armored Division had moved out of Texas, headed for embarkation points in Georgia; five other divisions were placed on alert. At noon Salinger announced that the President would speak on television at 7:00 P.M.; the topic, he said, would be "of the greatest emergency." Precisely on the hour Kennedy appeared on television to tell his countrymen that within the past week "unmistakable evidence has established the fact that a series of offensive missile sites is now in preparation on that imprisoned island. The purpose of these bases can be none other than to provide a nuclear strike capability against the Western hemisphere." He explained the quarantine and called it the first step in a plan with the "unswerving objective" of removing the nuclear menace. If necessary, other, stronger measures would follow.

The blockade line was drawn at 10:00 A.M., Wednesday, October 24. A Russian tanker, with petroleum as her only cargo, was permitted to pass through it, but the latest U-2 flights were alarming: work on the missile sites was continuing at an extraordinarily rapid pace. Another Russian ship, challenged by a U.S. destroyer, stopped and submitted to search. The inference was that Moscow had instructed Soviet captains to observe the blockade. At 6:00 P.M. Friday a long, emotional letter from Khrushchev came clattering over the Teletype linking the State Department with the American embassy in Moscow. The Chairman agreed to all the American terms. On Sunday, October 28, at 9:00 A.M. Radio Moscow announced a Soviet capitulation. "In order to eliminate as rapidly as possible the conflict which endangers the cause of peace," the official declaration read, "the Soviet government . . . has given a new order to dismantle the arms which you described as offensive, and to crate and return them to Soviet Russia." Castro declared that he had been betrayed, but he was helpless; the missiles were in Russian hands, and Cubans didn't know how to fire them anyway. The Ex Comm was jubilant. The President told them to exercise restraint. He pointed out that backing down must have been agony for Khrushchev, and warned that there must be no claims of an American victory. That evening the Kennedy brothers reviewed the thirteen days of crisis. At the end Jack said, "Maybe this is the night I should go to the theater." They both laughed uproariously. Then Bobby said, "If you go, I want to go with you."

Others saw triumph and a release from strain; the President saw opportunity. After his brother had left, and before retiring, Jack wrote a careful letter to Khrushchev, ending: "I think we should give priority to questions relating to the proliferation of nuclear weapons, on earth and in outer space, and to the great effort for a nuclear test ban." Somewhere in the universe, he felt, a gear had shifted. This was the chance for a great turning. And he knew how to start it. Presidential addresses, Dean Acheson once observed, are "often where policy is made, regardless of where it is supposed to be made." A speech by a chief executive is, by its very nature, a statement of national intention, addressed, not only to his countrymen, but to the entire world. This was the right time. After the missile crisis the last thing the Russians would expect from Kennedy would be an olive branch. At another time — in Vienna, say — they would have interpreted it as a sign of frailty. But now, having felt his strength in Berlin and Cuba, they would be attentive, and could respond without sacrificing their own self-respect. After the speech he wanted to fly to Europe. He had some things to say there, too.

His address was to be delivered at the commencement of American University on Monday, June 10, 1963. He had hoped to devote Sunday to revisions of his first draft, but presidential schedules are subject to change hourly. In this instance, the civil rights crisis in the South convinced him that he must address the U.S. Mayors' Conference on Sunday, at the end of a long western tour. He reworked the text on the ride back, introducing the balanced sentences and staccato phrases which had become Kennedy trademarks. Reaching Andrews shortly before 9:00 A.M., he went straight to the White House, changed his shirt, and arrived on the commencement platform at 10:30. Although dead tired and sweating in the sweltering amphitheater, he knew that Soviet officials had been alerted and were in their seats. In the United States the press missed the significance of his message; the *Times* ran it on page 16, and most other papers skipped it entirely, thereby overlooking one of his three greatest addresses, ranking with his talk to the Houston ministers and his inaugural.

At the outset he committed himself to an enduring peace, "not a *Pax Americana* enforced on the world by American weapons of war . . . not merely a peace for Americans, but a peace for all men; not merely peace in our time but peace for all time." Some people, he observed, said it was pointless to work toward this until the Russians changed their policies. "I hope they do. I believe we can help them do it. But I also believe that we must reexamine our own attitude." It was sad to read Soviet propaganda, he said; sad to contemplate the gulf between the two forms of government. "But it is also a warning — a warning to the American people not to fall into the same trap as the Soviets, not to see only a distorted and desperate view of the other side." Americans, he declared, "must conduct our affairs in such a way that it becomes in the Communists' interests to agree on a genuine peace. . . . If we cannot now end our differences, at least we can help make the world safe for diversity. For, in the final analysis, our most common basic link is the fact that we all inhabit this planet. We all breathe the same air. We all cherish our children's future. And we are all mortal." He reminded his audience that U.S. weapons were nonprovocative and carefully controlled: "The United States, as the world knows, will never start a war. We do not want a war. We do not expect a war. This generation of Americans has already had enough — more than enough — of war and hate and oppression. . . . We shall be alert to try to stop it. But we shall also do our part to build a world of peace where the weak are safe and the strong are just. We are not helpless before that task or hopeless of its success. Confident and unafraid, we labor — not toward a strategy of annihilation but toward a strategy of peace."

England's Manchester *Guardian* described his speech as "one of the greatest state papers of American history." Khrushchev later told Averell Harriman that he thought it "the best speech by any President since Roosevelt." It was the first significant U.S. address which, for as long as anyone could remember, was not jammed when broadcast by the Voice of America to Russia and Eastern Europe. *Izvestia* and *Pravda* printed the full text. Envoys in Moscow reported the thaw to their home governments, and the Kremlin awaited the President's next move. He had it ready — a proposal for a limited test-ban treaty between the nuclear powers. Khrushchev had been alerted. The Chairman immediately announced agreement in principle, and diplomatic negotiators began toiling over drafts.

Less than two weeks later Kennedy was in Godesberg. You were staying not far from there, in Essen, investigating the Nazi pasts of German industrialists. Ken O'Donnell phoned — it was astonishing how that White House switchboard always knew where to find you — and asked if you would like to come down. You explained that you had a problem. When your findings were published, they would upset many powerful German businessmen. If they remembered having seen you with the President, certain inferences might be drawn. You didn't want to become a source of embarrassment for Jack, so it seemed wiser to take a rain check. Ken understood. Perhaps, he said, you would be in the crowd. The prospect was, in fact, irresistible. If you knew the SS agents in the White House detail, they would find you a good spot in the crowd; they did, and you were close enough for Jack to recognize you outside the Köln cathedral and flash that dazzling smile. You had come early, and a good thing, too; over 400,000 Germans were gathered there to watch the President attend mass with Adenauer. Thousands of them were children waving tiny American flags. The President asked *der Alte*, "Where did the flags come from? Don't tell me these families just happened to have American flags in their homes." The old man chuckled. "Oh, we arrange things as you do in your election campaigns. But we didn't arrange this huge crowd. The cardinal is wishing right now that he could attract this many people to the cathedral for one of his masses."

On the previous July 4, Kennedy had issued a "Declaration of Interdependence" in Independence Hall, Philadelphia, looking toward a new union between Europe and the United States. *Le grand Charles,* in response, had called a press conference, attacking the concept in savage words, and excluding from his own grand design not only the United States but also Britain. It was in Frankfurt's Paulskirche (Saint Paul's Church) that Kennedy replied to de Gaulle. He had done all he could to convince *le grand Charles* that America's intentions were honorable and its motives in the best

interests of France. He had promised de Gaulle that should Russia prepare an attack on France, the United States would not hesitate to strike the first nuclear blow. De Gaulle had seemed impressed. But as Kennedy and Khrushchev approached agreement on nuclear test bans, the president of France informed the American President that he wanted no part of it; his participation, he said, would violate the sovereignty of France. In Paris *L'Express* attacked de Gaulle, accusing him of adopting the Communist slogan "U.S. Go Home." Kennedy finally discovered that his hero's feet were ceramic. He told David Brinkley: "Charles de Gaulle will be remembered for one thing only: his refusal to take that treaty."

Now in the Paulskirche, in the stark chamber where the first German parliament had met in 1848, with sunlight streaming through the high windows, illumining the old Teutonic banners, Kennedy reaffirmed the American commitment to European security. "My stay in this country will be all too brief, but in a larger sense the United States is here on this continent to stay so long as our presence is desired and required. Your liberty is our liberty, and any attack on your soil is an attack on our own. . . . The first task of the Atlantic Community was to assure its common defense. That defense was and still is indivisible. The United States will risk its cities to defend yours because we need your freedom to protect ours."

You took the Frankfurt shuttle to Tempelhof, stayed in an inexpensive little hotel you knew just off the Kurfürstendamm, and were part of the dense mass of some 1.5 million Germans who had turned out to greet him and demonstrate that Berliners are a breed apart. Later you learned that as Air Force One was arriving at Tegel Airport, Kennedy had asked Ken O'Donnell, "What was the proud boast of the Romans? *Civis Romanus sum?* Send Bundy here. He'll know how to say it in German." Bundy came and translated "I am a Berliner" as *Ich bin ein Berliner.*" Jack wrote it down and then asked: "Now tell me how to say in German: 'Let them come to Berlin.'" Having committed these to memory, Kennedy was ready for the city, which, he quickly discovered, was more than ready for him. It had, in fact, become an emotional maelstrom. People of all ages stood four deep all along the route of his motorcade, perched in every window and on every rooftop, chanting, "Ken-ah-dee! Ken-ah-dee! Ken-ah-dee!" German crowds, when mesmerized by a strong leader, are unlike any others on earth. You were part of the seething, impassioned, semihysterical multitude packed in the Rudolph Wilde Platz outside Schöneberg Rathaus, and you felt drained of your identity as an individual, part of an enormous, swelling, heaving, delirious multitude that was capable of almost anything — at which point it occurred to you that German mobs, at one time or another, had proved themselves capable of just about anything. And when Jack appeared on the platform, looking twelve feet tall, handsome, virile, and — yes — Aryan, he was not entirely familiar to you. He had been transformed by them. His speech, moreover, was unlike any he had ever delivered. He had just seen the wall, an affront to every believer in liberty, and he was aroused. So were the Berliners. You could almost feel their rage; it was as though a gigantic thermostat of mass emotion had suddenly been turned up. Freedom has many flaws, he said, and democracy is imperfect. "*But,*" he cried, "*we have never had to put a wall up to keep our people in!*" The Germans bellowed,

**THE
BERLIN
WALL**

howled, roared. He quickly caught their mood; there was a new cadence in his voice which the printed word can never convey and he flung his rhetoric at them like a lash on salted wounds, each stroke biting deeper than the last.

> There are many people in the world who really don't understand, or say they don't, what is the great issue between the free world and the Communist world.
>
> Let them come to Berlin!
>
> There are some who say that communism is the wave of the future.
>
> Let them come to Berlin!
>
> And there are some who say in Europe and elsewhere that we can work with the Communists.
>
> Let them come to Berlin!
>
> And there are even a few who say that it is true that communism is an evil system, but it permits us to make economic progress.
>
> *Lass' sie nach Berlin kommen!* Let them come to Berlin!

Then he cried: "All free men, wherever they may live, are citizens of Berlin, and therefore, as a free man, I take pride in the words: *Ich bin ein Berliner!*"

Semihysteria had become hysteria. The crowd had become a rabble, swaying as it bayed, and you were wedged between a workman and a hausfrau, struggling to breathe, baffled and apprehensive. This wasn't Jack's style. As he said later, he had simply fallen into it. As he finished, he confided, he had felt exhilarated, then troubled, then alarmed. He felt that if he had said, "March to the wall — tear it down!" the mob would have done it. You were afraid they were going to do it anyway — and so, you later learned, was Mayor Willy Brandt, who was holding troops and tanks nearby, to intervene should his people, or the East Berliners who were listening on the other side, lunge toward the barrier separating them. Jack shouldn't have been surprised. He had often argued that crowds were irrational and easily stampeded. This one was in a lynching mood. They needed only a spark to erupt into flame, and he had come perilously close to arson. As his own pulse returned to normal, he realized it. The East Berliners were cheering; one of them threw a bouquet over the wall. He smiled, waved, and left quickly. That afternoon, at the Free University, he was himself again, quiet and reflective. Of social progress and human rights he said: "The very nature of the modern technological society requires human initiative and the diversity of free minds. So history, itself, runs against the Marxist dogma, not toward it." Yet some of the fever he had felt in Rudolph Wilde Platz was still in Berlin. As his motorcade returned to the airport, Germans were still there on both sides of the road, hoarsely chanting, "Ken-ah-dee!" To those around him he said: "We'll never have another day like this one." He did not sound regretful.

The President and his party flew from Tegel to Dublin Airport. There was no justification for this visit. O'Donnell had pointed that out: "If you go to Ireland, people will say it's just a pleasure trip." Kennedy had nodded. "That's exactly what I want," he had said. "A pleasure trip to Ireland." Before leaving the White House, he had read several books of Irish history. Dave Powers did a little research at the Library of Congress and reported that he had traced the President's branch of the Kennedys from a member of the royal Brian Boru family named Cinneide, which, translated, meant "Helmet Head." ("Let's keep that quiet," Jack said quickly.) Kennedy himself had found that his bloodline had been forced to flee abroad in the seventeenth century. He had also taken to quoting the last stanzas of Thomas Davis's "Ballad of Eoghan Ruadh O'Neill," an Irish patriot ambushed by the British in the seventeenth century:

We thought you would not die — We were sure you would not go:
And leave us in our utmost need to Cromwell's cruel blow —
Sheep without a shepherd when the snow shuts out the sky —
Oh, why did you leave us, Eoghan? Why did you die?

Nearly a year later, on a sunlit Saturday at Hickory Hill, sitting on the edge of Bobby's pool, you told him that ever since Dallas you had been unable to get those lines out of your head. He was crouched over, in that way he had, and he gave you one of his upward, swift looks, said he had the same problem, and quickly changed the subject.

Of Kennedy's two June days in Dublin, Wexford, Cork, Galway, and Limerick, it is difficult to say who was moved most, Jack or his audiences, descendants of people his great-grandfather Patrick Kennedy had left to sail for Boston. Patrick had lived in New Ross, near Dunganstown, and on arriving there Jack saw white-sweatered students lying on a New Ross slope to spell out *Failte*, the Gaelic word for "Welcome." Standing on the wharf whence Patrick had left a potato famine for the promise of the United States, he said: "It took a hundred and fifteen years to make this trip and three generations. When my great-grandfather left here to be a cooper in East Boston, he carried nothing with him except two things: a strong religious faith and a strong desire for liberty. I am glad to say that all of his great-grandchildren have valued that inheritance." Then came the witty twist. He looked around and his eye lit on a large ugly building bearing a huge sign identifying it as the Albatross Fertilizer Plant. "If my great-grandfather had not left New Ross," he said, pointing at the building, "I would be working today over there at the Albatross Company." If you were standing two feet from him you heard him add in a low voice, "Shoveling shit."

He spoke to the combined houses of parliament, the first Dáil session to be televised throughout Ireland, and he quoted James Joyce's description of the Atlantic as "a bowl of bitter tears" — the first time, the *Irish Times* noted, that Joyce's name had been mentioned in the Dáil except during debates over censorship. From there he was driven to the Catholic National University of Ireland and the Protestants' Trinity College. Both awarded him honorary degrees. He said: "I want to say how pleased I am to have this association with these two great universities. I now feel equally a part of both, and if ever they have a game of Gaelic football or hurling, I shall cheer for Trinity and pray for National."

"Terrific!" was Kennedy's answer to everyone in the White House when asked how the trip had gone. They wanted details, but he was impatient for word of the test-ban negotiations. Harriman, Gromyko, and Britain's Lord Hailsham were hard at work, and their progress was amazing. A treaty unthinkable only a few months ago had become possible, and now seemed inevitable, because the shrewd peasant in the Kremlin and the cool patrician in the White House had decided that an escalating arms race was unreasonable and unacceptable. Kennedy's American University speech had been the catalyst. The more Khrushchev studied it, the more impressed he became. On July 2, describing it as "notable for its sober appraisal of the international situation," he took the great step, proposing that all nations outlaw nuclear-weapons tests in the atmosphere, in outer space, and underwater. Such an agreement, "combined with the simultaneous signing of a nonaggression pact," would create "a fresh international climate." He was told that the nonaggression pact, like the test ban, would require consent by the American Senate, and it was wiser to take one step at a time. Moreover, inspections, to make sure neither side was cheating, would be necessary. Khrushchev had suggested that be left out. His generals, he had explained, would fume. Now, feeling it imperative that the world "be relieved of the roar of nuclear explosions," he agreed to two or three annual inspections.

Quite apart from the Soviet military establishment, Khrushchev's position was far more difficult than Kennedy's. It meant an open rupture with his great ally to the south. The West had not grasped that when, on July 4, Khrushchev publicly declared that "only madmen could hope to destroy capitalism by nuclear war; a million workers would be destroyed for each capitalist. . . . There are people who see things differently. Let them. History will teach them." The following day a delegation arrived from China to discuss ideological stances which should be adopted by the two great Communist powers. From all reports the two delegations were savaging each other, with nuclear warfare as the bone between them. The Central Committee of the Soviet Communist party issued a statement which provided an inkling of the growing rift. It quoted Mao Tse-tung's declaration that he was prepared to sacrifice millions of his people in a nuclear conflict. The Russians could not "share the views of the Chinese leadership, about creating 'a thousand times higher civilization' on the corpses of hundreds of millions of people."

Kennedy's feelings on nuclear weapons had surfaced when, as President-elect, he had been briefed on U.S. nuclear capabilities. He had loathed everything he heard and particularly detested first-strike weapons, which, he felt, invited a preemptive strike. Then he learned about fallout. Outside the scientific community, few Americans then had more than a vague idea of how thermonuclear tests could poison the air for generations. Jack called in Jerry Wiesner, his science adviser. Wiesner explained the nature of fallout, the degrees of danger, the deformities it could create in unborn infants. Jack asked how it came down. One way, said Wiesner, was rain. Rain washed radioactive debris from the clouds and brought it to earth. Outside the Oval

Office a light drizzle was moistening the rose garden. Jack walked to one of the tall French windows and looked out. He asked, "You mean that stuff is in the rain out there?" Wiesner said, "Yes." Kennedy stood silent, staring out, his face heavy and grave.

In both countries the proposed test ban was controversial. Information about Soviet protests is sketchy, but a spasm of heavy tests in September suggests that Khrushchev's generals and scientists were blasting as fast as they could; they could analyze the data after the deadline. The Americans supporting the ban were allies Kennedy did not need — Humphrey, Galbraith; bogeymen to the conservative nationalists, suspect even to the center. Edward Teller was against it, of course, and Barry Goldwater. Admiral Lewis Strauss said: "I am not sure that the reduction of tensions is a good thing." Nelson Rockefeller, regarded as a liberal Republican, denounced the test ban. Admiral Arthur Radford, a former chairman of the Joint Chiefs, saw peril in every phrase of the treaty and predicted that it would "change the course of world history." Kennedy read that aloud from the *Times* and told a friend, "I hope he's right."

The treaty was initialed, and Khrushchev invited Harriman to join him for dinner. Kennedy, facing ratification in Washington, told his staff that this, like civil rights, was an issue more important than reelection. He needed the support of the Joint Chiefs, and he got it, though they exacted their price, or, to use their word, "safeguards." On September 24 the Senate voted its approval. After 336 nuclear explosions in the atmosphere — a thirteen-year accumulation of radioactive poisons in the world's air — U.S., U.K., and USSR testing had come to a complete halt. Signing the treaty, the President used sixteen pens, handing them out to those who had negotiated the treaty and then fought for it. He drew a firm line under his signature with a seventeenth pen and pocketed it. He smiled and said, "This one is mine."

To him this was only the beginning. He announced that the "hot line," an emergency link between the White House and the Kremlin to lower the risk of accidental war, had been in service since August 30. On the very day of the treaty's ratification, the President, learning of a poor harvest in the Soviet Union, prepared to sell sixty-five million bushels of wheat to Russia. It was a daring move then. Americans from Eastern Europe would be resentful, and both O'Donnell and Lyndon Johnson thought it bad politics. Afterward, the Republicans charged that Kennedy had failed to "consult" the congressional leadership. They were right; anticipating endless quarreling, he had told them about it after it had been done. At his next press conference he was asked if he expected "political repercussions." Yes, he said; there would be "some who will disagree with this decision. That is true about most decisions. But I have considered it very carefully and I think it is very much in the interest of the United States."

Kennedy's view of the national interest, however, differed radically from the consensus which had been reached by both parties when Stalin showed his fist after the war. Almost no one in Washington had noticed it, but since his inaugural Kennedy, quietly challenging that consensus, had eliminated cold-war bromides from his speeches. His vision was the creation of a new *Weltpolitik,* beginning with a dramatically altered relationship between the United States and the Soviet Union. He would never convert the Tellers, Strausses, Goldwaters, and Radfords. But, he argued, he had something his adversaries lacked. He had youth; he had time. "Look at their ages," he told you one evening, "and look at the actuarial tables. Halfway through my second term, at the very latest, I'll be the senior statesman of the West — maybe of the world." His superannuated critics on the Hill would go to their graves, he said, mouthing tired clichés about the Free World ("Always capitalized," he said, "a telltale sign of shabby pomposity") and the Communist World, maintaining that all countries must ally themselves with either the white hats or the black hats. This was the magic kingdom of John Foster Dulles. He would rave on and on about it. You told Jack of one stifling morning you spent in New Delhi with Foster when he was Ike's secretary of state, and how he kept insisting that Nehru *had to choose*, that this was a struggle between good and evil, and no one had the *right* to remain neutral. He overdid it once with Winston Churchill, who went off muttering, "Dull, Duller, Dulles."

Kennedy had no patience with Dullism. He believed in pluralism, in the right of every nation to seek its own destiny without deferring to or even consulting the superpowers. At the University of Washington he said: "We must face the fact that we are only six percent of the world's population — that we cannot impose our will upon the other ninety-four percent of mankind — that we cannot right every wrong or reverse each adversity — and that therefore there cannot be an American solution to every world problem." The United States could not remake the world in its image, he concluded, and shouldn't try. Every nation was entitled to form a society true to its people's traditions, their genius, their instincts for survival.

Although his critics would have been outraged by the very idea, Kennedy's concept of diversity was deeply rooted in American tradition. Pluralism is a political expression of pragmatism, the oldest U.S. philosophical position. Despite its debt to British empiricism, the word *pragmatism* was coined by one Harvard man, C. S. Peirce, while another, William James, became the leader of the movement. James believed no one could find absolute truth, but thought free men could find fragments of it. By assembling them they would form, not a dogma, but a makeshift arrangement that would get them through life. The excitement of pragmatism, and its great attraction for Kennedy, is that it is vested in action. James wrote: "The issue is decided nowhere else than *here* and *now*. *That* is what gives the palpitating reality to our moral life and makes it tingle."

One day Jack dumped a pile of newspapers from his lap to the floor and announced: "I'm tired of headlines. All they describe is crisis, and they give the impression that we have our backs against the wall everywhere in the world. But this is illusion. Look at it from Khrushchev's viewpoint. He has headaches in China, Albania, agriculture, the intellectuals, Eastern Europe, and I'll bet he feels just as harried as we do — probably more so. The fact is that the world has changed a lot in the last decade, and most of the change has been in our favor." There was more, he continued. The Soviet position in Berlin had shrunk. They had bungled in Africa and the Middle East. Though untidy and at times exasperating, pluralism passed the pragmatic test — it worked. And as he told students at Berkeley, "No one can doubt that the wave of the future is not the conquest of the world by a single dogmatic creed but the liberation of the diverse energies of free nations and free men."

Harry Truman, who would have dismissed pluralism as hogwash, believed that the Communist bloc was not only monolithic but also conspiratorial — that a central intelligence guided all Red activities. Truman wrote in his memoirs of how he saw "a pattern in Indochina and Tibet timed to coincide with the attack in Korea," and that both actions in these two widely separated theaters of the world were "a ruse to bring to a halt American aid in the rebuilding of Europe." He was merely summing up the bipartisan consensus, but had he been right, American troops would never have been sent to Vietnam. The dimensions of his error may be traced in the cable traffic between Washington and Moscow after the Cuban missile crisis. Khrushchev, at Kennedy's urging and with Harriman as midwife, had persuaded the Pathet Lao to accept a neutral regime in Laos. Thus, the commitment of U.S. infantry to the defense of Vientiane, which Eisenhower had regarded as almost inevitable, proved unnecessary. Early in 1963 Kennedy asked the Chairman to join him again in reaching a similar solution to the growing crisis in Vietnam. Khrushchev tried; he tried very hard. But while it was in his interests to improve his relationship with the Kennedy government, it was not in Mao's. And Mao's respect for Khrushchev was gone. The Chairman's humiliation in Cuba, observed by the entire world, had cost him a terrible loss of prestige. Jack gloomily told you: "I cut his balls off."

Thus a series of what Churchill called "terrible Ifs" had accumulated. If there had been no Bay of Pigs fiasco, Khrushchev would not have concluded that Kennedy was a weakling; if Khrushchev had not regarded the President as weak-kneed, he would not have risked the Berlin crisis; if the Chairman hadn't been the loser in Berlin, he wouldn't have tried to recoup by installing the missiles in Cuba; if there had been no missile crisis, Khrushchev would have had the muscle to suppress the Communists in South Vietnam, a country virtually useless to the Soviets then except as a bargaining chip. And if all these events — together with nuclear testing, the space race, Big Steel, de Gaulle, Latin America, and civil rights confrontations in the South — had not required the undivided attention of the President, he might have thought twice about sending his idle, restless vice-president into a delicate situation where a commitment by Johnson might have consequences extending beyond the lifetimes of both men.

Ever since the War of Independence it had been the proud boast of U.S. schoolboys that "America has never lost a war." Long after Kennedy's death, when it became clear that a U.S. defeat in Vietnam was inevitable, everyone involved scurried about in a desperate effort to cover his tracks, and admirers of Lyndon Johnson and Richard Nixon, the chief culprits, started trying to spread the blame backward. They could not tar Franklin Roosevelt, who, in March 1945, had tried to stop the return of French colonists to Southeast Asia by withholding military supplies from French forces in that part of the world. To Asian patriots, FDR's death was a disaster. His successors lacked his vision. They believed they needed France as a NATO ally, and when the French told them the Indochinese insurgents were all Communists, they appropriated funds to pay for French troops fighting the Viet Minh, as the native rebels were then called.

As relations go between Presidents and vice-presidents, Kennedy's and Johnson's had gone well. To be sure, that is not saying a great deal. Any President feels uncomfortable with his understudy. The man next in line is a reminder of his own mortality. He is more; he stands to inherit the President's most cherished possession, his high office. To put him out of sight and keep him busy, JFK sent LBJ abroad on various pretexts. The results were often amusing, for LBJ was an exuberant, comical prodigy. He was always campaigning — "My God!" gasped an American doctor in Pakistan. "He's shaking hands with a leper!" — and his decision to transform a Karachi camel driver into an ambassador of goodwill delighted the press. But LBJ was still a masterly politician. He knew what he was doing. Ahmed's trip to the United States was a great success. "If it had been me," Kennedy told you, "I'd have wound up with camel shit all over the White House lawn."

It is one of history's Rabelaisian touches that the trip which appealed to Johnson least looms largest in retrospect. Accompanied by Jean and Steve Smith, the vice-president glumly flew to Asia, instructed by the White House to bolster the self-confidence of non-Communist regimes, notably that of Chiang Kai-shek. He was not, as in Berlin, a symbol of America's resolve to fight alongside South Vietnamese troops. At that time U.S. commitments had not gone that far. Nevertheless, his pledge in Saigon was far stronger than anything the President intended. Greatly taken with President Ngo Dinh Diem, Johnson exceeded his authority by asking him if he needed U.S. troops. Diem said he didn't, although money was always welcome. The vice-president called a press conference to hail Diem as "the Winston Churchill of South Asia." After his plane had left Vietnam, a writer asked Johnson if he really believed that. "Shit, man," LBJ replied, "he's the only boy we got out here."

The Winston Churchill of South Asia was a dark, stubby, chain-smoking, aloof mandarin, an archetype of the strong man in power. His critics were sent to concentration camps, freedom of the press was unknown, and any proposal for reform was angrily rejected. Diem ruled the country with his fanatical brother, Ngo Dinh Nhu, and Nhu's lovely, venomous wife. They scorned the Buddhist masses and particularly the young Buddhist priests and monks, who were poor, militant, and distrustful of everything Western. None of the Saigon dissidents were Communist then. The Communists, soon to unite as the Viet Cong, were sons of the Viet Minh, now guerrillas in the bush.

Congressman John F. Kennedy had been among the few who had studied the Vietnamese problem on the spot and returned convinced that Roosevelt was right. "Without the support of the native population," he had declared on "Meet the Press" in 1951, "there is no hope of success in any of the countries of Southeast Asia." He modified his view somewhat when, after the United States and other French allies had refused to aid the natives, the Viet Minh had turned to the Communists for help. Kennedy didn't want a Red Vietnam. But he believed that Indochina would never again be French. The only acceptable alternative, he felt, was an independent, democratic native state.

In the 1950s information about Vietnam was hard to come by. As a foreign correspondent in those days, you had covered the French foreign legion's fighting in the Red River delta, west of Hanoi, and the only way you had been able to send honest accounts home had been to board a Hong Kong flight and file your dispatches from there. Censorship, rigid under the French, tightened under Diem and the Nhus. This lack of hard facts explains one of the great mysteries about the Vietnam War: why it became a grave-yard for experts' reputations. In 1954, Kennedy had diverted his Senate colleagues by reciting some earlier appraisals of it: "The military situation appears to be developing favorably" (Dean Acheson, 1952); "In Indochina we believe the tide is now turning" (Walter Robertson of the State Depart-ment, 1953); a French victory "is both possible and probable" (Secretary of Defense Charles E. Wilson, 1954); and "The French are going to win" (Ad-miral Radford, 1954). The French lost after sacrificing nineteen thousand volunteers, which would seem to have vindicated the skeptical young New England senator. Kennedy's skepticism grew during his first months in the White House. De Gaulle had warned him against jungle fighting, and Ken-nedy knew, from his wartime service in the Solomons, that de Gaulle was right. Even more persuasive was the advice of Douglas MacArthur. The old soldier was contemptuous of the Pentagon's new breed of generals, and he told Kennedy, as he had told others, that "anyone who wants to commit American ground forces on the Asian mainland should have his head ex-amined."

The President kept trying to find out what the real situation was over there. One of his first moves, on assuming office, had been the appointment of a State-Defense-CIA–White House task force to recommend U.S. moves in Vietnam. As MacArthur had predicted, the task force's report called for the commitment of U.S. combat troops. Kennedy vetoed that, but agreed to an increase in the number of military advisers. His decision was influenced by a Senate committee report, issued the year before, which predicted that "on the basis of the assurances of the head of the military aid mission in Vietnam . . . the U.S. military . . . can be phased out of Vietnam in the foreseeable future." With more volunteer advisers, the President was told, the war would be won in eighteen months. In his 1954 Senate speech, he had been critical of French and American generals for what he had then called "predictions of confidence which have lulled the American people." Now, on the strength of just such a forecast, he drew closer to the Diem regime. Talk of abandonment "only makes it easy for the Communists," he said. "I think we should stay."

Congressman Kennedy in 1951, and Senator Kennedy in 1954, would have been appalled. Why did President Kennedy disagree with them? The answer is political. The congressman and the senator were confident of reelection; the President couldn't be so sure. The Republicans' most pow-erful postwar campaign issue had been the charge that Truman had "lost" China to the Communists. If possible, Kennedy wanted to avoid "losing" Indochina. Men were determined to disassociate themselves from Cham-berlain's sin of appeasement. "The cause in Vietnam," wrote Theodore H. White, was "the cause of America." *Time* told its readers: "South Vietnam must be defended at all costs."

It was assumed in most of official Washington that an exchange of letters between Eisenhower and Diem had formally committed the United States to support of the government in Saigon. Kennedy believed it; so did Johnson. "Ike made a promise," Johnson would say later. "I have to keep it." A withdrawal of American support, wrote Ted Sorensen, would have caused "the world to wonder about the reliability of this nation's pledges." Arthur Schlesinger went farther: "Whether we had vital interests in South Vietnam before 1954, the Eisenhower letter created those interests." He added that Kennedy "had no choice but to work within the situation he had inherited." Johnson argued that to "cut and run" would have been to "say to the world in this case that we don't live up to our treaties and don't stand by our friends." McNamara and Generals Maxwell Taylor and Lyman Lemnitzer said that if American draftees weren't sent to Vietnam when Diem said he needed them, the United States would have broken its sacred word and, as a result, "we would lose Asia all the way to Singapore."

There was no sense in any of this. The Eisenhower letter had declared that the United States would "assist the government of Vietnam in developing and maintaining a strong, viable state, capable of resisting subversion or aggression through military means." But Ike made this agreement — and this was also in the letter — with the understanding that it would be accompanied "by performance on the part of Vietnam in undertaking needed reforms" and that Diem would hold free elections on July 20, 1956. Eisenhower's letter had no validity now because Diem had openly flouted his obligation to introduce reforms, "needed" or otherwise, and he had refused to consider holding elections at any time. In the light of this performance it would have been absurd for him to have invoked the sanctity of treaties, even if the United States had been bound to him by a legal treaty — that is, one ratified by the U.S. Senate — which, of course, it wasn't. The real pressure on the administration was the fear that Ngo Dinh Diem might become another Chiang Kai-shek. It is all the more tragic, then, that they repeated the very mistake the Americans counseling Chiang had made. In both cases the problem was political and the aid sent was military.

Vietnam had been comparatively quiet during the later Eisenhower years. A month before Kennedy's inauguration, Diem's enemies formed the National Liberation Front (NLF), which soon became known as the Viet Cong. Diem wasn't concerned. Some U.S. help would be welcome, he admitted, and Kennedy approved the dispatch of four hundred more advisers. By May 1961, however, the VC were on a rampage. As the situation deteriorated, a State Department minute urged the President to accept defeat of the VC as "a real and ultimate objective." The Joint Chiefs told him that 40,000 U.S. troops would "clean up the Viet Cong threat," and another 125,000 would be enough to turn back any further intervention by the North Vietnamese or Chinese.

Kennedy again vetoed troops. As the weeks passed, it became clear that Diem's forces were retreating everywhere. He asked for more help, and the President responded by sending two of his most trusted advisers, Max Taylor and Walt Rostow. It was an unbalanced team: a general and a militant civilian, a disciple of Dullism. On the eve of their departure they were waiting in the corridor outside the oval room, Rostow fiddling with the spinet as they discussed what lay ahead. Theirs would be the President's last appointment that afternoon. Jackie and the children were away; as often happened in such circumstances, Jack planned to spend the evening with you. You were sitting in the west sitting room, reading, and without intending to eavesdrop you overheard the conversation between Taylor and Rostow. Later, after a light meal, you told Jack that high-level missions to totalitarian countries learned little, and you reminded him that you had been in Vietnam on a very low level under the French until Dien Bien Phu, after which you had left deeply depressed. He gave you a long sideways look and said he wanted to hear more about that after Taylor and Rostow returned.

Their report was a shocker. To arrest the decline in Diem's fortunes, the commitment of American ground troops was now absolutely necessary. They proposed a vanguard of eight thousand infantrymen to leave at once, and Taylor asked Kennedy to make Vietnam the subject of a national telecast. As other advisers were called in, you became aware, for the first time, of the split between what were later called "hawks" and "doves." In the subcabinet the leading critics of the Taylor-Rostow report were Chester Bowles, George Ball, and Averell Harriman. The only senior man to question it, however, was Kennedy himself. He wouldn't go on television, and he wouldn't send American soldiers. Sorensen wrote: "All his principal advisers on Vietnam favored it, calling it the 'touchstone' of our good faith, a symbol of our determination. But the President in effect voted 'no' — and only his vote counted."

Now Jack wanted to hear about your adventures with the foreign legion, and you told him, sitting on a white love seat in the oval room while he rocked in his rocker, his back to the fireplace. It is a good rule, when reminiscing of things past, not to lock eyes with the other man. Instead, you looked out over the Truman balcony toward the Washington Monument and went through the whole sad story of cocky French colonels who liked to sing "Contre les Viets" when drunk but scorned the enemy's soldierly qualities — until, to their surprise and dismay, they realized that while they might rule the country by day, by night it belonged to the native guerrillas, who became so strong that when the sun set every sane Frenchman made sure he was safe inside one of the string of Beau Geste forts between Haiphong and Hanoi. Now and then Jack would interrupt with his sharp, quick questions, but mostly he rocked, his chin supported by one hand. Once you reached Dien Bien Phu, with fifteen thousand Frenchmen parachuting down there on an autumn day in 1953, it all came back to you: the building of the airfield, the construction of the *porcs-épics* (porcupines) as strongholds to harass the enemy, and the growing consensus among the foreign correspondents that the position the French had chosen for their stand was extremely vulnerable. It was in a natural basin, or saucer, surrounded by a rim of crests. The French hadn't taken the rim. If the enemy hauled heavy artillery there, the correspondents reasoned, their muzzles would look down on the *porcs-épics* and the new blockhouses, and the Viet gunners could pin down the defenders while their infantry shoveled away, digging zigzag trenches toward the French strongpoints: little hills with names like Anne-Marie and Claudine, and for the twin hillocks in the center, Elaine One and Elaine Four, a memorable sobriquet — "the Lollobrigidas." Christian de Castries, the senior French officer, was asked if that possibility had been considered. He replied disdainfully that French artillery was superior to anything the natives had, and besides, the question was academic; natives were incapable of manhandling heavy weapons over the rugged terrain beyond the basin. But de Castries was wrong. His opposite number, Vo Nguyen Giap, using ninety thousand Vietnamese peasants, hauled batteries of 105-millimeter field guns into position on the crest, and when he opened the siege of Dien Bien Phu with a dawn bombardment the following March 13, every foreign correspondent except the poor Agence France-Presse man, a government employee, boarded the next plane to Hanoi. Less than two months later, on May 7, Dien Bien Phu fell to the Viets.

Kennedy, always the pragmatist, asked what it had meant. You cited the maxim that any military force, however superb, is at a crippling disadvantage when the population sympathizes with the enemy. "Remember Lee," you said. "He was unbeatable as long as he stayed in Virginia. But when he crossed into Pennsylvania, he lost."

Jack rocked a little and tapped his teeth with his fingernails. "I can't act without information," he said. "And I can't seem to get it. I send a list of specific questions. State answers every one. Then I pick up the next day's *Times* and there's a big fat story by Halberstam contradicting everything in the State report." More teeth-tapping. Then: "They keep telling me to send combat units over there. That means draftees. Even the French didn't send draftees. I'll never do it." Another pause. He was tucking in his tie now. "I ask them, 'Why troops?' And they say, 'For confidence, for morale.' But you know what would happen. The troops would march in, the bands would play, the crowds would cheer, and in four days it would be forgotten. Then they'd tell me they needed more troops, for confidence and morale. It's like taking a drink. The effect wears off, and you have to take another." He rocked some more. "As long as it remains *their* war they should be able to win it. If white soldiers went into action, the people would think, 'The French are back.' And then, like the French, we'd lose." But, you pointed out, any U.S. presence — even volunteer advisers — represented a commitment. How would he pull them out? "Oh, that's easy," he said with a grin. "I'll support a government that'll ask me to leave." He rose. When a President stands, it's a signal for you to leave. As you parted, he was standing there, nursing his elbows, and he was saying, "But we'll never send troops. Not on my watch."

Kennedy did temporize, however, agreeing to a new exchange of letters with Diem. The president of South Vietnam would concede the need for reforms, and the President of the United States would assure him that U.S. assistance would be forthcoming, though no limits were to be set on the amount of it, its nature was unspecified, and dates and deadlines were unmentioned. George Ball predicted that Diem would keep pressing until he got U.S. troops. And the commitment, he predicted, would not stay small. Within five years, he told the President, there would be 300,000 U.S. troops in Vietnam. Jack laughed and said, "George, you're crazier than hell."

The two senior Americans in Saigon were Ambassador Frederick E. Nolting, Jr., and General Paul D. Harkins. Both choices were extremely unfortunate. Nolting, an anti-Communist hard-liner, would back Diem to the end. And although the President made it clear that he wanted to know everything, the bad as well as the good, Harkins didn't like to relay bad news. He thought it might reflect on him. As a result, the ambassador and the general became a kind of public-relations team. The tough and dedicated Diem, they said, was the key to success; he would be his country's savior. Lacking good news, Harkins simply invented it. When American foreign correspondents cited facts and figures which discredited the general's reports, he called them sensation-mongers and liars.

Here another Churchillian If arises. If the VC eruptions had continued, Harkins's press-agentry would have soon been exposed. Keeping two sets of books cannot go on for long when it is bodies that are being counted. But a sudden drop in guerrilla activity seemed to confirm Harkins. General Taylor said he sensed "a great national movement" in Vietnam to crush the VC. McNamara said, "Every quantitative measurement we have shows we're winning this war." Kennedy, surprised and pleased, opened his State of the Union message on January 14, 1963, by reporting: "The spearhead of aggression has been blunted in Vietnam." The lull in the conflict continued through the early months of the new year — his third in office. The VC were husbanding their strength, waiting to strike, and Diem's generals, knowing the low morale of their troops, were idle. But even without those omens, the country was seething. Both the privileged upper-class Catholics and the underprivileged Buddhists were in a belligerent mood, awaiting only an incident to touch off a struggle between them. On June 11 a bonze — a Buddhist monk — dramatized the protest by drenching himself with gasoline and then striking a match. After he went up in flames, other suicidal bonzes followed his example. Mme Nhu demonstrated the ruling family's genius for public relations by telling reporters she clapped her hands each time one of these "so-called holy men" put on a "barbecue show." Buddhist demonstrations followed. American correspondents and cameramen covering them were badly beaten by thugs on Diem's payroll.

By early July, the President knew that his Vietnam policy, or lack of it, was in deep trouble. Diem was almost entirely under the influence of his brother, who was usually under the influence of opium, and Mme Nhu was packing for a speaking tour of the United States to denounce Kennedy. The beatings of American newspapermen continued, evidence of government corruption was mounting, and, to cap it all, when the President tried to consult Nolting he learned that the ambassador to Saigon was absent on a two-month cruise of the remote Aegean and could not be reached. Kennedy fired him and sent as his replacement Henry Cabot Lodge. Lodge's arrival was observed by what could only be interpreted as a studied act of contempt for the Americans. In violation of every recent agreement, including a personal pledge to Nolting, government troops seized all Buddhist pagodas, arrested the priests and monks, and began a reign of terror for their followers.

In Washington, Dean Rusk declared that the American presence must remain in South Vietnam until the war had been won. McNamara and Taylor agreed. Ball and Harriman said that was absurd. Autumn was approaching, and each day the split between the two camps widened. It became an abyss in September, when the National Security Council sent another fact-finding mission to Saigon. The investigators were a Marine Corps general and a senior foreign service officer of comparable rank. When they returned, Kennedy reconvened the National Security Council to hear their reports. The general said the war was being won and Diem's performance could hardly be improved upon. The foreign service officer said the Diem regime was at the point of collapse. There was a silence. The President asked politely: "Were you two gentlemen in the same country?"

Astonishingly, General Harkins seems to have known nothing of this. Momentous events were in train, but the senior U.S. military commander in the country, cheerfully ignorant, continued to type out his press releases. Not only were they taken seriously; they served as the basic source for a report submitted by McNamara and Taylor. Diem's army, this rich document opened, "has made great progress and continues to progress." The report dismissed a heretical suggestion of Robert Kennedy, the first senior government official to visit Vietnam and return with the recommendation that all Americans posted there be recalled at once. ("What is all this doing to the *people* of that little country?" he kept asking, and the generals and diplomats stared at him as though he had created a public nuisance.) Writing of a feudal nation which was seven thousand miles from the United States, a primitive land of rice paddies and dense jungle curled around the remote Indochinese peninsula, McNamara and Taylor declared: "The security of South Vietnam remains vital to United States security. For this reason, we adhere to the overriding objective of denying this country to communism and of suppressing the Viet Cong insurgency as rapidly as possible."

In Saigon Nhu seemed to be losing touch with reality. He threatened to drive the Americans out of the country by forming an alliance with Ho Chi Minh in Hanoi. In a series of incomprehensible raids, Diem's secret police jailed college students, then high school students, and finally children in the elementary schools. Even Catholics weren't safe from persecution. Vietnamese of all faiths and persuasions were appealing to General Duong Van Minh, "Big Minh," the most prestigious officer in the army, begging him to oust Diem and Nhu. At a secret meeting Lodge assured Minh that the Americans would do nothing to impede a coup, and on the evening of Friday, November 1, a day of stupefying heat, the siege of Diem's palace began with an artillery and mortar barrage. At dawn a white flag appeared in a first-floor window, but Diem and Nhu were not there. Disguised as Catholic priests, they had fled through a secret tunnel. Precisely what happened after that is unknown, but they had been picked up by a squad of Big Minh's soldiers in the Chinese suburb of Cholon, and were gunned down, on whose orders we shall probably never know. Diem's corpse had also been stabbed repeatedly.

Awakened with the news in her Beverly Hills hotel, Mme Nhu sobbed that President Kennedy was to blame. In most of official Washington the news was accepted with resignation, even relief. There was one significant exception. Lyndon Johnson was bitter. The vice-president had given Diem his hand, had been his friend, and in Johnson's view that friendship had symbolized the American commitment to Diem. The same men who had been Diem's critics in Washington were also critical of the vice-president. He knew it, and knew them, right down to their Cardin shirts and PT-109 tie clasps. Later, in his 1971 memoirs, LBJ would write that the Saigon coup was "a serious blunder which caused deep political confusion," and would charge that Kennedy aides had been responsible for it. Actually, Diem's overthrow was inevitable, and if any American was involved, it was Lodge, a Republican, who simply told Minh and those around him that the United States would remain neutral. But in the world of presidential action, what is true is often less important than what men in high office believe to be true. Johnson regarded the assassination of the exotic, enigmatic little president of South Vietnam as a personal affront. If ever he had a chance to make amends in Vietnam, he told friends, he would seize it, with a vengeance.

Mme Nhu's accusation of Kennedy was absurd, but then, so was she. The President was in fact shaken, depressed for the first time since the Bay of Pigs. Diem had always been difficult to deal with, and lately he had become impossible, but he certainly had not deserved butchery. In matters of high politics, Kennedy, unlike Johnson, was not guided by his like or dislike of individuals. He measured men by their competence and judgment. His own judgment of character was not flawless. In assigning presidential priorities — deciding which issues had the highest claim on his time — he put Vietnam too low because of his confidence in McNamara, which, in this instance, was undeserved. But one must remember that in 1963 Vietnam was not the great national issue it later became, eclipsing reason and distorting the perspective of a new lost generation. Its grisly slaughterhouse years lay ahead. The first American battle deaths there occurred on July 9, 1959, midway in Ike's second term. Kennedy had been in the White House over nine months when, on October 31, 1961, another U.S. military adviser was shot. During his years as President, not a single American bomb was dropped on Vietnamese soil, and when he was slain in Dallas, the cumulative total of U.S. soldiers killed in Vietnam, beginning with the Eisenhower administration, was 108, all of them professionals; all volunteers. Every death is a private tragedy, but even in peacetime people are dying all around us; on an average day, 314 American motorists are killed in traffic accidents. Moreover, in the Kennedy years his countrymen gave little thought to Southeast Asia. It was so remote. Television, which brought it into American living rooms after Johnson sent the first U.S. troops there in April 1965, played a much smaller role then. The networks' daily news telecasts were limited to fifteen minutes, all black-and-white, with no direct telecasts from Vietnam, only tapes made the day before with hand-held cameras and flown to New York overnight.

In charting his course there, Kennedy had been guided by two imperatives: the country must not fall to the Communists, and he would send no American troops there. The possibility that the two might become mutually exclusive did not occur to him until 1963, but when it did, he decided that he would rather lose Asian territory than American lives. This meant ignoring the advice of his key aides and his cabinet, but the responsibility was his, not theirs. Looking ahead, he saw how Vietnam could become a running sore, dividing his party and turning American youth against the government. Before it got that far, he was determined to solve it or write it off.

He made his own decisions, but men he respected could influence his judgment. That happened here. His counselor in this case was not a member of the administration, and that very fact may have added weight to his advice. Late in 1962 the President asked Mike Mansfield, the tall, gaunt Senate majority leader, to tour Southeast Asia and return with his impressions. At that time Mansfield was perhaps the most respected man on Capitol Hill. He was also an orientalist. He had served three Presidents in Asia. Normally he was a quiet and thoughtful man. The President was therefore surprised when, during the Christmas holidays of 1962, which he was spending in Palm Beach with the rest of the Kennedy family, he was told that Mike, back from Vietnam, was flying straight to Florida with urgent advice.

Jack had never seen him more intense. Mike had put it all on paper, and he stood in silence as the President read his report. Not another U.S. military adviser should be sent to Saigon, it said. The country was racked by civil war. Americans could do nothing to help. If they remained, their presence would lead to insistent demands for still more U.S. troops, until an American army wound up fighting someone else's war. The prestige of the United States in Asia would suffer. The South Vietnamese would also be discouraged from doing what they must learn to do — stand on their own feet. Jack reddened and snapped, "Do you expect me to take this at face value?" The majority leader puffed on his pipe and mildly replied, "You *did* ask me to go out there." Jack, icy now, said, "Well, I'll read it again." Afterward, he told O'Donnell that he had been too disturbed to comment. He said: "I got angry with Mike for disagreeing with our policy so completely, and I got angry with myself because I found myself agreeing with him."

The following spring Mike spoke up again, this time during a White House breakfast for the congressional leadership. He wanted a complete, immediate withdrawal of all U.S. military advisers in Vietnam. The President suggested that the two of them move into the Oval Office for a private talk. When they were alone, Jack told Mike he agreed with him. Every American must be brought home. But not now. "I can't do it until 1965, after I'm reelected," he said. Any evacuation before the election would strengthen the Republicans, trigger a revolt by several Democratic leaders — who might be joined by the vice-president — and turn the campaign into a fight which would rock U.S. allies and inflict irreparable damage on America's reputation. Mike reflected, puffed on his pipe again, and finally said he agreed. After he had left, Kennedy told O'Donnell, "In 1965 I'll become one of the most unpopular Presidents in history. I'll be damned everywhere as a Communist appeaser. But I don't care. If I tried to pull out completely now from Vietnam, we would have another Joe McCarthy Red scare on our hands, but I can do it after I'm reelected. So we had better make damned sure I *am* reelected."

In '64 he wanted a landslide victory, of course — any President standing for reelection does. Then he could phase out U.S. commitments in Southeast Asia until, by the end of '65, the last technicians, Green Beret advisers, and helicopter pilots were safe at home. Meanwhile, he had to be candid. It would be disastrous later if he were vulnerable to charges that he had deceived the country. It was important that he clarify his position. To this end, he granted two television interviews in the waning months of 1963. American combat units, he said on both programs, would not be sent to Vietnam. On September 2 he told Walter Cronkite that the outcome of the war depended on South Vietnamese troops and their commanders. He explained: "It is their war. We can help them, we can send them equipment, we can send our men out there as advisers . . . but in the final analysis it is their people and their government who have to win or lose this struggle. All we can do is help."

In his last three public speeches that fall he discussed the Vietnam dilemma and reaffirmed his determination never to send an American draftee to solve problems only Vietnamese could solve. And, noting criticism of the United States in Saigon, he said that Americans would leave the instant they learned they were unwanted. On October 2, one month after his Cronkite interview, he presided over a National Security Council meeting convened to review the McNamara-Taylor report. As the members rose from their chairs, he asked the secretary of defense to announce to the waiting press that a thousand U.S. advisers were to be brought home from Vietnam before Christmas, and that he expected the last American to leave there before the end of 1965. While McNamara was still in earshot, Kennedy added: "And tell them that means all of the helicopter pilots, too." The secretary rephrased this message, thereby altering its meaning. He merely said that in his opinion "the major part of the U.S. military task" could be "completed by the end of 1965." But the President's verbatim instructions remain in the records of the National Security Council. And he followed them up. McNamara having weaseled presidential words, the President un-weaseled them. On the last day of October he told the nation: "Our object is to bring home every American technician, helicopter pilot, and military adviser by the end of 1965, permitting the South Vietnamese to maintain themselves as a free and independent country." Nor did he stop there. Two weeks later, on November 14, 1963 — eight days before he died — he announced that the first thousand men were already packing and would be on their way home by Christmas.

In light of these clear, unequivocal, public policy statements, together with his private assurances to Mansfield and the proceedings of the National Security Council, it is astonishing that hostile commentators, both Left and Right, have attempted to rank him as a warmaker comparable to Johnson and Nixon. They have yet to produce the flimsiest piece of evidence. Among informed, responsible critics of the American experience in Vietnam, David Halberstam is surely the most unsparing. He leaves few Kennedy advisers unscathed. Yet Kennedy himself, Halberstam concludes, "had a sense of being able to handle it, of having time, that time was somehow on his side. He could afford to move his people slowly; too forceful a shove would bring a countershove. It was late 1963, and since 1964 was an election year, any delay on major decisions was healthy; if the Vietnamese could hold out a little longer, so could he." Before leaving for his Texas tour, Kennedy cabled Lodge, suggesting he come home for a long talk. The President was impatient; he wanted to accelerate the withdrawal. Lodge replied that he was making arrangements to leave Saigon as soon as possible. That would be on Thursday, November 21. He would be in Washington, waiting to join Kennedy for lunch when he returned from the LBJ Ranch on Sunday.

Ordinarily, the White House is very quiet. Occasionally there are exceptions — once you arrived in the presidential apartment to behold Caroline, stark naked, streaking down the great corridor with her nanny, Maude Shaw, in embarrassed pursuit — but most of the time it is as silent as a well-run library. In fact, newcomers often respond to it in the same way: they speak softly. One of Jackie's icebreakers, when she heard a couple mumbling to each other, was to come over with her loveliest smile and say: "You're talking the way we did our first month here."

During that destroyed weekend after Dallas, however, when one would have expected hush, the mansion was noisy. The explanation for this incongruity was television. All seven of the White House sets seemed to be on most of the time, usually with the volume turned high. The networks had decided to omit all commercials for four days and show nothing but Kennedy. A loud White House was one consequence of this; another was that programmers, hard-pressed to fill the time, dug into their videotape libraries, running and rerunning every reel which was remotely relevant. One moment a viewer might see a still photograph of Jack Kennedy in his Harvard swimming suit (1940). Moments later Lieutenant (j.g.) Kennedy was being decorated for valor in the Pacific (1943). Congressman Kennedy would be campaigning in Boston (1946), Senator Kennedy would be moving for Estes Kefauver's vice-presidential nomination by acclamation (1956), and President Kennedy would be informing the nation of the Cuban quarantine (1962). The sequence might be reversed, scrambled, or interrupted by films of Franklin Roosevelt's funeral, which, in turn, might be succeeded by an amateur cameraman's record of the attempt on President-elect Roosevelt's life in 1932, or even the wounding of former President Theodore Roosevelt twenty years earlier.

The producers did what they could with what they had, fighting their way from one improvised schedule to another. But had footage existed for every memorable moment of the Kennedy presidency, and had talented network men been given adequate time, they might have provided the vast audience with a valuable memoir and a definitive answer to the jaded college student, quoted in the *New York Times* ten years later, who reduced the significance of those years to "glamour, Jackie, and football at Hyannis Port." It would have included glimpses of the inaugural, the missile crisis, the talks with de Gaulle, beleaguered Berlin, the Vienna confrontation, nuclear tests, the roaring welcome and the brilliant confetti in Costa Rica, the President staring down the governors of Alabama and Mississippi and then warmly welcoming Martin Luther King to the White House, violence in the streets of Saigon, and certain other moments, public and private, which may be briefly encapsulated here.

This much *was* on film: the joint sessions of Congress, awaiting the President's annual State of the Union address; the practiced cry of the House doorkeeper, William "Fishbait" Miller, "Mistah Speekah, the President of the United States!" and then the speech itself. What would be more stirring, and closer to the elusive essence of history, would be Jack's informal comments back in the mansion. "Have you ever tried to talk to Charlie Halleck?" he asked of the Republican leader in the House. "It's like trying to pick up a greased pig." The average congressman, he had calculated, was ten years older than he was, the average senator even older, "and that's a real problem. Let's face it. For this President, the champion of the teeming masses and suffering multitudes, Congress is absofuckinglutely *impossible.*" His greatest disappointment was the narrow rejection of Medicare, by a 52–48 vote. He went on television to tell the country that it was a "most serious defeat for every American family" and would be a major issue in the next election. He had at least introduced Congress to the idea of Medicare, and the next time it would pass, but he was unconsoled. He could never be resigned to defeat. Fortunately he retained his most effective shock absorber, his wit. One day, when he was beset by congressional critics of his economic program, he turned to Walter Heller, his chief economic adviser, and said, "Walter, I want to make it perfectly clear that I resent these attacks on you."

On the Hill, of course, they saw things differently. Everett Dirksen, a.k.a. the Wizard of Ooze, arranged the wrinkles and seams of his ruined face into what was meant to be an expression of concern, and warbled: "At the rate he's going, I wouldn't be surprised if this Democratic President didn't ask us to pass a hundred-billion-dollar budget." More appealing was a congressman from rural Tennessee who shook his head over "all that Mozart string music and ballet dancing down there and all that fox hunting and London clothes. He's too elegant for me." Looking back, it is surprising that the President and his emissaries on the Hill — led by the seductive Larry O'Brien — did as well as they did. Of the 107 recommendations Kennedy sent to the Eighty-seventh Congress, 73 were enacted into law, and when the Eighty-eighth session adjourned the Kennedy record of legislative achievement would include more health legislation than that passed by any two Congresses in history, including measures dealing with water pollution, hospital construction, mental health care, mental retardation, drug safety, and medical schools.

Yuri Gagarin's orbital flight of April 12, 1961, brought Kennedy to the Hill again with a special message on "urgent national needs." He asked Congress to accept "a firm commitment to a new course of action which will last many years and carry very heavy costs. . . . I believe we should go to the moon."

Paradoxically, the very fact that the Russians had larger rockets than the United States was evidence of their technological inferiority. In the missile race — which is what this was really all about — the Americans had found a way to design H-bomb warheads which were only a fraction of their former size and weight. Therefore they had no need of the powerful rockets Soviet scientists were building. In later phases the superiority of American technology would pay off. Everyone in the White House knew it. So did everyone in the Kremlin.

The man in the street did not know it, however, and Kennedy's space program was undoubtedly popular in the country, evidence that Americans were still ready to meet any challenge — "to invoke the wonders of science instead of its terrors . . . to explore the stars," as Kennedy had put it in his

*Meeting with the Atomic
Advisory Group*

*Observing missile
test flights*

inaugural. Congress approved his proposal by a thundering majority. Ground was broken at Cape Canaveral and the mission control center established in Houston. The aerospace industry was on its way.

The pilot chosen for the first U.S. human orbital flight was a forty-year-old marine lieutenant colonel named John H. Glenn, Jr. At 10:00 A.M. on February 20, 1962, while the President anxiously watched his television set in Palm Beach, Glenn lifted off the Cape Canaveral pad with a great gout of yellow-white flame licking out from his Atlas D rocket, orbited the earth three times in his Mercury capsule, *Friendship* 7, and returned spectacularly, with clouds of sizzling steam erupting as the capsule hit the waters of the Atlantic. A waiting carrier picked him up, and Kennedy arrived to congratulate him. There was a bit of byplay as Glenn, knowing JFK's aversion to funny hats, tried and failed, as so many had failed before him, to put a hard hat on his head. This *is* on film, but the sound is disappointing. Thus, you cannot confirm the story that Jack's first words to Glenn were: "You're doing pretty well for someone who's not in the family."

Glenn's presidential greeting was telegenic. Most Kennedy appearances were. And this, perhaps, was the richest paradox in his public career. The most literate President of his time, who relied upon newspapers for his information, cherished his friendships with journalists, and had even briefly been one himself, covering the first UN session and the British elections of 1945 as a Hearst correspondent (he had predicted Churchill's defeat), owed his success — his very office — to television, the new, unstable, and unpredictable medium whose power was literally visible in forty-four million homes — nearly 90 percent of America's families — across the nation.

Most Washington correspondents don't know the circulation of their papers; Kennedy did — and rationed his time with them accordingly. Like all leaders of his party, he enjoyed slim support among publishers (16 percent had endorsed him in 1960) and overwhelming backing from the working press. Yet despite his sophistication and insider's knowledge of the press, he never developed an immunity to critical columnists and editorial writers. At one time he regarded the New York *Herald Tribune* as his chief tormentor. Reading what he considered a slanted piece there one morning, he muttered that he never wanted to see the *Trib* again. Jack McNally, an aide with more loyalty than discretion, took him at his word and canceled all twenty-two White House subscriptions to the paper. Then Kennedy became annoyed with *Time*. He had been delighted by the newsmagazine's gibes at Eisenhower, but now Henry Luce was goring *his* ox, and he was furious. The unhappy, innocent man in the middle was Hugh Sidey, *Time*'s White House correspondent. Like many newsmagazine journalists, he found his copy unrecognizable when set in type. Jack came to understand. "Every week Sidey sends them the Bible," he told you, "and they print the Koran."

But neither the *Herald Tribune* nor *Time* was the force it had once been. As the President had observed six days after his election, "It was TV more than anything else that turned the tide." If there had been no debates, Nixon would have been living in the White House. Kennedy's sixty-three formal, televised press conferences proved him to be, as ABC-TV's Howard K. Smith put it, a "brilliant commentator." But his exploitation of the new medium wasn't limited to the conferences. On December 17, 1962, for example, he went on television live with Sandy Vanocur of NBC, Bill Lawrence of ABC, and George Herman of CBS. Ben Bradlee, watching the program, felt "professionally threatened as a man who was trying to make a living by the written word." After it was over he phoned Kennedy and told him so. "Well," Jack said pitilessly, "I always said that when we don't have to go through you bastards, we can really get our story over to the American people." The television commentators, like the correspondents, suspected that he was exploiting them but couldn't think how to avoid it. They proposed that the President sit for long, taped sessions, with a producer deciding later which footage would be used. Kennedy agreed. He came across better than ever. Years afterward, a commentator, rescreening the tapes, realized that whenever Jack was asked a question he disliked, he simply gave a long, involved, dull reply, knowing it would wind up on the producer's cutting-room floor.

Martin Luther King, who in these years dominated the struggle of American blacks toward equality, later called Kennedy the movement's best and strongest friend. As a matter of principle he and most senior members of his administration had resigned from Washington's exclusive Metropolitan Club, which would not allow blacks on the premises, even as guests. Among the consequences was one of his wittiest exchanges with the press. Arthur Krock of the *New York Times* approved of the club's segregation policy and remained a member. At the same time, he took up the cause of Moise Tshombe, the rebel Congolese leader whom Kennedy had refused to admit to the United States. Krock pestered the President about this until Kennedy turned and said, "Arthur, we'll make a deal. I'll give Tshombe a visa if you'll take him to lunch at the Metropolitan Club."

On this issue Jack Kennedy was a typical liberal of his generation, and his position must be understood before the flaw in it can be isolated. Throughout his presidential campaign he had reminded audiences, in the South as elsewhere, that a black baby born in America faced crippling handicaps in education, health, income, and even longevity. As President he had pledged himself to programs aimed at correcting those injustices. In 1961 it was considered brave just to endorse racial equality before an audience of southern whites. Bob Kennedy did it in his first major speech as attorney general, in Athens, Georgia, on May 6. If blacks were not treated equally, he said, "the Department of Justice will act. We will not stand by or be aloof." Of course, as he and his brother had privately explained to black leaders, these things took *time*. They couldn't expect it all *now*.

That was the flaw: the blacks wanted it now. They knew the Kennedys' hearts were in the right place, but they had been listening to promises year after year, and nothing had happened. It had become clear to them that racial prejudice was far more powerful than white liberals realized; that it was impervious to reason; and that if it was to be routed, some people, probably their own people, were going to have to die. The time had come for action — not filing motions, and issuing subpoenas, which is what Bobby meant — but physical action: white flesh against black flesh, black flesh against clubs, police dogs, fire hoses, even bullets. And the vanguard of their crusade was already on the move. Two days before Bob spoke in Athens, seven black and six white members of the Congress of Racial Equality (CORE) had left Washington by bus for an expedition through the Deep South, challenging segregation in interstate bus terminals — in waiting rooms, restaurants, and toilets. They called themselves "freedom riders."

Later, southern leaders and southern editorials would charge that they had been sent by "the Kennedys." Actually, neither Jack nor Bob nor anyone else in the government knew anything about them. CORE had sent an announcement of the expedition to the Department of Justice, but it had wound up on the desk of Burke Marshall, chief of the Civil Rights Division, who was home with the mumps. The White House first learned about their journey when stories erupted in the press, and Washington's reaction was anger — directed at the riders. This was the last thing the new administration needed now. Kennedy was still reeling from the Bay of Pigs disaster, the Russians had just won the race for the first manned space flight to encircle the earth, and in less than a month the President would confront Khrushchev in Vienna. From Jack's point of view, almost nothing could be worse than the prospect of ugly racial incidents. The Russians were still exploiting Little Rock, portraying America as racist. Any further evidence of that would be a humiliation for the United States. So the White House first regarded the rides as an embarrassment. The riders had expected that. They knew that their timing was, from the government's point of view, awkward. But to blacks, freedom for their people was more important than any issue in Cuba, Vienna, Vietnam, or outer space.

In the beginning the riders, ignoring the signs for WHITE and COLORED at each stop, merely drew ugly looks and muttered obscenities from white bystanders. But as they progressed, headlines about their journey appeared in newspapers farther along their route. Dixie's reaction began to build. Riders were clubbed and jailed. Policemen refused to intervene; in Montgomery, Alabama, ambulance drivers agreed to ignore all appeals from the injured. Neither the President nor the attorney general could reach Alabama's governor, John Patterson, by phone; Patterson had supported Jack in '60 but he owed his own election to Ku Klux Klansmen. Finally an intermediary told them that the governor would receive a personal envoy from the White House. The Kennedys chose a southern patrician, John Seigenthaler, a Tennessean, Justice Department official, and Bobby's best friend. At the bus terminal in Montgomery, John found mayhem: beatings; broken legs; riders doused with lighter fluid and set afire; and one rider, a white girl, battered to the pavement by a swarm of middle-aged women. She appealed for help. John stopped, but before she could get into his rented car, he was dragged from it and slugged unconscious. The personal representative of the President of the United States lay in his own blood for twenty-five minutes before help arrived.

Bob, livid, sent Deputy Attorney General Byron White to assemble four hundred federal officers trained in riot control. The governor announced that federal men who broke state laws would be arrested by Alabama police. Meanwhile, the nation was electrified by news that Martin Luther King had landed in Montgomery and would address a rally that evening in the First Baptist Church. An armed mob of white Alabamians gathered in a park across the street. Facing them was a skirmish line of White's federal officers. The mob charged, hurling stones and broken bottles. The governor called Bob and protested that Alabama was being "invaded." He had called out the National Guard, which was dispersing the mob with tear gas, but — he said this in a shrill yell — "You're destroying us politically!" Bobby said quietly, "John, it's more important that these people in the church survive physically than for us to survive politically." That ended it. The National Guard moved in and encountered no opposition, King spoke and left, and Montgomery returned to normal.

The freedom riders were accounted a success. No one had been killed, and Jim Crow had been routed. Segregation in airports and bus and train stations, theoretically outlawed by the Supreme Court in 1950, now ended in fact. By the end of the year you could travel coast to coast without seeing WHITE or COLORED in waiting rooms. In a Voice of America broadcast Bob declared that racism was ending in the United States. Most members of the Justice Department agreed with him. Burke Marshall was an exception. As evidence he cited Mississippi, the poorest, most ignorant, and least literate state in the union. Most Mississippians hadn't even heard of the civil rights movement. When they did, Marshall predicted, the dying would begin.

James Meredith, a Mississippi black and a nine-year veteran of the air force, had heard President Kennedy's inaugural address over the radio and, inspired by it, had written the University of Mississippi in Oxford — "Ole Miss" — that same evening, applying for admission. Since he had identified himself as "an American-Mississippi-Negro citizen," he was inevitably rejected. Medgar Evers, the state director of the NAACP, had taken up his cause in June, and on September 10, 1962, after a year of verdicts, appeals, and reversals, Supreme Court Justice Hugo Black, a native Alabamian, ordered the university to admit Meredith at once. "Never!" cried Governor Ross Barnett, and two days later he went on statewide television to declare: "We will not surrender to the evil and illegal forces of tyranny."

An intricate minuet followed, conducted by telephone, with the President, the attorney general, and the governor participating. Barnett always managed to be out of step. The Kennedys would propose a series of intricate moves, the objective being the quiet registration of Meredith. The governor would agree, change his mind, change it back, give his solemn word that he would keep his solemn word, and then break it ten minutes later. Hanging up after one mad conversation, Jack turned to those standing around him in the Oval Office and asked, "Do you know what that fellow said? He said, 'I want to thank you for your help on the poultry program.'" Another time Bob, trying to persuade the governor that Meredith's enrollment would work, asked, "Why don't you try it for six months and see how it goes?" Barnett said, "It's best for him not to go to Ole Miss." Bob replied softly, "But he likes Ole Miss."

Events were closing in on the governor. A federal judge found him in contempt of court, ruling that he would be fined ten thousand dollars a day if Meredith were not registered in four days. At the same time, the President announced that he would explain the situation over national television. Meanwhile, Barnett's equivocations and delays had created a political climate which could be resolved only by violence. On the Oxford campus alarmed faculty members noted a growing swell of visitors from all over Dixie, led by former Major General Edwin A. Walker — sinister, hard-bitten men with brushfire eyes who carried rifles and shotguns and asked: "Where's the nigger gonna come from?" Byron White having moved up to the Supreme Court, Nick Katzenbach was now deputy attorney general, and Nick flew down to supervise the operation. Barnett was in hiding. Accompanied by four hundred federal marshals, Meredith was quietly taken to Baxter Hall, at one end of the university grounds, while Nick and the marshals established a command post at the other end in the lovely old red-brick Lyceum Building.

Aware that it had been foiled but lacking details, the mob prepared to assault the Lyceum. Chanting, "Two-four-one-three, we hate Kennedy!" the rabble pelted the marshals (all of whom were white southerners) with stones and bricks, while others attacked swinging pieces of pipe. At 7:58 P.M. Nick authorized the firing of tear gas. Two minutes later the President, unaware of these developments, went on television. He revealed that Meredith was already on the Ole Miss campus, explained the need to enforce court orders, and appealed to Ole Miss undergraduates to uphold "the honor of your university and state."

In Oxford the students watching him jeered. The attackers threw Molotov cocktails, chunks of concrete, and bricks, and here and there the crack of rifles could be heard as invisible snipers zeroed in on the Lyceum. Two men were killed, 28 wounded, and 166 gravely injured. At 10:00 P.M. Katzenbach called for troops. Sixty National Guardsmen arrived; before daybreak sixteen of them would be casualties. The main body of troops included an MP battalion, which arrested two hundred members of the mob. Only twenty-four were students. Governor Barnett blamed the riot on "inexperienced, nervous, trigger-happy" marshals. The next morning, shortly before eight o'clock, three marshals accompanied Meredith to the Lyceum, where he was admitted by the stony-faced registrar. As he left the building a white student yelled, "Was it worth two lives, nigger?"

In the third year of the Kennedy presidency Martin Luther King zeroed in on Birmingham, "the most segregated city," he said, "in the United States." Police Commissioner Bull Connor liked to quote him on that, and it was true. Not only were the city's schools segregated; so were its public toilets, drinking fountains, theaters, parks, playgrounds, restaurants, and even churches. Federal rulings did not intimidate Connor. To him they were just bureaucratic red tape from "the Kennedys," attempts to disrupt law and order in Birmingham and, as such, opposition to be ruthlessly crushed. King's campaign opened April 2 with sit-ins and marches. Connor swiftly arrested four hundred blacks. King then sent groups to worship in white churches; with few exceptions, they were turned away. Mayor Arthur Hanes told the press that "this nigger" had been sent by the President and the attorney general, of whom he said, "I hope that every drop of blood that's spilled he tastes in his throat, and I hope he chokes on it."

The number of young blacks — all nonviolent, on King's stern instructions — swelled until the memorable morning when over two thousand surged into downtown Birmingham. Connor met them with police dogs and fire hoses. On May 4 newspaper readers around the world were shocked by a brutal photograph showing a huge, snarling dog lunging at a frightened black woman. The President said the picture made him "sick," and he said, "I can well understand why the Negroes of Birmingham are tired of being asked to be patient."

Jack was in the thick of it now, emotionally committed as his brother had been for nearly two years. On May 11 crude bombs demolished, first, the home of a black leader, and then a desegregated hotel. The next day enraged blacks erupted in the streets, and this time they were too much for Bull Connor's policemen, dogs, and hoses. He called on the new governor, George Wallace, for reinforcements. Wallace had been expecting an appeal and he was ready with a motley force — seven hundred deputy sheriffs, game wardens, liquor agents, and highway patrolmen. Shouting threats, they stormed around the city, shoving blacks into doorways and snapping the safety catches of their pistols menacingly. This was the first step in a carefully planned program of escalating intimidation, but Wallace never reached step two, because the President flew three thousand troops to an air base near Birmingham. "This government," Kennedy said, "will do whatever must be done to preserve order, to protect the lives of its citizens, and to uphold the law of the land." Wallace, furious, appealed to the Supreme Court, charging that the troop movement was "unconstitutional and void," an act of "military dictatorship" which "must be nipped in the bud." The Justice Department replied that as commander in chief of the nation's armed forces, a President could order soldiers moved to any base he wished.

In his quiet, persuasive way, Burke Marshall reconciled the city's black and white leaders, and lasting peace returned to the littered but integrated streets of Birmingham. The outcome was another triumph for King. Its implications reached far beyond the jurisdiction of Bull Connor. Here, as in Montgomery and Oxford, the conscience of millions of American whites had been stirred, and elsewhere protesting blacks were marching in Selma, Alabama; Albany, Georgia; Shreveport, Louisiana; Jackson and Philadelphia, Mississippi; and, to the north, in Chicago. "The fires of frustration and discord," the President said, "are burning in every city . . . where legal remedies are not at hand." In a phrase which would be remembered, Ken O'Donnell predicted "a long, hot summer." Before autumn ended fourteen thousand demonstrators would be in southern jails.

Wallace was now a national figure, and he meant to ride the tiger of racism as long and as hard as he could. His next step put him in Bobby's path. During his campaign the governor had repeatedly vowed to stand in the doorway of any white Alabama school to block black children. The attorney general flew down to Montgomery to talk to him. It was a strange meeting. The statehouse, inexplicably, was ringed by state troopers, and

CIVIL
RIGHTS

Roy Wilkins and Martin Luther King meet with UN Ambassador Adlai Stevenson and JFK to urge a greater role for American blacks in U.S. African policies

JFK meets with the leaders of the March on Washington (left to right, front row): Whitney Young, Martin Luther King, Rabbi Joachim Prinz, A. Philip Randolph, JFK, Walter Reuther, and Roy Wilkins; behind Reuther is Lyndon Johnson

pickets carrying such signs as KOSHER TEAM: KENNEDY KASTRO KHRUSHCHEV. Bob told Wallace that the most urgent legal problem in Alabama, which he hoped local officials would help him meet, arose from court orders ruling that the state university must admit black applicants. Over and over he emphasized that the law must be enforced; over and over the bantam governor said that this would mean violence and the blood would be on the hands of the Kennedys.

The President was determined to prevent another Oxford. Flying down to Muscle Shoals, he spoke from the same platform as Wallace and elliptically warned him not to defy the law. Under the terms of a court order three blacks had been declared eligible for the university's summer term. Wallace, more audacious than Barnett, said he not only meant to bar these applicants; he intended to force federal officers to arrest him, too. Nick Katzenbach devised a scheme to make Wallace look foolish. The governor had ordered a white line painted outside the building where students would register. A lectern had been placed there; he intended to stand at the lectern and make his speech. But Katzenbach had reached an understanding with the university authorities. The blacks had not only been admitted; they had been assigned to dormitories. Nick left them in the car, walked up to the line, and, when Wallace strutted out, escorted by towering state policemen wearing helmets, sidearms, gas guns, and truncheons, the governor was informed that his token resistance was meaningless; there was nothing to resist; it was all over. However, if the governor refused to meet his official obligations and guarantee the safety of the students, the Alabama National Guard would be federalized.

Wallace looked ruptured. He raved on about "Yankee justice" and the "force-induced intrusion" of the "central government," but only the press and the state policemen, sweating in the hundred-degree heat, were there to hear him. Katzenbach had returned to his car, and driven the blacks to their residence halls. That evening the President went on television to tell the nation that the racial issue was a moral issue "as old as the Scriptures and . . . as clear as the American Constitution." He said, "A great change is at hand, and our task, our obligation, is to make that revolution, that change, peaceful and constructive for all." To that end he was asking Congress to enact a broad, sweeping civil rights bill committing it to the premise "that race has no place in American life or law." Eventually most Americans would accept that, but in that first of the long, hot summers, racism at times seemed infinite, lurking everywhere in the dark corners of the American mind. Even as Kennedy spoke, Medgar Evers of the NAACP, James Meredith's friend and adviser, was returning to his home in Jackson, Mississippi, after attending a civil rights rally in a church. He never reached his front door. A sniper ambushed and killed him. Discouraged and gloomy, the President said, "I don't understand the South. I'm coming to believe that Thaddeus Stevens was right. I had always been taught to regard him as a man of vicious bias. But when I see this sort of thing I begin to wonder how else you can treat them."

When Kennedy learned that civil rights leaders were planning an enormous peaceful demonstration in Washington, he was dismayed. "We want success in Congress," he said, "not just a big show." But the March on Washington of August 28, 1963, was a high point for those who believed that the grievances of blacks could be redressed by working within the system, and that the marchers were more civilized, and better behaved, than those who had sneered at them. Nothing like it had ever been seen in the country — over 200,000 Americans, and all of them orderly. They sang hymns and spirituals and:

Deep in my heart,
I do believe,
We shall overcome
One day.

Their self-discipline was a marvel. The District policemen had nothing to do but direct traffic; four thousand soldiers standing by were never called. The President was profoundly affected. In the White House he received King and all the leaders of the march, telling them how he had been "impressed by the deep fervor and quiet dignity" of their people. To the press he said, "This nation can properly be proud." Afterward, with his brother, he discussed the political implications of their civil rights bill. The polls, Bob said, showed the beginning of what Eliot Janeway, the syndicated economic columnist, called white "backlash." In the huge ethnic wards of northern cities, King was anything but a hero. Every study showed that the President's stands in Alabama and Mississippi had cost him popularity among blue-collar workers. Jack put on his glasses, studied the poll figures, removed his glasses, and looked up. "Well, if we're going down," he said, "let's go down on a matter of principle."

On Wednesday, May 29, he had become forty-six years old. It was a relief to realize that this year there would be no repetition of last year's present from Frank Sinatra — a rocking chair covered with yellow chrysanthemums and white carnations, which the staff had dispatched to the Children's Hospital before Jack could even see it. But René Verdon was again whipping up one of his chocolate cakes, a Kennedy favorite, and the staff had planned a surprise birthday party for the man still known to some of them as the Tiger. He was lured to it on the pretext that a call awaited him on the scramble phone in the Situation Room, but not much surprised this President, and he was grinning broadly when Mac Bundy led him into the White House mess. Pierre Salinger, acting as master of ceremonies, handed him a speech which began, "Twoscore and six years ago there was brought forth in Brookline, Massachusetts . . ." Kennedy was then handed a satellite model with a card reading, "Hope you have a good trip, Barry," and Jackie, teasing her husband over his pride in the new flower garden outside his office, gave him an enormous basket of dead grass. "From the White House Historical Society," the card read, "Genuine Antique Grass from the Antique Rose Garden."

The real birthday celebration was held that evening, a cruise down the Potomac with Bobby and Ethel, Teddy, the Shrivers, and such close friends as Bill Walton, the Bradlees, the Fays, the Bartletts, Jim Reed, the

David Nivens, and Senator George Smathers and his wife. It was rather grand. A three-piece band played all night; cocktails were served on the fantail, followed by dinner below. Jack enjoyed himself hugely. He had ordered the skipper to be back at the dock by 10:30 P.M., but when the yacht was back at her mooring, Kennedy ordered another cruise, and another, and another, and another. The weather was shocking — bolts of lightning and sheets of hurrying rain — but if you had complained, you would have lost face with these promoters of Kennedy *machismo*. Everyone was slightly smashed when the time came for toasts. Teddy did his imitation of Honey Fitz, which puzzled everyone who hadn't known the old man, and Red Fay, after much urging, did his soft-shoe, boater, and malacca cane vaudeville act, which dated back to PT days in the Solomons and always put Jack in stitches:

> *Hooray for Hollywood . . .*
> *That screwy-bally-Hollywood,*
> *When any office boy or young mechanic*
> *can be a panic*
> *with just a good-looking pan,*
> *And any barmaid*
> *can be a star maid*
> *if she dances with or without a fan. . . .*

By 1963 the twist had become outmoded, but no one had had the temerity to tell the President of the United States, who loved it, so you heard Chubby Checker over and over. Jack decided to postpone opening the pile of presents until tomorrow at Camp David. Unfortunately they were unsheltered, and the guest list included Clem Norton, a last-minute guest of Teddy's who dated back to Jack's congressional campaign in '46. Norton, absolutely crocked, staggered and put his foot right through Jackie's gift to her husband, a rare, priceless, irreplaceable old engraving. This was disaster, but Jackie had been bred to control herself in such circumstances. She said, with studied nonchalance, "Oh, that's all right. I can get it fixed." It certainly didn't look fixable, and you felt that Jack's casual response — "That's too bad, isn't it, Jackie?" — bordered on the insensitive. But that may have been a misreading. As Ben Bradlee once observed, the President and his wife rarely displayed emotion, except in laughter.

Hung over, a much smaller group assembled on the south lawn of the White House Thursday noon for a helicopter ride to Camp David. There each guest or couple was assigned a lodge, and after a visit to a skeet-shooting range nearby, which revealed that there wasn't a marksman in the group, followed by a swim in the heated pool and a tray of marvelous Bloody Marys on the terrace, everyone's spirits rose. Jack's birthday presents were stacked around his chair, and except for the ruined engraving — you could see now that it was, in fact, quite hopeless — the rite went pleasantly. Like a child he would rip the paper off one gift, glance at it, put it aside, and turn to another. The one which delighted him most was a scrapbook from Ethel, a takeoff on White House tours with Bob and Ethel's Hickory Hill madhouse substituted for the executive mansion.

Doubtless none of this appears fascinating now. Neither does a magician's sleight of hand once he has explained it. A survivor can only affirm that there was a kind of enchantment about the Kennedys then, a rare quality investing all their festivities, and since you still don't understand how the trick was done, the charm lingers among the bric-a-brac of treasured memories. Your common sense kept reminding you that laughter and shining triumph cannot last forever, but somehow you felt, against all reason, that these people were going to be an exception. In those days, before the elegiac dark, it seemed that no problem, here or abroad, could defy solution by the American people under this President. The idea of anyone else presiding over Washington never crossed your mind. You assumed that nothing would change, that the whole veteran generation would never age. The Victorians had called bright, cloudless spells "Queen's weather"; in Wilhelmine Germany they were *Kaiserwetter*. Beginning in the '60 campaign those around Jack called such splendor "Kennedy weather." As 1963 wore on you didn't know how very few such days were left. Now you can be grateful, at any rate, for that innocence.

Toward the end of the summer the couple living at 1600 Pennsylvania Avenue celebrated their tenth wedding anniversary at Hammersmith Farm. Jack presented Jackie with a list of antiques from antique dealers, none costing less than a thousand dollars, and told her she could take her pick. He had only glanced at the list before, but now, as he went down it and saw some of the really expensive items, expressions of faint alarm crossed his face, and he whispered to you, "Got to steer her away from that one." She chose a simple serpentine bracelet. Her gift to him represented a lot of work; it was a before-and-after scrapbook of rose garden pictures. Each photograph was accompanied by a copy of his schedule that day and a quotation in her own hand. He was elated. He liked all the quotations and read them aloud.

In retrospect these celebrations seem to have been a high tide for the Kennedys and those of us who were minding the jibs, hitchhiking along as the skipper flew before the wind and toward glory. Jack, of course, anticipated even higher tides in his second administration and brisk sailing afterward. (Jackie once said she wanted him to be President for life; he stared at her in mock horror.) After the five White House years left to him, he planned to found and edit a new Washington newspaper. It would be a great one; all the best newsmen would want to write for it. But in '63 all that lay hull down. Justice, peace, and youth continued to be the soaring themes of the administration. The Kennedys' life-style was in many ways that of those who were then called "the young marrieds." All three wives, Jackie, Ethel, and Joan, were pregnant that spring. Baby carriages and playpens had become familiar furniture in the homes of senior government officials who in other administrations would have been grandfathers. That was part of the Kennedy ambiance; like the Peace Corps, it reminded young Americans that this was their President. You remember his concern, in that last June of his life, over a very small matter. He learned that the John Burroughs High School prom in Los Angeles had reserved the Beverly Hilton ballroom long ago, and now the prom committee had been told they must look elsewhere because the local Democrats planned a thousand-dollar-a-couple dinner in the President's honor. Jack ordered this reversal reversed. During the fund-raising dinner he left the head table to visit the prom, bringing Jack Benny with him. The students roared when, presenting Benny, he said, "I want you to meet my kid brother, Teddy," and Benny, for once, was speechless. To be sure, a President has other generational constituencies. Celebrating the end of his six-year term as a Harvard overseer, he held a stag dinner at 1600 Pennsylvania Avenue for distinguished Harvard alumni. But even then he was conscious of his age. "It is difficult to welcome you to the White House," he told them, "because at least two-thirds of you have attended more stag dinners here than I have."

Yet he was completely comfortable in the presidency, reconciled at last to his loss of privacy and freedom of movement. At some point — your impression is that the turning began in Vienna — he had stopped thinking of himself as a Democratic politician and became, in his own mind, President of all the people. That was both statesmanlike and good politics; the next time he ran, the people would be less interested in campaign tactics than in his White House record. He had aged visibly, as Presidents do. He had, you estimated, about thirty years ahead of him, but already he was becoming sedate, and, yes, dignified. His mind was as alert as ever, perhaps more so. In the west wing his thoughts raced ahead of his words; without bothering to finish one sentence he would break off and start the next, and since his staff had learned how his intellect worked, they could respond to this verbal shorthand. He now read at such speed that he could get through his daily paperwork and still read for pleasure; he recommended that you read Emmet John Hughes's inside account of the Eisenhower years, *The Ordeal of Power* — "It's a terrific book." Plainly he loved his job more and more. Jackie now called O'Donnell "the Wolfhound," because when she saw his unsmiling face appear in the second-floor elevator vestibule, she knew her husband had to leave her, and neither knew for how long. However tired, Jack always rose eagerly to new challenges. He could imagine nothing so appealing as the presidency. Even when things went wrong, he would say, "It's still the best White House I've ever worked in." Like all chief executives he knew moments of loneliness, but when the solitude ended he could turn to his family. In a sense that had always been true, though in 1963 Jack's family was no longer the same clan that had celebrated inaugural day.

The great Kennedy then had been his father. The bond between the old ambassador and the new President had still been powerful. Through most of Jack's first presidential year they had talked on the phone almost daily and, though they rarely agreed on foreign policy — Joe thought his son's defense of Berlin a great mistake — the old man had made an excellent sounding board, if only because the echo was so loud. Yet that first summer it was already clear that the power of decision was gradually moving toward Jack. Obviously he was now the most important man in the Hyannis Port Compound. The play area between the three houses was smaller because a pad had been constructed for the presidential helicopter. Whenever it came whirling down, the ambassador was there waiting at the edge with his broad, loving smile. Out of consideration for Jack's back, Joe had acquired a light blue electric golf cart that would carry the President anywhere he liked — frequently it was to the nearby candy store, with shrieking Kennedy children clinging to the side as passengers — and the old man's masseur was available at any hour, day or night, when his son was in pain.

Their relationship was forever altered in December 1961, when Kennedy had been in the White House less than a year. After Thanksgiving he confided in friends that he was worried about his father's health. Jack's concern was swiftly vindicated; returning from a Latin American trip six days before Christmas, he stopped in Palm Beach and found the ambassador in fine form, but an hour later the old man was stricken while playing golf. The White House was notified. In a strangled voice Jack called Bob: "Dad's gotten sick." Air Force One bore the President back to Florida that night, but there was nothing he could do. At Saint Mary's Hospital in West Palm Beach his father hovered on the brink of death. Last rites were administered; then, slowly, he came back. When Cardinal Cushing called and told him he would get well, he responded haltingly, "I . . . know . . . I . . . will." But he didn't. He became a vegetable. His vocabulary dwindled to two words, "out" and "no," and then simply to "no." He understood you, but when he attempted to reply, he said "no" over and over.

You had last seen him two weeks before his stroke. He had never appeared more alert. Over a year later you saw him again at a small White House dinner with Jack and Jackie, Bobby and Ethel, Teddy and Joan, Eunice, and Ann Gargan, the Kennedy cousin who now devoted every waking hour to the care of her uncle. It was difficult to stifle an expression of dismay. He was thin and twisted, paralyzed from head to toe on his right side. It seemed impossible to believe that the old spirit was there beneath this caricature of what he had been. But it was. Everyone was cheerful — no family could be cheerier — and the ambassador responded. You could see it in his eyes, in his crooked smile, and in the startling strength of his handshake. In the rose garden that afternoon the President had completed the ceremonies making Winston Churchill an honorary citizen of the United States, and now he told his father, "All your old friends showed up, Dad," reeling off the names of men Joe detested, beginning with Bernard Baruch and Dean Acheson. The family had been planning little reunions like this for him, making sure he wasn't lonely on special days, like Saint Patrick's Day, when they stood around him belting out "The Wearin' o' the Green." Jackie was marvelous this evening. She chatted on, apparently idly but actually with great skill, reminding him of all the happy times they had spent together, and telling him how much she appreciated the way he and his crony Frank Morrissey had worked on Jack, persuading him to propose to her.

When the Kennedys were together their energy seemed to increase by a kind of geometric progression, or, even more dynamically, like a nuclear pile when they start to pull the rods out. They began by exchanging gossip about celebrities and politicians, some of it shocking, some very funny. Each would interrupt the others, but the one interrupted would cut back in, so you were getting several stories at once. It is difficult to explain but eventually you *did* get *all* of them. The only Kennedy who could have the floor whenever he wanted it was Jack. Always working at his job, he had been sizing up Nelson Rockefeller, and, knowing you knew him slightly, he asked if you had any dirt on him. That is not the kind of question one is usually asked, even by a friend, but still, there it was. Luckily the answer was easy.

Your acquaintance was really very slight, and apart from his relationship with Happy Murphy, which was not news, you had heard nothing. But he persisted; he was under the quite erroneous impression that voters disapprove of candidates who should have had combat records and didn't. "Where was old Nels when you and I were ducking bullets in the Solomons?" he asked. The implication, that Rockefeller had been dodging the draft, was unjustified; at FDR's request he had served the United States well on delicate wartime missions in Latin America.

It was a source of continuing wonder that members of the family never stopped competing; with one another, with anyone. One evening when the President and his wife were watching the television news with a friend, the screen showed a nine-year-old boy mugging for the camera. "My God, that's Bobby Shriver!" Jack cried. "He's the biggest publicity hound we've got around here!" And with that he told the White House switchboard to get the boy's parents on the line. He told them to lower Bobby's profile. Judging from the conversation on his end, and knowing Eunice's fierce affection for her young, the seed fell on barren ground. Your favorite story of Kennedy competitiveness, which amounts to chutzpah, involved a professional entertainer, Marian Anderson. Ethel had picked her up at the airport for the inaugural. Because Marian was in the business, her driver thought she might like to hear a really outstanding voice. So Ethel sang to her all the way.

During his first weekend in the White House, Jack had given his younger brother a small case inscribed: "And the last shall be first." Teddy, or "Eddie," as Jack always called him, took the initial step toward being first on March 14, 1962, twenty days after his thirtieth birthday (and constitutional eligibility for the upper house), when he declared his candidacy for the U.S. Senate. This was a clarion call to the tribe, and all rallied to the standard. The ambassador was still articulate then, and in words which would have staggered outsiders, and even stunned friends of the family, the old man said to Jack and Bobby: "You boys have what you want now, and everyone worked to help you get it. Now it's Ted's turn." The help they gave did not involve patronage, foreign policy, or matters of state. Mostly it was political advice. Ted was the only Kennedy with a tendency toward fat, so he was given a calorie chart and warned he would be weighed frequently, without notice. Then Bobby and Ted Sorensen flew up to coach him, as any young performer would be coached, on how to move, gesture, and use his hands while on camera. Once Jack, watching Ted field questions from a television panel, became so nervous that he switched the set off.

Once Ted had been elected, Jack naturally left him on his own. You saw the two of them laughing at a family gathering and walked over to ask why. Teddy said, "I'm supposed to have a pipeline to the White House. Some pipeline. I tell him a thousand men are out of work in Fall River, four hundred men out of work in Fitchburg. And when the army gets that new rifle, there's another six hundred men out of work in Springfield. And do you know what he says to me? 'Tough shit!'" That was the right presidential response. Later, though, another exchange with Teddy was one of those rare occasions when Jack disappointed you. After eight years in the White House, he said, he might like to return to the Senate. Would Teddy resign so he could regain his seat? Ted said yes, of course, although he was understandably upset. Bobby wasn't ruthless. But Jack could be, and this seemed to be an example of it. And yet . . . with the family you could never tell. The lengths to which they would go in making one another uncomfortable, and the joy that discomfort gave them, were absolutely extraordinary.

If the ambassador had been his old self, that would have brought him roaring into action, but by the time you saw him after his stroke, when he could speak but one word, he was beyond coping with family problems. He sat immobile, his bright eyes searching the room, his ears cocked to pick up low voices. The family's gaiety seemed genuine, even infectious. But it was all show. Later, when he was alone, Jack's mask fell away. You saw his eyes fill with tears. "He's the one who made all this possible," he said, choking up, "and look at him now." Later he told you that frequently, when his phone rang, his heart would lurch as he heard Ann Gargan tell him that his father wanted to come on the line and talk to him. Then after a pause he would grit his teeth and grind them together while the voice on the other end said, "No, no, no, no, no, no, no, no."

Jack's extraordinary control of his emotions — at the height of the Cuban missile crisis, leaving the Ex Comm to a dusk-to-dawn session, he calmly said at the door, "Gentlemen, the President of the United States is going to get a good night's sleep" — seemed inhuman only to those who never saw him with his children. When with them he was transported; he couldn't have masked his rapture had he tried. Caroline — in her early years he called her "Buttons" — was three when the family moved into the old mansion at 1600 Pennsylvania Avenue and six when they moved out, and at any given time during those thousand days of occupancy she could make your heart leap with a gesture, a smile, or a shy glance from beneath those quite remarkable eyelashes. Before then, she had seen her father only intermittently; their real binding had begun when, at the end of a year of almost uninterrupted campaigning for the presidency, he had arrived in the Compound one afternoon lugging an enormous sack of toys, including a cellophane-wrapped pink teddy bear almost as large as Caroline herself and a stuffed giraffe that was actually larger. You recall the fragrance of brown Betty drifting over from the kitchen in the Big House, and the curious way the ambassador and his son greeted each other — Joe's cupping grip on Jack's clenched fist — but mostly you remember how father and daughter exchanged looks. He had been smitten the first time he saw her newly born. He began to know her during the transition, when he was President-elect, and in the White House they really discovered each other. He would open his arms and she would rush into them, into joy.

He rarely disciplined her, or even raised his voice. Once, looking out the tall windows from his Oval Office desk and noting a suspicious movement in her jaw, he called, "Caroline, are you eating candy?" There was no answer. He repeated, "Caroline, are you eating candy?" Again, silence. Finally, in exasperation: "Caroline, answer me; are you eating candy? Yes, no, or maybe?" But if she wept, he dissolved. He found it hard to correct her; you remember the presidential voice, now plaintive, coming from an

BROTHERS

adjacent room, pleading, "Caroline, please hang up. I have to use the phone." And if she was away, he worried. He would call her every evening in Palm Beach, Hyannis Port, Hammersmith Farm, wherever. Once Miss Shaw told him she was at a friend's birthday party and had not returned. Her father, sounding as though she were a wayward teenager, said, "She's got to start staying home at night." He wouldn't agree to her spending a weekend away from home until she was nearly six. She, the pink bear, and her Raggedy Ann would be staying with little Agatha Pozen, whose father was in the Department of the Interior. Agatha's mother was to pick her up at the White House early in the afternoon of Friday, November 22, 1963.

Her first word had been "plane." It was followed by "Daddy," "car," and "shoe" — at least two denoting action. Her parents were determined to shelter her from publicity, but they were fighting, at best, siege warfare. She was still tiny on that morning in Georgetown when Jack was soaking in the bathroom and she raced in, threw a copy of *Newsweek* with his picture on the cover into the tub, shouted, "Daddy!" gleefully, and sailed out. Her public appearances were few but memorable. She first emerged at a diplomatic-corps reception, where she greeted guests in a fancy party dress. (Admirers of it were told, "It's my very best.") She was marvelous with old European aristocratic diplomats; her curtsy was deep and graceful, a sweeping movement from another age. She and her little brother probably met more heads of state than most cabinet members. They would watch ceremonies on the south lawn from the Truman balcony, shouting "bang" to echo each shot in a twenty-one-gun salute, and one hot day they outwitted Miss Shaw, escaped from the mansion, and were found, naked as jaybirds, bathing in the south-lawn fountain. By then Caroline had become a celebrity. The entire country knew that her pony's name was Macaroni, that she had asked Sam Rayburn why he didn't have any hair, had wandered into the press lobby to tell reporters her father was "sitting upstairs with his shoes and socks off not doing anything," and had been photographed leaving church with her father, clutching her rag doll. (Jack told a friend, "I don't mind them taking pictures after mass, but I sure as hell don't want them around after confession. I feel humiliated then, and I know I look it. A Catholic likes to confess to a priest who doesn't know him. It's very disconcerting to sit in the booth and hear the voice from the other side of the screen saying, 'Good evening, Mr. President.'")

In the presidential apartment, unpenetrated by the press, the family's life differed little from their Georgetown days. Caroline watched her father shave and bathe each morning; then she, and later John, would patter off to watch animated cartoons on television. At the end of the afternoon she and the dogs would wander over to the west wing. If he was busy she could chat with Evelyn Lincoln or explore the cupboard of toys and games Evelyn kept for this very purpose. Jack was allergic to dogs, but Caroline loved them, and that, for him, was that. Jackie had set up a small schoolroom on the third floor of the mansion for Caroline, Agatha Pozen, and other children of New Frontiersmen, and she had also established a play area, with a sandbox, slides, and swings, on the lawn near the Oval Office. Caroline, and then her toddling brother, would spend hours there, accompanied by Charlie; Shannon, an Irish cocker spaniel; and Pushinka, Khrushchev's gift. Between appointments the President would often step outside, clap his hands, and then brace himself for two hurtling children and three charging dogs. There were times when it hurt. You could see his face whiten, but knew that the pang was a small price for this full moment.

Caroline acquired her mother's love of horses, her father's love of the sea, and from both, a love of books. Daughter and son bore the unmistakable Kennedy stamp: they were friendly but reserved with strangers, alert, bright, possessed of immense curiosity, and fired by awesome energy. In the press they sounded angelic. In fact, they weren't. Their mother, while reading Dr. Spock's book, told a friend that it was "a relief to know that other people's children are as bad" as hers "at the same age." In time Jackie sensed that Caroline's daddy's zeal to preserve the child's privacy was less than her own. The appeal of little children is powerful political capital, and at times he succumbed to its temptation. Jackie fought publicity down to the last desperate inch. To get her young away from the White House, she would pile them into her blue Pontiac station wagon and spend hours in parks or shops or the homes of understanding friends. Halloween was the perfect answer. Not only could they wear masks; so could she. Thus, Arthur Schlesinger, Joe Alsop, and Dean Acheson answered the door to greet a pair of unrecognizable little hobgoblins, bounding up and down and extorting treats by threatening tricks. Unfortunately, the voice of the costumed demon could not be disguised, and when she told the children that it was time they moved on to the next house, the dispensers of candy corn identified the First Lady in drag.

As a father, Jack was at his best telling stories. He had the usual repertoire: the amnesia of Bo-peep, the trespassing of Goldilocks, and the London Bridge disaster. But he also had tales of his own, of a little girl named Maybelle who lived in the woods; of a giant named Bobo the Lobo; and of the eccentric appetites of the White Shark and the Black Shark. The White Shark's diet was limited to people's socks. You recall one afternoon when Jack was sitting in the stern of the *Honey Fitz* beside Frank Roosevelt. Frank was reading. His legs were crossed, his shoes were off, and he was wearing a filthy pair of sweat socks. Jack was talking about the White Shark and how, for him, the dirtier a sock, the more relishing a *bonne bouche* it became. As he told the story, he reached down, pulled off one of Frank's socks, and tossed it over the stern. Then he explained that the only thing the White Shark liked better than one filthy sock was two filthy socks, and reaching down again he yanked off Frank's other sock, and threw that, too, into the river. Frank never looked up. Caroline's eyes couldn't have been wider. She was utterly captivated, convinced that the instant the socks disappeared into the Potomac they were devoured by the Shark following the boat.

By her sixth year her father had decided it was time she took a long step up to poetry. She adored a couplet which he had attributed to Emily Dickinson (he blushed when she found it in a volume of Edna St. Vincent Millay) and loved to hear it from him:

Safe upon the solid rock the ugly houses stand:
Come and see my shining palace built upon the sand!

At her repeated insistence he promised to include it in a speech, and did so, on the spur of the moment, while addressing a group on the south lawn. To his delight he found that she possessed a retentive memory, and he would sit back proudly, chewing a cigar, while in her clear sweet voice she recited from Shakespeare:

> *Where the bee sucks, there suck I*
> *In a cowslip's bell I lie;*
> *There I couch when owls do cry.*
> *On the bat's back I do fly*
> *After summer merrily:*
> *Merrily, merrily shall I live now*
> *Under the blossom that hangs on the bough.*

Young John was never "John-John" to his parents. Here is the origin of that myth. One day the President left his Oval Office and called his son, who was playing nearby: "John!" There was no response. Kennedy raised his voice: "John!" This time the boy heard him, jumped up, and came on the run. A minor aide recounted the episode to a reporter, who asked: "And what were the President's exact words?" The aide replied: "John! John!" By the time this reached print it had become "John-John." Reading it, Jack caustically remarked: "I suppose if I'd had to call him *three* times, he'd have become 'John-John-John.'"

Kennedy had established a gentle relationship with his daughter, but boys are different; they are expected to be more physical, and fathers are supposed to be more active with them. One of the pleasanter of such activities, for most men, is throwing their sons in the air. Jack's back ruled that out, however. Adenauer, at the age of eighty-six, tossed young John up, and the delighted child giggled and begged for more. Jackie said this was the first time anyone had thrown him up. Jack made sure it wasn't the last; his friends were drafted as substitutes. "John doesn't know it yet," he told them sadly, "but he's going to carry me before I carry him." On Squaw Island that last summer, as Jackie sat nearby, drawing plans for a new country retreat, Jack would fall to the grass in the area behind the house, facing the sea, and, with the ground supporting his back, pull John down with him. His hope was that the boy would accept this as a substitute for tossing, but he didn't. Jack would say, "John, aren't you lucky to have a dad who plays with you like this?" Sadly, the boy didn't answer. When he found he wasn't going to be tossed, he would turn to another man present and say, "Throw me up."

But that was a minor disappointment. Father and son were a source of boundless merriment for each other. They teased each other endlessly. Even teasing was unnecessary. If their eyes met, it was enough; both would be convulsed. Sitting in the Squaw Island cottage, Jack would make a motion toward the boy showing he meant to catch him, and John, almost immobilized by his giggling, would totter away, complaining when caught, "Daddy, let me go. Mommy, make Daddy let me go." They would race on hands and knees, the father shouting, "I'm going to get you!" and grabbing and tickling his son. In Palm Beach, he would pursue John to the pool ladder and pull down his little swimming trunks, the boy yelling, "Silly

FAMILY LIFE AT
THE WHITE HOUSE

Bobby Jr., RFK's son, on his first official visit to the White House gave the President a salamander as a gift

The family after mass

AT HYANNIS PORT

Daddy!" or "Naughty Daddy!" During their last Palm Beach vacation, John somehow picked up what he considered an outrageous insult. Crouching just out of his father's reach, he would call, "Daddy, you are a foo-foo head!" Kennedy's jaw would sag, his eyes would bulge, he would tremble with mounting outrage and rise, crying: "John Kennedy, how dare you call the President of the United States a foo-foo head? Wait till I get hold of you!" And the chase would be on. One evening, when the grown-ups were all sitting around the pool, and the children were saying their good-nights, John leaned toward his father and said in a stage whisper, "Foo-foo head!" The President froze in an attitude of total shock, and the exultant little boy darted off to bed, convinced that he had won a famous victory.

It is a scene witnessed a thousand times a day, in homes or parks or on beaches. But in this instance it had special significance. After his futile attempt to stare down Khrushchev in Vienna, Jack told you: "It doesn't really matter as far as you and I are concerned. What really matters is the children." He was preoccupied with the rising generation. On a trip to New Mexico he looked down into a huge crater, the result of an underground blast. Two physicists explained enthusiastically that they were perfecting a much smaller bomb that could produce a larger crater. He frowned, perplexed. Afterward, he asked you: "How can they be so damned cheerful about a thing like that? They keep telling me that if they could run more tests, they could come up with a cleaner bomb. If you're going to kill a hundred million people, what difference does it make whether it's clean or dirty?" And another time, talking of the need to ban tests, he told you: "On this issue I'm also President of generations yet unborn — and not just American generations."

Because Caroline and John were such a source of joy for him, the loss of the baby Patrick, in the summer of 1963, plunged him into grief. Patrick would have been their brother. He lived for thirty-nine hours. He wasn't expected for another five weeks, but on the morning of August 7, after taking Caroline to Osterville for riding lessons, Jackie was stricken by labor pains. The birth was imminent. Dr. John Walsh, her Washington obstetrician, happened to be vacationing nearby, and he accompanied her in the ambulance from Hyannis Port to Otis Air Force Base. The President arrived at 1:30 P.M. By then Walsh had delivered Jackie, by cesarean section, of a son weighing less than five pounds. The base chaplain immediately baptized him Patrick Bouvier Kennedy. Patrick had difficulty breathing, and Walsh and a consulting physician decided to move him by ambulance to the Children's Hospital Medical Center in Boston. Jack visited Caroline and John on Squaw Island, visited Jackie, and spent the night in Boston's Ritz-Carlton, studying test-ban documents.

In the morning the news was bad. The infant had developed a lung affliction. They moved him again, this time to Harvard's School of Public Health. There he was put in a high-pressure oxygen chamber. Jack decided to spend the night in a vacant hospital room. At 2:00 A.M. a Secret Service agent woke him; Patrick had taken a turn for the worse. The President paced the corridor for two hours. Then his tiny son's heart failed and he died. Later his father said simply: "He put up quite a fight. He was a beautiful baby." At the time he couldn't talk at all. He didn't want anyone to see him weeping, so he went upstairs, to the room where he had slept, and sat on the bed, sobbing.

The funeral mass was celebrated by Cardinal Cushing and attended only by members of the family. Later the cardinal told you how, after the others had gone on to the Brookline gravesite, he had remained behind with Jack. In his grief Kennedy tried to take the little coffin with him. He could put his arm around it — it was that small — but he couldn't lift it, and the old prelate rasped, "Jack, you'd better go along. Death isn't the end of all, but only the beginning." At the grave the President again lingered until nearly everyone had gone. Dave Powers watched him lean over and touch the ground and say softly, "It's awfully lonely here." Then he returned to comfort Jackie. She wanted to stay with him and the children; normality, routine — that seemed the best way to cure depression. He had a different idea. Aristotle Onassis, the Greek shipping tycoon, had suggested she take an Aegean cruise on his opulent yacht, the *Christina*. So at Jack's urging she went, with her sister, Lee, and Frank Roosevelt. As Jack had anticipated, there was substantial press criticism of her trip. The papers were full of stories about the "brilliantly lighted luxury yacht," described as "gay with guests, good food, and drinks," with "lavish shipboard dinners" and "dancing music," a "crew of sixty," including, for the First Lady, "two coiffeurs."

To Jackie's astonishment, Jack had been right about the trip. The diversion actually worked. The voyage was so unreal, such a complete cut-off, that she seemed to be on another planet. She couldn't even talk to Jack by phone; she would place a call in one of the little places where the yacht stopped, wait three hours, and then learn that the operators had "lost the connection." Eventually it occurred to her that calls might be indiscreet anyway, since every word would be overheard, so she wrote him ten-page letters, punctuated with dashes like everything she wrote. She told him how much she loved him, and missed him, and wished he could be with her to share the tension-free atmosphere of the Mediterranean. Dispatches traced her progress from Istanbul to Lesbos, Crete, Delphi, Marrakesh, and Skorpios, the island in the Ionian Sea that Onassis owned. Royalty, beginning with the king and queen of Greece, entertained her, toasted her, admired her, and presented her with exotic gifts. When she returned to the White House on October 17, one member of the White House staff said, "Jackie has stars in her eyes — Greek stars."

She invited friends over for cocktails, to hear about her trip. Onassis, she said, was "an alive and vital person." She talked about the Moors, the palaces, how she had to eat with her hands — one hand, actually, the other being considered soiled — and the dances. Disappearing briefly into her bedroom, she reappeared wearing the embroidered, stone-studded white silk Moroccan caftan King Moulay Hassan had given her, and after putting some Moroccan music on her record player, she demonstrated the native dances. Later she seemed somewhat remorseful about the publicity in the United States, which, she acknowledged somewhat sheepishly, was no recipe for votes. Kennedy told a friend that he had vetoed any Onassis visit until after 1964, clear evidence that he thought the trip had been damaging politically. But in an aside to Ben Bradlee he noted that what he called "Jackie's guilt feelings" might work to his advantage. They did. Smiling, he suggested that she join him in a whirlwind tour of El Paso, Houston, Fort Worth, and Dallas, winding up at the LBJ Ranch, where the vice-president would encourage them to feast upon the culinary specialties of his house. She replied, "Sure I will, Jack. We'll just campaign. I'll campaign with you anywhere you want." And flipping open her red 1963 appointment book she scrawled "Texas" across November 21, November 22, and November 23.

More and more often you heard the battle cry: "Wait till '64!" On November 13, exactly one week before his departure for Texas, the President convened his first strategy meeting for the reelection campaign in the Cabinet Room. Bobby was there, and Larry O'Brien and Ken O'Donnell, and other veterans of '60. They talked for over three hours, with the President in absolute control. In many ways this session resembled the Palm Beach and Hyannis Port meetings of April and October, 1959. "As usual," Jack said, "the campaign will be run from here." On Monday next he would speak in Tampa and Miami; then, after a brief layover in Washington, he and Jackie would head for El Paso and his big swing through LBJ's home state. Texas was a problem; he needed its electoral votes, but the party was split between Governor John Connally, a right-wing Democrat, and the liberal senator Ralph Yarborough. Lyndon seemed helpless, so Kennedy was going to use his presidential prestige to bring Connally and Yarborough together, at least until November 3, 1964.

He wanted a livelier convention this time. "For once in my life," he said, "I'd like to hear a good keynote speech." Afterward, he would debate his Republican opponent on television. That was confidential for the present, but definite. The big question was: who would he be running against? There was no doubt about the Democrats' favorite Republican. They wanted Goldwater, the only politician in either party who would, literally, rather be right than President. Jack was sure he could bury Barry. The strongest candidate the GOP could nominate, Jack said, was Nelson Rockefeller. But then the governor had divorced his wife to remarry. Jack shook his head in bewilderment. He was the last man to slight the joy of sex, but political suicide was beyond his comprehension.

Actually, he was already running. His every action as President would be an issue next year, but the more recent an event, the greater its visibility. Prosperity, or the lack of it, was a major issue in any election. He had chuckled when Eisenhower, baffled by Keynesian economics, had cried out in a magazine article: "What can those people in Washington be thinking about? Why would they deliberately do this to our country?" What Kennedy was deliberately doing to the country's economy, with the help of Douglas Dillon and Walter Heller, was producing the longest peacetime expansion in history. And if Congress accepted his recommendation of a tax cut, he believed there would be no recession in 1964.

The most exciting and most unexpected new issue was the nuclear test ban. To the President, the test ban had been a matter of conviction. He assumed it would lose votes. In the treaty hearings Edward Teller had declared: "If you ratify this treaty . . . you will have given away the future safety of this country." It wasn't true; Maxwell Taylor and an array of scientists had testified it was untrue, but Kennedy didn't doubt that in some parts of the country the arrow had found its mark. One such part was the block of eleven mountain states, eight of which had been carried by Nixon three years before. On the day of ratification, Kennedy flew west for a swing through the block. His justification for the trip was that it was a conservation tour. But everyone knew it was political. Ten Senate seats would be at stake there next year, the John Birch Society was active in all of them, and Jack wanted to cut his, and his party's, losses. He didn't plan to talk about the test ban unless challenged. His first speeches, as billed, were on the preservation of natural resources. But on the second day, in Billings, Montana, he struck a deep chord. It was pure chance. Mike Mansfield was on the platform, and in his third sentence the President commended him for his role in guiding the treaty through the Senate. To his astonishment, this touched off long and sustained applause. A few minutes later, he decided to test the mood of the audience again. It was his hope, he said, that he had decreased the "chance of a military collision between those two great nuclear powers which together have the power to kill three hundred million people in the short space of a day." This time the crowd's enthusiasm was unmistakable.

That evening he thrust the rough drafts of his other conservation speeches in the back of his briefcase and set to work on new ones. He would talk about his "Strategy of Peace." In Great Falls, Montana, he declared that the job "isn't going to end. . . . We have to stay at it. We must not be fatigued." The contest with the Soviet system must not become "a competition in nuclear violence." There, and in Hanford, Washington, audiences gave him standing ovations. But his great test came in Salt Lake City, a stronghold of the Radical Right. There Kennedy dealt, not only with the test ban, but with his policy of pluralism. It was understandable, he said, that in confused and perplexing times Americans should look back to earlier days with nostalgia. But the achievements of science and technology were irreversible. The wisest course, he said, was to preserve and protect "a world of diversity," in which "no one power or combination of powers can threaten the security of the United States." At the end the crowd stood on their chairs cheering. Until now, he had thought only later generations would understand pluralism. That night, before that immense crowd at the Tabernacle of the Latter-Day Saints, he began to realize that they understood him now. And the test ban wasn't the political sacrifice he had thought it to be. Gallup reported that 80 percent of the electorate approved of the test-ban treaty.

If he overwhelmed Goldwater, a Kennedy landslide would bring him the congressional majorities he needed for a triumphant second term, when the legislative promises of the first term could be redeemed. The administration bills now clogging calendars on the Hill, or mired in committees, would become law — laws on mass transit, conservation, civil rights, employment of youth, education; the tax cut, his war on poverty, and Medicare. Congressional attempts to curb his distribution of foreign aid and thwart his wheat sales abroad would die unmourned by the White House. Despite conservative protests, the wheat sales to Russia had proved a thundering success. The Russians seemed grateful, Western Europe was once more aware of American generosity, and according to the polls, Americans thought the agreement admirable. Kennedy wondered if donations of grain could lead to an "open door" relationship with isolated China. "If it would lessen their malevolence," he said privately, "I'd be for it now." He knew the risks. Richard Nixon would attack any trafficking with the Chinese. Moreover, there would be no way to make sure that the food went to those who most needed it, no guarantee that the Chinese people would know who had sent it. "And let's face it," he said. "That's a subject for the second term."

By then he hoped to have a better grasp of the Orient. Ever since his return from Europe he had been planning an extensive visit to the Far East with Jackie, followed, before the '64 election, by a tour of Russia. Already the governments of Japan, the Philippines, India, and Pakistan had been alerted; the President and the First Lady would be arriving in the immediate future. Kennedy had considered a departure shortly after New Year's Day, but this would have meant an advance trip by Ken O'Donnell over the Christmas holidays, and for once Ken threatened mutiny. So Jack put off the advancing until January. "But are you sure I'll be leaving Texas in time to have lunch here with Cabot Lodge on Sunday?" he asked. "Don't worry about it," Ken said. "It's all set." The President had already signed and announced the order bringing the first thousand U.S. military advisers home from Vietnam. American participation in the war, for good or for bad, would end the year of his second inaugural, and Lodge should plan accordingly.

A number of people, none of them alarmists, were concerned about the President's decision to drive through downtown Dallas on Friday in a convertible. Byron Skelton, the Democratic National Committeeman for Texas, felt strongly that the city should be omitted from Kennedy's itinerary. He wrote Bob Kennedy and Walter Jenkins, Lyndon Johnson's chief aide; then he flew to Washington to talk to John Bailey of the Democratic National Committee and to Jerry Bruno, who was advancing the Texas trip. Skelton described the political climate in Dallas. It wasn't safe, he repeated; regardless of previous commitments, it should be avoided. They told him Kennedy's mind was made up. He considered the possibility of assassins simply "one of the more unpleasant aspects of the job." If the time came when a President was afraid to enter any American city, he should move out of the White House. That had been Kennedy's reply when Senator J. William Fulbright, a liberal from a state which borders Texas, had told him that "Dallas is a very dangerous place," that "I wouldn't go there," and "don't *you* go."

Dallas was not wicked, nor were a majority of its people sympathetic to the extremists among them. Kennedy's following there was tremendous and enthusiastic, as the turnout for his motorcade would demonstrate. But its leaders were hospitable to, and often members of, the Radical Right. In that third year of the Kennedy presidency the impression grew that a kind of political pestilence had infected the city. The homicide rate was appalling. Billboards demanded, IMPEACH EARL WARREN! Major General Edwin A. Walker had bought a home there, and in his yard he flew the American flag upside down. Radical Right polemics were distributed in the public schools; the President's name was booed in classrooms; junior executives were required to attend Radical Right seminars. Dallas had become Mecca for the political evangelists of Welch, Hargis, Schwartz, the Patrick Henry Society, the Sons of the American Revolution, the Minutemen and Minutewomen, and the National Indignation Convention, which held that those advocating the impeachment of Earl Warren were suspect — by an overwhelming vote, the convention demanded that the chief justice be lynched.

Stocky, cowboy-booted executives affixed K.O. THE KENNEDYS stickers to their chrome bumpers. Handbills were circulated with photographs of the President of the United States — full-face and profile like the posters of fugitive criminals displayed on post-office walls — with the message: WANTED FOR TREASON. THIS MAN IS WANTED FOR TREASONOUS ACTIVITIES AGAINST THE UNITED STATES. On the morning of Kennedy's visit to Dallas, a slick variation of this would appear in the Dallas *Morning News*, whose publisher had accused the President of riding around on Caroline's tricycle. Stanley Marcus of Neiman-Marcus had assembled his executives and told them he hoped Kennedy would give Dallas a miss. "Frankly," he said, "I don't think the city is safe." More recently — less than a month before — Adlai Stevenson had come to Dallas to speak on UN Day. As he stepped down from the platform, he was mobbed and spat upon. Wiping his face with a handkerchief, Adlai asked coldly, "Are these human beings or are they animals?" When Jack read of it in the *Times*, he phoned Arthur Schlesinger. "Call Adlai," he said. "Give him my sympathy, and tell him we thought he was great." Naturally there was no doubt now that Kennedy would ride through Dallas in an open car. If Adlai could take it, so could he.

It was a time of last things, of goodbye hugs and farewell handshakes, though of course, no one knew that then. You recall them now with almost unbearable poignance, with a dark tug in your chest, as though you are watching a tragic play about someone who once lived, who was almost a part of you, and was greatly beloved. Your affection is rekindled as the scenes gather momentum, but unlike the figures on the stage you are alert to the approaching disaster. You yearn to warn the hero and can't and so you sit, horrified and helpless as the climax approaches and you await the entrance of the last character — now in the wings — Death. So it is now as you see Jack then, in 1963. There was his parting with his parents, his last glimpse of the Cape, Teddy singing "Heart of My Heart" while Joan played the piano; and on Sunday, November 10, entertaining friends at Wexford, as Jackie called their new home-away-from-home on a tract of land bought from Bunny Mellon in the rolling terrain west of Middleburg, Virginia. All this was pleasant, but the memory now is heavy.

Kennedy spent the last weekend of his life in Florida. He had flown down to campaign and loaf with Torbert Macdonald, once his Harvard roommate and now a Democratic congressman, and the inseparable Dave Powers. They were to be together from Friday through Monday, when Jack would return to the White House, wade through paperwork, and then fly to Texas with Jackie. Jack and Torbey rode through Tampa and Miami in motorcades, two aging roommates standing together, acknowledging the cheers with practiced grace, but mostly they were in the ambassador's home. Usually Palm Beach is at its most unattractive in November; the wind blows hard and relentlessly; you have to hide from it. But during these four days there was no wind, none at all, just a cloudless sky — in short, Kennedy

A LOVE OF
THE SEA

Mrs. Kennedy enjoys a good book as well as sailing

weather. Jack said his back hadn't felt better in years. Torbey remembers, "It was like being back in 1939, where there was nothing of moment on anybody's mind. Sure there was some talk about politics . . . but it wasn't the usual tension-filled weekend."

Saturday morning they watched the firing of a Polaris missile at Cape Canaveral, and, after lunch, sprawled around a television set watching Navy play Duke. Jack picked Navy, giving Torbey and Dave ten points. He won; Roger Staubach passed the midshipmen to a 38–25 win. Had Jack lost, he would have all but declared himself bankrupt, but having won, he demanded an immediate payoff, and by immediate he meant *now*, so Torbey and Dave had to trot upstairs and fetch their wallets. Most of Sunday was also spent on the patio. Jack picked the Chicago Bears over the Green Bay Packers, and luck held, permitting him to fatten his savings account, which now stood somewhere on the opulent side of fifteen million dollars. That evening they saw *Tom Jones.* He loved it. And before turning in, he sang a song, in that impulsive way Kennedys had. For once his voice was, not toneless, but reedy and clear:

> *Oh, it's a long long while from May to December*
> *But the days grow short when you reach September*
> *When the autumn weather turns the leaves to flame*
> *One hasn't got time*
> *For the waiting game.*
>
> *Oh, the days dwindle down to a precious few*
> *September, November!*
> *And these few precious days I'll spend with you*
> *These precious days I'll spend with you.*

Back in Washington, he toiled through documents and executive orders, bowed over his nautical desk in the Oval Office, singling out papers from the Hill for special attention. Congress was restless, but the President had made it clear that both houses would remain in session until their job was done. At his last press conference he had predicted: "By the time this Congress goes home, next summer — in the fields of education, mental health, taxes, civil rights — this is going to be a record. However dark it looks now, I think that 'westward, look, the land is bright.'" Wednesday evening the annual judiciary reception was held in the East Room. Bobby was there, of course. It was his thirty-eighth birthday, but he would celebrate that later in the evening at Hickory Hill.

Next morning, after breakfast and bath, Jack went through his morning ritual, drawing on his back brace, lacing his shoes — the left one with its quarter-inch medical lift — and slipping into the clothes George Thomas had laid out, anchoring his tie with a bright PT tie clip. He inspected his face in the cluttered mirror. Thrust in it at strange angles were a picture postcard of the Kennedy "ancestral home" in Ireland; a postcard from Amalfi, Italy

("I like Italy better than Hyannis but I like Hyannis a little bit more because there's fairs. I miss you daddy very much X Caroline"); a scribbled schedule of Washington masses at Saint Stephen's and Saint Matthew's; a snapshot of Caroline standing in her mother's shoes; a Polaroid shot of Jackie; and an old photograph of Jack, Jackie, Ethel, and Bob.

"Caroline!" he called, clapping his hands. "John!" Both came running, John in plaid short pants and his sister in blue tights and dark blue velvet dress. Their mother was having her hair set, so he had them to himself at breakfast. He telephoned an instruction to the Pentagon; then it was 9:15 and time for his daughter to leave for school. She embraced him, whispered, "Bye, Daddy" (*"Bye, Caroline"*), and was gone in a twinkle of blue-clad legs. John played with toy planes while his father went over to the Oval Office for a crowded hour, then strolled into the Cabinet Room and admired the new draperies. They had been hung only yesterday. Fingering the red border of one, he called to Evelyn, "When do we get ours?" "While we're in Texas," she called back. "Rugs, too?" he asked. "Rugs, too," she assured him. He said, "Good. When we get back we'll have new offices."

Returning to the mansion he overruled Miss Shaw's objections to exposing his son to the drizzle outside and ordered Provi, Jackie's maid, to ready John for the helicopter ride to the airfield. The departure of the choppers — there were three this morning — was always a spectacle. Like great brown wasps they trembled on their pads, rose, and dipped toward Andrews Field, a twelve-minute ride to the southeast. John, snug in a little London Fog raincoat and a sou'wester hat, was aboard the presidential helicopter in the lap of a friend who would be joining the presidential party later. The boy had set his heart on making the Texas trip. "I want to come," he told his father, his voice beginning to break. "You can't," Jack said gently. His mother hugged him, but he began to cry. Then Kennedy told the friend, "Look after him," and taking John in his lap the friend said, of course he would, and began diverting the boy with stories about Bertram the Beaver, and Jaggy the Jaguar, and Jasper the Jet. The vice-president had already boarded another of the President's 707s. At 11:05 A.M. Kennedy's flagship zoomed upward as Jim Swindal quickly raised the great ship to its cruising speed of 550 miles per hour, lifting the graceful white fuselage into the murky sky, its blue flashings vanishing in scudding clouds. The little boy in the chopper sighed. He always loved to watch that plane.

"Westward look, the land is bright," Jack had said, quoting Clough, but looking westward from Andrews the skies were a sullen, roiling mass of storm clouds. Swindal, of course, would ride above them. Air Force One was the safest, most prestigious airplane in the world. All other flights, military and civilian, deferred to it. Its progress was monitored on radar screens, and a chain of SS checkpoints was established on the ground beneath its aerial route. Should it make a forced landing, an agent in a souped-up car could reach the spot quickly. Indeed, the failure of the ranking agent aboard to report that he was passing checkpoint Able or Baker would have been enough to start the sirens screaming. Before Swindal landed or took off from any airport, the field was unavailable to other aircraft for fifteen minutes. You had to hand it to the Secret Service. They thought of everything.

THERE THOU LYEST

At 12:30 P.M. Texas time, on the afternoon of Friday, November 22, 1963, President Kennedy was killed by a sniper as his motorcade crawled through downtown Dallas. Back in McLean, Virginia, Bobby was in the middle of a working lunch at his Hickory Hill poolside when J. Edgar Hoover — briskly, without a word of sympathy — phoned him the news. A friend raced across the Potomac from downtown Washington, hoping to be of help, and together they walked back and forth in the Hickory Hill yard. Bob recalled Byron Skelton's warnings that the President should avoid Dallas at all costs. Jack, unlike Bob, had never worried about assassination attempts, but both had agreed that Bobby was the likelier target for a fanatic. The friend, desperately searching for a bright thread, said, "Maybe this will reduce hate." Bob shook his head. He said: "In a few months it will be forgotten."

Among those whose business it is to forecast the public mood, nearly all agreed that while the assassination would be remembered, it would soon recede in the public consciousness. The adoration of Franklin Roosevelt had been unmatched by that of any other President in this century, and the nation had been grief-stricken at his loss in the spring of 1945. Yet by summer the catharsis had run its course. Harry Truman had settled down in the White House, and the country felt comfortable with him there. There was no reason to expect that the Kennedy–Johnson transition would be any different. After the burial in Arlington, Kennedy aides rushed to finish their memoirs before their audiences dissolved. When Jackie asked you to write an account of the President's last days and his funeral, with the understanding that it could not be published for another three years, your literary agent, who was rightly regarded as the best in his craft, predicted that by then the public would have lost interest in Jack.

Officially the period of mourning was to last thirty days. That is less impressive than it sounds. It merely meant that flags would be flown at half-staff and no social functions would be scheduled by or for members of the government. Elsewhere business opened as usual on Tuesday, November 26, the day after the state funeral. Television commercials resumed, the stock market rose sharply, theater marquees were lit up. The thirty days passed, the flags were hoisted to the top of their poles, Washington hostesses started entertaining again — and then you discovered that the mourning hadn't ended at all. In New York a thousand people, sheep without a shepherd, walked slowly up Fifth Avenue, each holding a candle in memory of their slain President. In Arlington on Christmas Day, 1963, a steady procession passed Kennedy's eternal flame all day, five abreast; a six-inch snow lay on the ground, yet the waiting line stretched the equivalent of several city blocks. Scotty Reston wrote: "The Kennedy Legend grows and deepens. It is clear now that he captured the imagination of a whole generation of young people in many parts of the world, particularly in the university communities. Even those who vilified him now canonize him, and many of his political opponents who condemned him are now seeking a candidate who looks and sounds like him."

Magazines began to issue JFK memorial editions, and every bookstore had its little corner altar of volumes by and about Kennedy. Auctioneers found that his letters were as valuable as Lincoln's. To emphasize the continuity of government, the White House staff began distributing photographs of both Presidents during Johnson's trips outside Washington, but the practice was quickly discontinued; for every LBJ picture, the public would take ten of JFK. The Secret Service seethed when Johnson rebuked an SS agent for wearing a PT-109 tie clip and tore it off his shirt. Yet Johnson's pique was understandable. He was overshadowed and sometimes eclipsed by his predecessor. Even the 1964 Democratic National Convention, which had been carefully planned as a Johnsonian festival, was stolen from under his very eyes. A month earlier he had scratched Bobby from his list of vice-presidential possibilities. Nevertheless, the most moving moment in Convention Hall was not LBJ's. It came when Bob stepped to the podium to introduce a film about his brother's presidential years. For fifteen minutes the delegates gave him a roaring, standing ovation, and then wept as he softly quoted Shakespeare in that inimitable voice:

> . . . *When he shall die,*
> *Take him and cut him out in little stars,*
> *And he will make the face of heaven so fine*
> *That all the world will be in love with night,*
> *And pay no worship to the garish sun.*

Bob had done nothing to encourage the demonstration. You watched through misted eyes as he repeatedly tried to interrupt it, and then, biting his lip, lowered his head as against a storm. You felt utterly shattered, for you were remembering that evening when you walked the Ellipse with Jack, talking of stars. He had asked you how well you remembered the sky over the Solomons. You could recall only the Southern Cross, but as a PT skipper he had been trained in celestial navigation. Speaking softly he had reeled off the names, one by one, of the bright guides that had twinkled each night in the vault above the islands — Apus was one; Pyxis may have been another — and he recalled how he had taken fixes on them and then felt his way back down the Slot to his Peter Tare base. The constellations had fascinated him and still did; he described their movements across the night sky and through the seasons down under. You remembered how, returning from the Ellipse, you and he had talked some of what you had felt your prospects would be then, whether you would even have a future. Your life expectancies, at that time, in that place, had been too short to be recorded on any actuarial table. And now he had been taken from us like this. It seemed so utterly monstrous, as you listened to Bob, at a convention his brother should have been dominating, that Jack had gone through all that in the Solomons Slot to die as he had, at peace under a bright noon sun in a boisterous American city. Sartre was right, you thought; life is a theater of the absurd. There was no other word for it.

At some point in 1964 you realized that other Americans, and many who were not American, were trying to do what you had done — to incorporate memories of him in their lives. The most obvious course was to name something after him. Cape Canaveral, New York's Idlewild Airport, and the National Culture Center in Washington were rechristened for Kennedy. So, all across the land, were countless bridges, highways, causeways, recreation centers, and schools. The U.S. Treasury minted fifty million Kennedy fifty-cent pieces. It couldn't keep them in circulation because they were being hoarded as souvenirs — and still are, nearly twenty years later. A Canadian peak became Mount Kennedy — the first man to climb it was Robert F. Kennedy, by then U.S. senator from New York — and the climax was reached when England set aside three acres of the historic meadow of Runnymede, where the Magna Carta had been signed in 1215, as a Kennedy shrine. The idea was Queen Elizabeth's. On May 14, 1965, she presided at the ceremony dedicating the tract to the President, "whom in death my people still mourn and whom in life they loved." Jackie replied that it was "the deepest comfort to know that you share with me thoughts that lie too deep for tears."

But the phenomenon was too deep for thought, too. It still is, for in the 1980s, despite criticisms of his policies and even of his character, his place in the hearts of his countrymen is secure. In 1982 a Harris survey asked the American people to rate the last nine Presidents, and Kennedy dominated the poll. He was, according to this nationwide cross section of the electorate, the President who inspired the most confidence, could be most trusted in a crisis, set the highest moral standards, and possessed the most appealing personality. Since the others being judged included Roosevelt, who led the country out of its worst depression and to victory in its greatest war, you begin to grasp why it is that the more men ponder Kennedy's hold on the people, the less they understand it. David Brinkley concluded that the assassination and its aftermath are unfathomable. "The events of those days don't fit," he told you. "You can't place them anywhere. They don't fit in the intellectual luggage of our time." To him the tragedy was "too big, too sudden, too overwhelming, and it meant too much. It had to be separate and apart." But events that cannot be accommodated in the intellectual luggage of our time may fit perfectly in kit which is not intellectual and whose force is therefore not recognized in our time. Brinkley is highly intelligent, articulate, and above all rational; so are our other social commentators. That has not always been true. In earlier eras their role was played by prophets, seers, and oracles, who found reason was weak when pitted against the tides of emotion. The terrific energy released by the death of the President would not have surprised them. They would have found the emerging Kennedy legend familiar — for though strange to us, it is as old as the human race — and they would even have known how it could be used to strengthen and invigorate the country.

There were a few who sensed this at the time. Senator Ralph Yarborough had been bred in the florid tradition of southern oratory, and when the President was pronounced dead at Parkland Hospital, Yarborough turned aside, whispering, "Excalibur has sunk beneath the waves." Jackie had not heard him, but several days later, talking to Theodore H. White, she too evoked Arthurian images, remembering how Jack had loved those lines: "Don't let it be forgot / That once there was a spot / For one brief shining moment / That was known as Camelot." Once, she said, she had thought of history as something that "bitter old men" wrote. "Then," she said, "I realized history made Jack what he was. You must think of him as this little boy, sick so much of the time, reading the Knights of the Round Table, reading Marlborough. For Jack, history was full of heroes. And if it made him this way — if it made him see the heroes — maybe other little boys will see. Men are such a combination of good and bad. Jack had this hero idea of history, the idealistic view." Other great Presidents would be elected, she said, "but there'll never be another Camelot again."

Actually, of course, there never was a Camelot. It exists only in legend. But that does not discredit it. Legends cannot be measured by dialectic. Biblical miracles are myths. If you dismissed them as lies, however, you would not only offend those who cherish them; you would also be wrong. When Jesus told Pontius Pilate that it was his mission "to bear witness to the truth" and that "everyone who is of the truth hears my voice," Pilate replied: "What is truth?" Men have been struggling to answer him for two thousand years. The first of the fourteen definitions of truth in the Oxford English dictionary is the character or disposition of being "true to a person, principle, cause, etc.; faithfulness, fidelity, loyalty, constancy, steadfast allegiance." Truth, in short, may be simple faith — faith in today's creeds; faith also in those creeds of the past which we call myths or legends. They are many. The legendary hero is found in all cultures — Vikramaditya in ancient India, for example, Siegfried of the *Nibelungenlied*, Frederick Barbarossa of the Teutons, Sigurd and Balder in Scandinavia, Cuchulain in Ireland, Arthur in Britain, and Roland in France.

Doubtless all of these champions existed in one form or another. The difficulty lies in sorting out the facts about them. Those who shape legends have never been content to leave substance alone. Roland, for example, deserves to be remembered for his stand at Roncesvalles. His lily needs no gilding. Nevertheless, the *Chanson de Roland* tells us that he fought with a magic sword and a wonderful horn that could be heard twenty miles away, both of which he had won from a giant. This sort of fictive embroidery is even more intricate in tales of the most remarkable of all legendary heroes, Arthur of England, though here, as in so many other particulars, exceptions must be made. The embellishments — the sword in the stone, the sacred sword Excalibur, the Round Table, the Holy Grail — are so consistent with one another, and so magnificent in their entirety, that they guarantee immortality in themselves. Arthur is unique. His fame is not confined to England; indeed, for several centuries he was better known on the Continent than in his own country. He is the only historic figure from England's Dark Ages to have emerged, radiant, into the Renaissance and then to have grown through the centuries that followed, until today he is as celebrated as the twentieth century's world leaders. He died 1,444 years ago. Yet his story runs through the tapestry of our literary inheritance like a golden thread, appearing in Chaucer, Malory, Spenser's *Faerie Queene*, Milton, Dryden, Fielding, Carlyle, Sir Walter Scott, Swinburne, Mark Twain, T. H. White, and John Steinbeck.

Who was he?

In the sixth century, England, no longer shielded by the Roman legions, was beset by Saxon invaders from Germany. The hordes from Saxony ("Sessoynes") were hated, and with reason: they were rapists, arsonists, carriers of disease; men who fought, as Tacitus observed, for pleasure and loot. Britons prayed for the preservation of what was left of their civilization. England had never been unified. It was a quilt of little kingdoms. The kings turned to Arthur, who was not royal himself but instead a *dux bellorum* — a military commander and cavalryman of great gifts and courage. Few records were kept in those dim, blurry centuries; fewer have survived. But some have, and they are priceless. Among those now in the British Museum are the so-called Easter Tables, contemporaneous documents prepared and updated in abbeys, and *Historia Brittonum*, set down by the eighth-century Welsh monk Nennius. In A.D. 488 an Easter Table reported that the English had fought a great pitched battle during which the Saxon chief had been killed. Of this clash, Nennius observes that "Arthur fought against them [the Saxons] in those days, with the kings of the Britons, but he himself was the leader of the battles."

Nennius then lists twelve Saxon defeats, all at the hands of Arthur. In the last engagement he led a charge which slew 960 Saxons. "No one overthrew them except himself alone," according to Nennius. "In all battles he stood victor." This final conflict is noted in the Easter Tables. The scribe's Easter calculations are confusing, but the year is either A.D. 499 or 518. The entry reads: "Battle of Badon, in which Arthur carried the cross of our Lord Jesus Christ on his shoulders [shield] for three days and three nights and the Britons were victors." Badon is one of the great battles in English history. The sixth-century Celtic monk Gildas, who was keeping his own record of the times, called Badon "almost the last slaughter of the enemy," and said Arthur's victory halted the Saxon advance for at least a generation. It seems incredible that anyone could have endured three days and three nights of combat, but Gildas clears that up; Badon, he says, was a siege — "*obsessio Badonici montis*." The last Easter Table citing Arthur is dated A.D. 539. It reads: "The Battle of Camlann, in which Arthur and Mordred perished."

Camlann was not a fight between Britons and Saxons. The need to drive away the Germans had united England's small kingdoms. The Saxon withdrawal had loosened the alliance. The allies quarreled with one another and then resorted to the sword. In their lethal struggle Arthur and Mordred may have been resolving a personal quarrel or championing different kingdoms. In any event only horsemen were involved; the peasants were undisturbed and unthreatened. The tremendous thing is that Arthur, by his skill and bravery, had brought Englishmen a lifetime of peace, and that was so unusual in the Dark Ages that he won what proved to be everlasting gratitude. Elizabeth Jenkins, after reviewing the brutal, almost genocidal conduct of the Saxons, writes that it "makes us see why the commander who routed them in a series of pitched battles . . . became the image of the hero and savior, whose death people refused to believe in, whose return was yearned for and expected throughout centuries."

After the Tables, Nennius, and Gildas, the documentary trail is faint. But we must remember that during those ages only monks could read and write. Even kings were illiterate. Nevertheless, men could speak. Thus, Arthur's story spread. Tales told by the fireside doubtless gained in the telling. By the tenth century it was assumed that Arthur had been a king, which he never was. Detailed accounts of his life did not appear until the early 1100s, and it is impossible to sort out the apocrypha in them, or to determine what was omitted. They carry no mention of Guinevere, for example. Yet she lived, and there can be little dispute over why she was remembered. To this day, in remote Welsh villages, a woman who breaks her marriage vows is called "a regular Guinevere."

In 1184 fire destroyed the last structure dating from Arthur's time, a small fifth-century wattle-and-daub church — the first Christian shrine in England — where he may have prayed before going into battle. Meanwhile, however, the Arthurian legend continued to grow, and not only in England. The prior of Tewkesbury noted that British pilgrims, returning from abroad, reported "winged praise of Arthur" in Egypt, the Bosporus, Carthage, Antioch, Armenia, and all the major cities of western Europe. Over the next two centuries writers added Lancelot and the Round Table — actually, peasants had spoken of them for hundreds of years — until, in the 1460s, Sir Thomas Malory wrote his superb *Morte d'Arthur*, establishing for all time the image of the noble king presiding over his chivalrous knights and slowly realizing that Camelot and all it represented were doomed because the two people he cherished most, his beautiful wife and his mightiest knight, had become lovers. After a great convulsion of violence Lancelot vanished, Guinevere closed her legs and entered a nunnery, Excalibur went its watery way, and Arthur departed to sleep beneath the inscription "*Hic jacet Arturus, Rex quondam, Rexque futurus*" — "Here lies Arthur, the Once and Future King." Thus, he joined that small circle of mythical heroes who can never die, who, in Steinbeck's words, have found "a seat of worth beyond the reach of envy, whose occupant ceases to be a man and becomes the receptacle of the wishful longings of the world."

Arthur lived, fought, and died when all his countrymen, including monks and nuns, believed in heroes. Kennedy's age was the age of the antihero, the victim. Alienation had become a cultural vogue. Great leaders belonged to the past; the leonine mold had been broken. It therefore followed that this young President who seemed to have been cast from it must be an imposter. Those who held this view were a minority, but they were immensely influential. Because of Kennedy's class, taste, and interest in the world of ideas, he had moved among them for years. Their modes were familiar to him but unacceptable. He continued to write of the gallantry they disparaged and spoke eloquently of the need for a new idealism. In Houston, the night before he was slain, he quoted the Proverbs: "Where there is no vision, the people perish." He saw his country threatened by a gray tide of mediocrity and an implacable enmity toward the concept of excellence which he exalted.

In his lifetime this was not always understood. His elegance, his sophistication, and his self-deprecating wit were effective camouflage. He needed that; he was a man of understatement. Nevertheless, the one illness which never afflicted him was cloying liberal piety. He felt neither alienated nor victimized. Duty, dedication, and devotion were the very essence of him, and if those words sound quaint, the fault lies with us and not with him. "Unless democracy can produce able leaders," he had written at Harvard in 1940, "its chances of survival are slight." That thought became his keel. He seemed taller than he was because he was reaching; and because he would never stop reaching, his grasp became extraordinary.

The tension between him and the intellectuals who should have identified with his presidency but didn't, became irrelevant in Dallas. Most Americans didn't know that heroism was obsolete. Their grief in November 1963 was like that of any people, at any time in history, whose champion has been slain. During the seventy-four-hour, fifty-four-minute telethon some seventy million people watched their TV screens, averaging nearly ten hours at a stretch. They were stricken. Some have never fully recovered. Some institutions are universal, and burial of the dead is one, but it can be done in various ways. The ritualistic splendor of these mourning ceremonies for Kennedy struck deep, atavistic chords, recalling ancestral memories older than the nation. For example, the riderless, caparisoned steed that followed the gun carriage, with boots reversed in their stirrups, a sign that the beloved rider would ride no more, goes back at least to the days of Genghis Khan and Tamerlane. Somehow Jack's young widow had reached back across the centuries and found the noblest of funeral rites, celebrating the sacrifice of fallen leaders; then, gathering that solemn aura into the prism of her own anguish, she refracted it into a radiant, penetrating beam of light that blinded a nation with its own tears.

One conclusion was predictable. The country's concept of President Kennedy had changed forever. Once a leader becomes a martyr, transformation naturally follows. Endowed with a nimbus, he must also be clothed in raiment which he would have found strange, but which satisfies the public eye. As Edmund Wilson pointed out, the Lincoln to whom Americans are introduced as children, and whom Carl Sandburg did so much to perpetuate, has little in common with the cool, aloof genius who ruled this nation unflinchingly as the sixteenth President of the United States. That man was destroyed on the evening of April 14, 1865. The urbane public man who became his nineteenth successor shared his fate. The real Kennedy vanished on November 22, 1963. The fact that Lincoln and Kennedy shared an abiding faith in a government of laws therefore becomes inconsequential; legends, because they are essentially tribal, override such details. What the hero was and what he believed are submerged by the demands of those who mourn him. In myth he becomes what they want him to have been, and anyone who belittles this transformation has an imperfect understanding of how the emotions of an entire nation may be moved. A romantic concept of what may have been can be far more compelling than what was. "Love is very penetrating," Santayana observed, "but it penetrates to possibilities, rather than to facts." All people ask of a legendary hero is that he have been truly noble, a splendid figure who was cherished and cruelly lost. Glorification follows. In love, nations are no less generous than individuals. In grief, they are no less stricken. And as the years pass their loyalty deepens.

The legendary Arthur, like the Jack Kennedy we knew, was in his element on seas and streams. He was said to have been conceived at Tintagel, where towering seas crash against cliffs and burst into billowing clouds of foam. Five of the great battles in which he rescued England from the swarming Saxon invaders were fought on the banks of rivers; he fell with his last wound on the shore of another stream; he returned his sacred sword to the Lady of the Lake, whose hand rose from the depths to receive it; and he was carried away by three queens on a royal barge.

But those who yearn for his strength and courage do not look seaward. Since the beginning of time men have sought the answer to profound mysteries in the sky. In various eras stars have been worshiped. Along the Euphrates, observations of them were recorded before 3800 B.C.; the Chinese had discovered the 365¼-day solar year by 2300 B.C.; the Egyptians laid out their pyramids and established the rules of surveying by charting celestial movements. Thus, those who seek Arthur search the stellar vault of the heavens, seeing him in Arcturus, the star said to have been named for him, or in the sparkling constellation Ursa Major, "Arthur's Wain."

If you were sitting beside Jim Swindal in the Air Force One cockpit during that flight home from Texas on November 22, hurtling eastward at a velocity approaching the speed of sound, goaded by a mighty tailwind, you became aware that night was approaching rapidly. Less than forty-five minutes after you left Dallas, shadows began to thicken over eastern Arkansas. In the southern sky you could see a waif of a moon, a day and a half off the quarter, hanging ghostlike near the meridian. Like you, Jim, near tears, was fighting to control himself. Conversation was out of the question; voices couldn't be trusted. Outside, twilight turned to olive gloaming and became dusk. You looked out upon the overarching sky and realized that in the last days of autumn the northern firmament is brilliant. Jupiter lay over the Carolinas, the Big Dipper beyond Chicago. Cassiopeia and the great square of Pegasus twinkled overhead. Arcturus was setting redly over Kansas. But the brightest light in the bruise-blue canopy was Capella, just beginning its annual five-month wintry cruise over the hemisphere. Always a star of the first magnitude, it seemed dazzling tonight, and as Air Force One rocketed toward West Virginia it rose majestically a thousand miles to the northeast, over Boston. Ever since then you have thought of Capella as Kennedy's star. It is brilliant, it is swift, it soars. Of course, to see it, you must lift your eyes. But he showed us how to do that.

The last time "Hail to the Chief" was performed for JFK it was played as a dirge

FAREWELL

A small hand, to get closer,
slipped under the flag

PICTURE CREDITS

Page 2, Paul Schutzer, Life Magazine, © Time Inc.; *12 top,* Cecil Stoughton, The John F. Kennedy Library; *12 bottom (left and right),* United Press International Photo; *13,* Cecil Stoughton, The John F. Kennedy Library; *19–21,* The John F. Kennedy Library; *22 top,* Stephen Halpert; *22 bottom (left and right),* The John F. Kennedy Library; *25 left,* Bachrach, Inc.; *25 right,* The John F. Kennedy Library; *26 top,* The John F. Kennedy Library; *26 bottom,* United Press International Photo; *27 top,* Richard Sears, Pathé, Boston; *27 bottom,* The John F. Kennedy Library; *28 (top and bottom),* Dexter School; *29 top right,* Choate Rosemary Hall; *29 bottom left,* Dexter School; *29 bottom right,* Pictorial Parade; *30–31,* Bachrach, Inc.; *34 left,* Elliott Erwitt/Magnum; *34–35 top,* The John F. Kennedy Library; *34–35 bottom,* Elliott Erwitt/Magnum; *35 right (top and bottom),* The John F. Kennedy Library; *37,* The John F. Kennedy Library; *40–41,* The John F. Kennedy Library; *42 top left,* United Press International Photo; *42 top right,* unknown; *42 bottom,* The John F. Kennedy Library; *43,* The John F. Kennedy Library; *48 left,* United Press International Photo; *48 right,* Pictorial Parade; *49 top,* The John F. Kennedy Library; *49 bottom,* Salamon/Magnum; *50–51,* The John F. Kennedy Library; *52 top,* Peter Hunter/Magnum; *52 bottom,* The John F. Kennedy Library; *53 top,* Pictorial Parade; *53 bottom,* The John F. Kennedy Library; *54 top,* The John F. Kennedy Library; *54 center and bottom,* Pictorial Parade; *57,* Look Magazine; *66–67,* unknown; *67 right,* Boston Globe Photo; *68,* United Press International Photo; *69,* Wide World Photos; *72,* The John F. Kennedy Library; *73,* Wide World Photos; *74,* The John F. Kennedy Library; *75,* United Press International Photo; *78 top,* Burt Glinn/Magnum; *78 bottom,* The John F. Kennedy Library; *79 top,* United Press International Photo; *79 bottom,* Cornell Capa/Magnum; *84 top (left and right),* United Press International Photo; *84 bottom,* Abbie Rowe, The John F. Kennedy Library; *85 top,* Abbie Rowe, The John F. Kennedy Library; *85 bottom,* United Press International Photo; *86,* Robert Knudson, The John F. Kennedy Library; *87 top,* Abbie Rowe, The John F. Kennedy Library; *87 bottom,* Robert Knudson, The John F. Kennedy Library; *88,* United Press International Photo; *94 top,* Wide World Photos; *94 bottom,* United Press International Photo; *95 top,* The John F. Kennedy Library; *95 bottom left,* United Press International Photo; *95 bottom right,* unknown; *96,* United Press International Photo; *97 top left,* unknown; *97 top right,* United Press International Photo; *97 bottom,* Look Magazine; *98 top,* Cornell Capa/Magnum; *98 bottom,* John Buckley; *99,* Wide World Photos; *105,* United Press International Photo; *108,* Cornell Capa/Magnum; *110,* United Press International Photo; *114,* The John F. Kennedy Library; *116,* The John F. Kennedy Library; *117,* United Press International Photo; *118 top,* unknown; *118 bottom,* United Press International Photo; *122–123,* Boston Globe Photo; *124–125,* Henri Dauman/Magnum; *126,* United Press International Photo; *129,* Henri Dauman/Magnum; *130 top,* United Press International Photo; *130 bottom,* Cornell Capa/Magnum; *131,* Henri Dauman/Magnum; *132–133,* Cornell Capa/Magnum; *134 top,* United Press International Photo; *134 bottom,* Abbie Rowe, The John F. Kennedy Library; *135,* Cecil Stoughton, The John F. Kennedy Library; *139,* United Press International Photo; *142 top,* Abbie Rowe, The John F. Kennedy Library; *142 bottom,* United Press International Photo; *143,* Wide World Photos; *145–147,* Abbie Rowe, The John F. Kennedy Library; *148,* Cornell Capa/Magnum; *149 top and bottom,* United Press International Photo; *149 center,* Cornell Capa/Magnum; *150 left,* Cornell Capa/Magnum; *150 top right,* Cornell Capa/Magnum; *150 bottom right,* United Press International Photo; *151–155,* Cornell Capa/Magnum; *155 right,* Abbie Rowe, The John F. Kennedy Library; *158 top,* Abbie Rowe, The John F. Kennedy Library; *158 bottom,* Cornell Capa/Magnum; *159 top,* Abbie Rowe, The John F. Kennedy Library; *159 bottom,* Cecil Stoughton, The John F. Kennedy Library; *162–163,* United Press International Photo; *169,* Cecil Stoughton, The John F. Kennedy Library; *170–173,* Robert Knudson, The John F. Kennedy Library; *174–183,* Cecil Stoughton, The John F. Kennedy Library; *184,* Bob Gomel, Life Magazine; *189–191,* Cornell Capa/Magnum; *192 left,* United Press International Photo; *192–194,* Abbie Rowe, The John F. Kennedy Library; *195 top left,* Abbie Rowe, The John F. Kennedy Library; *195 top right,* Cecil Stoughton, The John F. Kennedy Library; *195 bottom,* Abbie Rowe, The John F. Kennedy Library; *196 top,* Abbie Rowe, The John F. Kennedy Library; *196 bottom,* Elliott Erwitt/Magnum; *197 top,* Cecil Stoughton, The John F. Kennedy Library; *197 bottom,* Abbie Rowe, The John F. Kennedy Library; *202,* United Press International Photo; *203,* Cecil Stoughton, The John F. Kennedy Library; *206–207,* Abbie Rowe, The John F. Kennedy Library; *208–209,* United Press International Photo; *211,* United Press International Photo; *214,* Abbie Rowe, The John F. Kennedy Library; *228–229,* Abbie Rowe, The John F. Kennedy Library; *230–231,* United Press International Photo; *238–239,* United Press International Photo; *248,* Cecil Stoughton, The John F. Kennedy Library; *249–250,* United Press International Photo; *253,* Cecil Stoughton, The John F. Kennedy Library; *254,* United Press International Photo; *255 top,* United Press International Photo; *255 bottom,* Robert Knudson, The John F. Kennedy Library; *256 top,* United Press International Photo; *256 bottom,* Elliott Erwitt/Magnum; *257,* Wide World Photos; *264,* The John F. Kennedy Library; *265 top,* United Press International Photo; *265 bottom,* Robert Knudson, The John F. Kennedy Library; *266–267,* Wide World Photos; *267 top right,* Cecil Stoughton, The John F. Kennedy Library; *267 bottom right,* Elliott Erwitt/Magnum; *278,* United Press International Photo; *279 top,* Wide World Photos; *279 bottom,* United Press International Photo.